AF531595

DUKKHA
Suffering in Early Buddhism

DUKKHA

Suffering in Early Buddhism

By

Dr. M.V. Ram Kumar Ratnam

M.A., M.Phil., Ph.D.
Centre for Mahayana Buddhist Studies
Department of Buddhist Studies and Philosophy
Nagarjuna University
Nagarjuna Nagar–522510
Guntur, A.P., India

Editor

Dr. Digumarti Bhaskara Rao

M.Sc., M.A., M.A., M.Ed., Ph.D.
R.V.R. College of Education
D-43 Srinivasa Nagar
Guntur–522006
A.P., India

2003

DISCOVERY PUBLISHING HOUSE
NEW DELHI–110002

First Published–2003

ISBN 81-7141-653-5

Published by
DISCOVERY PUBLISHING HOUSE
4831/24, Ansari Road, Prahlad Street,
Darya Ganj, New Delhi-110002 (India)
Phone: 3279245 • Fax: 91-11-3253475
E-mail:dphtemp@indiatimes.com

Printed at Tarun Offset Printers, Delhi

Contents

Preface

Man from times immemorial has been striving hard to make his life happy *(ananda)* and avoid suffering *(dukkha)*. But a look at human existence does show that man is exposed to suffering, physical or mental or spiritual. It is physical, in the sense, it springs from the body. It is mental in that, it has its genesis in man's unfulfilled desires and other cravings. It is spiritual in that, man suffers from ignorance concerning the true nature of the "Self". Philosophers who have been sensitive to human suffering, want to discover the causes of human misery and the means for its elimination. In fact, the perception of 'universal' suffering has formed the motivating factor for philosophical inquiry.

Philosophical inquiry in Indian tradition arose in man's endeavour to extricate himself from pain. The sensitiveness of the Indian mind to suffering was so intense that Professor Hiriyanna goes so far as to say that 'Philosophy in India did not originate in wonder or curiosity as it seems to have done in the West, but originated under the pressure of a practical need arising from the presence of moral and physical suffering, *(Outlines of Indian Philosophy)*. Philosophical inquiry and resultant wisdom are used as means to attain freedom from the bonds of dukkha. Freedom from dukkha i.e., *moksṣa,* the *paramapurusartha,* is the ultimate goal of all forms of inquiry, philosophical and non-philosophical, in Indian tradition.

The Indian philosophers knew that this ideal cannot be achieved without meeting the requirements of the sense of curiosity i.e., knowledge and the sense of perplexity i.e., clarity. Sankara observes in his *Vivekachudamani (verse175):* Knowledge and ethical perfection constitute the two wings, for the self in its spiritual flight. Since the requirements for *moksha* necessitate the fulfillment of such requirements as knowledge and clarity, the Indian philosopher did not institute them as the 'Ideals' as such, they have done in the case of mokṣṣa.

Being alive to the fact of suffering the systems of Indian philosophy have addressed themselves to the origin and annihilation of suffering. Īsvara Kriṣṇa in his *Sāmkhya Kārikā,* in the very *first Kārikā* state that it is *dukkha* which motivates man for philosophical inquiry. He observes that man is tormented by a three-fold pain, viz., *Ādhyātmika, Ādhibhautika* and *Ādhidaivika.* He is convinced that no other means except philosophical inquiry can redeem man from this three-fold dukkha. Philosophical inquiry enables man to gain the requisite discriminative wisdom (*tattva-jñāna*) that *purusa (man)* is different from prakṛiti. It is prakṛiti which suffers and is of the very nature of suffering, whereas puruṣa is pure, eternal consciousness and is never in bondage or misery. It is always free. It is the appropriation of the suffering of *prakṛiti* nature by the *puruṣa* owing to its beginningless ignorance that is at the root of man's suffering. Philosophical inquiry dispells this ignorance and restores the *puruṣa* to its natural state of isolation *(kaivalya).*

The *Yoga* philosophers apart from accepting the three-fold dukkha of *saṁkhya,* speak of another four types of duhkha, viz, *duhkha of change (Perinama duhkha), duhkha of anxiety (tāpa duhkha), duhkha of habituation (saṁskāra duhkha)* and *duhkha of qualities (guna duhkha) (Yoga sutras, 11.5).* The systems of *Nyaya and Vaisesika* agree that earthly life is full of suffering. Bhasaravajāña in his *Nyāyasāra* identifies twenty-one types of duhkha which man encounters during his empirical existence. The *Naiyayikas* are convinced that liberation *(mokssa)* from duhkha is possible only through right knowledge which is provided by philosophical inquiry.

The instruction in *Vedanta* aims at leading man from duhkha to ananda. Śaṅkara contends that philosophical inquiry based on *Sravana, Manana* and *Nididhyasana* is the means for producing the discriminative knowledge of the self as being different from body and that all suffering pertains to the body. He also advises man to take refuge in God *(brahman)* in order to put an end to the circles of birth and death, which is the source of all suffering. In his *Bhajagovindam* he observes, Being born again and again, dying over the over again; and getting in to mother's womb over the over again; it is hard to cross this ocean of repeated birth and death *(saṁsāra);* save me from it, O Merciful Lord (*punarai jananam punarapi maranam ... ... paahi muraaree...)*

The general spirit that runs through all orthodox schools (including Jainism among heterodox schools) is that the genesis of human suffering lies in man's ignorance concerning the true nature of the self. It consists in his identification of the self with body and appropriating its properties. Hence, ignorance concerning the true nature of the self is at the root of human suffering. In order to overcome this suffering, man should overcome ignorance. The antidote for ignorance is knowledge. Therefore, it is knowledge and knowledge alone that can lead us to immortality.

The environment of Indian philosophical tradition at the time of Buddha was too idealistic to be practical. Buddha felt that these idealistic dispositions will not provide a remedy for man's suffering. Just as man struck by an arrow should first get his wound medicated before embarking on an inquiry regarding the type of arrow or the person who has shot it, man should address himself to the immediate problem of suffering without wasting his time in questions that land us in interminable disputes. Buddha gave Indian philosophical inquiry a more practical orientation, which is aimed at providing tangible solutions to the problems confronting man. The transition was from idealism to realism to pragmatism and humanism.

No other thinker was as sensitive as Buddha to the fact of dukkha. Buddha says: 'O Monks, two things only do I teach, dukkha and the cessation of dukkha' (*Cullavaga IX, 1.4.)*. He could see suffering *(dukkha)* at every moment of his life. 'Birth is suffering, decay is suffering, disease is suffering, death is suffering. Coming into contact with those who are not liked is suffering. Separation from those who are liked is suffering, not to get what one desires is suffering in short, the five aggregates that conduce to clinging are suffering' (*Digha Nikaya* II, 304). It is this sensitivity to suffering *(dukkha)* that forms the 'guiding ideal' for his philosophical inquiry. Philosophizing for him consists in the inquiry into the very causes that give rise to dukkha and the factors that annihilate it. To quote Dr. Radhakrishna: "The melancholy foreshadowed in the upanissạds occupies the central place here" *(Indian Philosophy, Vol. I)*

Buddha, realizing the fact that 'to live is to suffer', started his inquiry into the causes of dukkha and after a great deal of agonizing experience, found a way out. In short, he arrived at the four noble truths *(ariya saccas),* which he expounded in his first sermon at Isipatana, modern Saranath, near Varanasi; *Dhammacakkappavattana sutta.* They are: 1. There is suffering *(dukkam ariyasaccam)*; 2. There is a cause for suffering, viz, carving (tanha) *(dukhasamudayam ariyasaccam);* 3. There is cessation of suffering *(dukkhanirodha ariyasaccam);* and 4. There is a path leading to the cessation of suffering, viz., eight-fold path *(ariyo attangiko maggo) (dukkhanirodhagamini patipada ariyasaccam)*.

'Dukkha' in Buddhism is a more comprehensive concept than that of suffering. It includes not merely physical and mental suffering, includes also such deeper ideas as imperfection, impermanence, emptiness, conflict, unsubstañtiality, unsatisfactoriness and ignorance *(avijja)* concerning the true nature of man and his existence.

Buddhism speaks of three types of dukkha confronting human existence: *dukkha-dukkhatā, vipariṇāma dukkhatā and sankhāra dukkhatā. Dukkha-dukkhatā* refers to all kinds of ordinary suffering in life such as birth, ageing, death, sorrow, lamentation, pain, grief, despair, etc., *vipariṇāma dukkhatā* refers to the suffering produced by change. The feeling of pleasure *(sukha)* or a pleasant condition in one's life is not permanent. Being ingrained with impermanence *(anicca)*, they change and fade out and can at times become a source of suffering. *Saṅkhāra dukkhatā* refers to the suffering arising in man due to his conditioned state of existence.

The universal causal law *(Praṭiccasamupāda)* states that the cause being present, the effect must originate. Buddha feels that everything in this world takes place in accordance with the causal law. The origin of everything is dependent, conditional and relative. Dukkha being an event, also depends upon some cause. The cause for suffering *(dukkha)* is craving *(tanha)*, it may be craving for sensual pleasures, carving for continued life or craving for power. It is impossible to satiate the ever-following desires of man. Unfulfilled desires, unsatiated cravings lead to disappointment, giving rise to suffering. This craving for things is rooted in the false notion that there is a permanent principle the 'I', which is sought to be satisfied and gratified by the objects sought by the craving. It is this false notion of a permanent 'I' or individuality' or 'personality' that is the root-cause of all suffering.

The cessation of suffering *(dukkha)* can be brought about by the noble eight-fold path *(ariyo attangiko maggo)*. It progressively dismantles the 'I' by showing its illusoriness. With the removal of this illusion, man gains freedom from suffering, i.e., liberation *(nibbāṇa)*. Liberation, for the Buddhist, is a state of freedom from rebirth, whereas for the other systems of Indian philosophy, it is a state of immortality.

The present study seeks to analyze and discuss the conception of dukkha with special reference to early Buddhism, for it is here that Buddhism manifests as that which was primarily concerned with the inquiry into the causes of human suffering and its removal. As we know that the later Buddhism with all its hair-splitting analysis found itself entangled in theoretical and intellectual discussions of different doctrines that have emerged from early Buddhism, than with the actual problem of suffering and its removal.

The concepts concerned to Dukkha are discussed in seven chapters. The first chapter, Introduction gives a brief introduction of the concept of dukkha. The second chapter, Duhkha in Indian Philosophy: An Analysis, deals with the analysis of duhkha in non-buddhist systems. In the third chapter, Dukkha in Early Buddhism, deals with the nature and analysis of dukkha as a motivating factor for philosophical inquiry in early Buddhism. The fourth chapter, The origin of Suffering, attempts a detailed analysis of the Buddhist view as to how the notion of an immutable 'self' is rooted in ignorance and that man is nothing but a complex of the five-fold fleeting aggregates. The buddhist doctrines of *kamma* and *praticcasamupāda* and their role in suffering have been highlighted. The fifth chapter, Means of Deliverance, is devoted to the study of the various components of the eight-fold part *(ariyo attangiko maggo)*. The early Buddhists have categorised these components under three heads: *Sīla* (morality), *Samādhi* (meditation) and *Pañña* (knowledge). An in-depth study of these three stages has been undertaken. The sixth chapter, Nibbāṇa: A State of Deliverance, is devoted to the study of the buddhist conception of Nibbāṇa as the ultimate ideal to the sought after. The concluding chapter, summary, summarizes the results of the discussion in the preceding chapters.

When Buddha teaches that craving is at the root of man's suffeirng, it must be noted that he only suggests that man should liberate himself from the cravings of his 'greed' and not his 'need' (for his survival) as such. This is reflected in his eight-fold path of dhamma as means for deliverance. As we know, Buddha is averse to the two extreme paths of self-mortification and self-indulgence and adopts the middle path.

Dr. Ram Kumar Ratnam
Dr. Bhaskara Rao
Sai Soudha
1-22-10, S.V.N. Colony
Guntur-522006 (A.P.)

Introduction

The study of human civilization is a story of Man's battle against pain and unhappiness. Man has been striving hard to make his existence happy. All Literature: Prose or Poetry, Logic or Grammar, Engineering or Medicine, Arts or Science; reflects man's endeavour in this direction. Man, naturally aims at a state of freedom from suffering, to put it positively achieve a state of happiness. Man is supposed to be exposed to suffering, physical or mental or spiritual or all the three put together. It is physical, in the sense, that it results from injury to the body arising due to one's own action or due to others' actions. It is mental, in that, it originates due to 'unfulfilled' desires. It is spiritual, in the sense, that it has its origin in man's ignorance of his true nature.

Thinkers, sensitive to suffering, have from times immemorial been struggling hard to unearth the causes of human misery and find a way out of it. In fact, it is the perception of 'universal' suffering along with the accompanying sense of curiousity and perplexity that formed the motivating factors for philosophical inquiry, especially in Indian tradition. Dr. S. Radhakrishnan observed that the suffering of the world provokes the problems of philosophy and religion.[1]

Philosophical inquiry in Indian tradition had its origin in man's need to extricate himself from suffering (*duḥkha*)[2]. The senstitiveness of Indian mind to the problem of suffering was so intense that Professor Hiriyanna goes so far as to say that "Philosophy in India did not originate in wonder or curiosity as it seems to have done in the West; but possibly originated under the pressure of moral and physical suffering."[3] Philosophical inquiry and resultant wisdom are tools for man's freedom from suffering. Philosophical wisdom (*tattva-jñāna*) is intended to help us to transcend the sphere of discord and disharmony, sorrows and sufferings of life and arrive at happiness.

The Vedas which form the source for all philosophical speculation in the Indian scene have primarily addressed themselves to the problem of suffering. The vedic sages prayed for a life free from pain in their day to day life. Rishi Gṛtsamada pleads Bṛhaspati in the Rig Veda[4] (II.23.7). "Lord, greatest of great, keep him away from our path, the fiendish shark who, with implacable rancour, tortures us despite our innocence, carve out for us the safe and smooth road to divine happiness". They sought health, happiness, long life endowed with freedom from fear and miseries. They thought that they have no say over these things and they owe these things to some deities behind the forces of nature. Their happiness depended on the propitation of these deities. Hence, they began to please the deities either through invocatory hymns (mantras) or through sacrifices or both. The aim was to attain a state of freedom from pain originating for want of day to day requirements such as food, progeny, gold, cattle; or pains caused by other human beings, animals and birds; Gods and evil forces, and positively, they are aimed at a state of happiness. Rishi Medhātithi addressing a hymn to Varuṇa and Indra observes. "Indra and Varuṇa, quickly bestow happiness (sukha) upon us; for our minds are devoted to you both."[5] Therefore, to ensure obtaining happiness and to avoid suffering they invoke the deities through offerings and sacrifices.

In the upaniṣadic period, a clear demarcation was drawn between the two forms of suffering, empircal and transcendental. Empirical suffering refers to suffering of the physical body and mind arising out of empirical factors such as fever, injury, and natural calamities like floods and storms. These can be overcome by empirical remedies prescribed by medicine and scientific techniques. Transcendental suffering is more threatening than the empirical one. Upaniṣads, therefore addressed themselves primarily for the elimination of transcendental suffering. This suffering arises due to ignorance (*avidyā*). Ignorance concerning the true nature of man. Whether he is of the nature of body or of the nature of the spirit (self). It is the convinction of the upaniṣadic seers that man is of the 'self' (ātman) as distinct from the body. The self is real. It never is born or dies; neither does it become non-existent nor coming into being; it is unborn, eternal, everlasting and primeval.[6] The self cannot be burnt, cut by weapons, drenched by water nor can it be dried by air. It is all pervading, stable, firm and everlasting.[7] It is the body (non-self) which suffers fever, headache and so on for the body by its nature is full of suffering and is the source of all suffering. Prajāpati says. "He who moves about adored in dreams, he is the *ātman,* this self is not blind when this body is blind nor one-eyed when the body is one-eyed not suffers defects of the body, nor is slain when the body is slain..."[8]. Self is free from sin, free from old age, from death and grief, from thirst and hunger[8a]. Suffering is attributed to the self on account of its association with body. It is only right knowledge, that is, discriminative knowledge that `Self' is distinct from the 'Body' alone that can remove all ignorance and thereby all suffering. It is this discriminative knowledge (soul-saving knowledge) that can put an end to the cycle of births and leads to immortality. The *Chāndogya upaniṣad*[9] also confirms that it is the knowledge of the 'self' that helps us overcome suffering. Nārada says to Sanat kumāra, "I know the Rg Veda, the Yajur-veda, the Sāma-veda...., the Itihāsa (the Bhāratha); the Veda of Vedas (grammar) .... I know the Mantras only, the sacred books, I do not know the self". He requests Sanata kumāra to impart the knowledge of the 'self' in order to overcome suffering. He observes: "I have heard from men like you, that he who knows the 'self' overcomes grief. I am in grief. Do, Sir, help me overcome this grief of mine."[10] Equipped with self-knowledge, one gains freedom from the cycle of birth and secures immortality. This is aptly reflected in the *Kaṭha upaniṣad*[11] wherein, Nachiketa realising the conditioned nature of human existence seeks from Yama the secret knowledge of immortality.[11a] The central theme and the watch word of all Upaniṣadic teaching is `know thy self' to overcome all suffering.

Being alive to the fact of suffering the systems of Indian philosophy have addressed themselves to the origin and annihilation of suffering.

Īsvara Kṛṣṇa in his *Sāṅkhya Kārikā* in the very first *Kārikā* states that it is *'duḥkha'* which motivates us for philosophical inquiry.[12] He observes that man is tormented by a three-fold pain namely, *'ādhyātmika'*, *'ādhibhautika'* and *`ādhidaivika'* duḥkha, from birth to death in one form or other. Ādhyātmika duḥkha are pains caused by intrinsic factors such as cold, fever and so on, whereas *ādhibhautika duḥkha* are caused by external agencies like fellow human beings beasts and birds. *Ādhidaivika duḥkha* are the pains that are caused by supernatural agencies. For him, liberation (*mokṣa*) is freedom from the three-fold pain. This freedom, he feels is possible only through philosophical inquiry, for it will enable man to gain discriminative knowledge (*vivekajñāna*) that the *'puruṣa'* is different from the '*prakṛti'*. It is *prakṛti* which suffers and is of the nature of suffering, whereas *puruṣa* is pure eternal consciousness and is never in bondage or suffering, it is always free. It is due to this ignorace that one thinks *puruṣa* is bound and thereby suffers.

In addition to the three-fold pain of *Sāṅkhya*, *Yoga*[13] speaks of another four types of pain namely, 1. *duḥkha* of change *(pariṇāma duḥkha)*, 2. *duḥkha* of anxiety *(Tāpaduḥkha)*, 3. *duḥkha* of habituation (*saṁskāra duḥkha*) and 4. *duḥkha* of qualities (*guṇa duḥkha*). The systems of Nyāya and Vaiśeṣika agree that earthly life is full of suffering. The *Nyāya sārah*[14] identifies twenty one types of *duḥkha*, which man confronts within his existence.

Adi Śaṅkara, the founder of *Advaita Vedānta* seeks refuge in the Almighty to save him from misery of the suffering of *saṁsāra.* "The suffering and sorrow of living as the embryo amidst urine and faecal matter, of disease, decay and death, are unbearable". "Other than you, O Merciful One, I see no other way of release from these". "Why are you not showing me mercy?"[15] The existence of man, recalls Śaṅkara, is comparable to that of 'drops of water' on a lotus leaf.[16] Man's mind dances around like the drop of water under the sway of unceasing desires, such as wealth, relatives, knowledge and others. He feels that the body is permanent and satisfying its requirements is primary. He seeks pleasure and happiness by identifying and attaching himself with the body and fleeting objects of the world. The cause for this suffering is ignorance (*avidyā*). It is the failure to discriminate the real, eternal 'self' from the apparent, impermanent 'body' The body is impure, non-eternal and destructible, that contains the germs of suffering, whereas the 'self' is pure and free from suffering, one should realise this self to be free from pain. It is only self-knowledge, which is self-realisation that can help man to attain freedom from suffering. To quote "Worldly happiness leads to sorrow. Try to know the real 'self', attain a state of freedom from all embodiment, for it points to attachment leading to suffering."[17]

The ideal of life was putting an end to the chain of births and deaths. The *Chāndogya Upaniṣad* VIII.15.1. concludes with the words "And he does not return", meaning he is not born again, since birth involves pain. The *Bṛhadāranyakas Upaniṣad*[18] and *Prasna Upaniṣad*[19] say the same. Kalidasa concludes his drama 'Sakuntala' with the prayer "may self-existent God Siva destroy for me rebirth."[20] Potana, the Telugu poet adducing reasons of undertaking the translation of the Bhagavatam says, that he wants this because it would put an end to his sufferings namely rebirth.

The same idea runs through all other systems, orthodox and heterodox, reaching its climax in Buddhism.

No other Indian thinker was so sensitive to the fact of suffering as Buddha. The Buddha says: "O Monks, two things only do I teach, suffering and the cessation of suffering."[20a] Birth is attended by pain, disease is painful, death is painful and decay is painful.[21] In fact, it was this sensitivity to suffering that forms the guiding ideal for his philosophical investigation. To quote Dr. S. Radhakrishnan, "The melancholy which occupies the foreshadow in the *Upaniṣads* occupies a central place in his philosophy."[22]

The Buddha started his inquiry into the causes for suffering and after a great deal of agonising search found a way out. In short, he arrived at the Four Noble Truths (*Ariya saccāni*):

1. There is suffering (*dukkha*).
2. There is a cause for suffering (*dukkha-saṁudayo*).
3. There is a cessation of suffering (*dukkha-nirodho*) and
4. There is a path leading to cessation of suffering (*dukkha nirodha gāminī paṭipadā ariyasaccaṃ*)[23]

These Four Noble Truths about suffering form the corner stone on which the whole edifice of Buddhist philosophy is founded. The Buddha's prime concern was towards making man aware of the magnitude of suffering dominating his life, realising which one should earnestly strive for the cessation of it. "In this long pilgrimage of repeated births and deaths, you have shed more tears than the waters in all the Four Great oceans, arising out of the various experiences of miseries, such as loss of father, mother, children, wealth or possessions."[24] Every living thing is subject to the six kinds of changes: 1. birth 2. being 3. change, 4. growth, 5. old age and 6. destruction is also subject to suffering (*dukkha*)[24a]. *Yadaniccaṁ taṁ dukkhaṁ*—anything impermanent is painful.[25] This suffering of man is not something which is arbitrary, but is governed by the law of causation, both physical and moral. The wheel of suffering turns around the axis of causation, which is the most intricate of all philosophical issues confronted by the seeking mind. Buddhist thought revolves round this axis to provide man with an enlightenment regarding suffering and its annihilation.

The universal causal law states that, cause being present, effect must originate. The Buddha opines that everything in this world takes place in accordance with the causal law. The origin of everything is conditional, dependent and relative. He feels that the *dukkha* being an event is also dependent upon some cause. It originates from craving (*taṇhā*), which leads man to seek attachment or develop aversion towards the objects of the world depending upon the experiences they generate in him. Man wants and seeks pleasure temporal or ephemeral, the craving for sensual pleasure, the craving for continuous life, the craving for power. It would be impossible to satiate the ever-flowing desires of man. Unfulfilled desires, unsatiated craving leads to disappointment which in turn leads to suffering. This eternal craving for things is rooted in the false notion that, there is a permanent principle the 'I', which is sought to be satisfied and gratified by the objects sought by the craving. It is this false notion of 'I' that is the root-cause of all suffering. The ignorance about the 'I' causes suffering. "No world or thing here below ever feel into misery without having first fallen from folly".[26]

Pain, being an effect produced by its attendant causes, can be eliminated with the removal of its causes. The cessation can be brought about by the Noble Eight-fold Path *ariyo aṭṭangiko maggo.* For, it progressively dismantles the 'I' by showing its illusoriness and with the removal of this illusion, man gains freedom from *dukkha.*

The Buddha affirms that the lack of enlightenment *(pañña)* is an ailment and hence leads to suffering. "He who is not enlightened is ill."[27] He who has not attained liberation *(nibbāṇa)*, therefore suffers. Hence, *'dukkha'* is used in a wide sense in Buddhism. Ignorance *(avijjā)*, absence of enlightenment is a state of suffering. The Buddha visualised 'good' life as that which is free from suffering. It is rooted in loving-kindness *(metta),* compassion *(karuṇā)*, sympathetic joy *(mudita)* and equanimity *(upekkha)*. These four *Brahma Viharas* form the guidelines for good life.

The scope of the book is limited to the analysis of the concept of *dukkha* with special reference to Early Buddhism. It is in the early Buddhism that the problem of suffering received complete attention and is analysed and discussed thoroughly. Early Buddhism refers to the period of Buddhist tradition starting from Sixth century B.C. to the First century A.D.[28] The philosophy of this period presents the analysis of the nature of man, the causes for the suffering and a way out of it. The basic doctrines of early Buddhist philosophy concerning the origination and annihilation of suffering have their basis in the three-fold Buddhist scriptural cannon known as *Tipiṭakas:*[29] *Vinaya, Sutta* and *Abhidhamma.*

There is controversy regarding the actual "teachings' of the Buddha: whether the contents of the *tipiṭaka* constitute the words of the Buddha or whether these are interspersed with the views of the followers of Buddha (elders-*Theravādins*). Soon after the Buddha's death, controversy set in amongst his followers regarding the Master's teachings. The first three councils[30], were held in order to isolate and identify the actual teachings of the Buddha from the interpolations. Some of the living disciples of Buddha such as Mahākassappa, Upāli[31] and Ānanda[32] did participate in the First Council held a little more than three months after the *parinibbāṇa* of the Buddha at Rajagaha, to rehearse and finalise the teachings of the Master.[33] Some disciples like Puraṇa preferred not to take part in the First Council and said that he preferred to stick to what he had heard from the Master's lips.

It is natural that when the discourses of the Buddha were handled and handed down, many changes, omissions and commissions, must have crept in. There is no doubt that it is difficult to isolate and identity the actual teachings of the Buddha, but it is not impossible to do it when we take an overall picture of the Buddhist teachings. Those that do not cohere with the fundamental tenets of the Buddhist doctrines could easily be eliminated. George Grimm[34] in his monumental work *'The Doctrine of the Buddha'* while aware of the difficulty in isolating the teachings of the Buddha from interpolations does not give up hope to identify them. He cites the instance of an archaeologist who reconstructs a dilapidated temple with the available stones, on the basis of a ground plan. It is true that the effort to isolate the teachings of the Buddha from those of the Buddhist is riddled with problems. It is for this reason that the councils were constituted. If there is doubt inspite of the Buddhist councils regarding the actual 'teachings' of the Buddha, perhaps, it is not possible to resolve them we may have to rely on the contents of the *tipiṭaka* as a whole and not on the basis of the views of any one particular doctrine to understand the teachings of the Buddha. The views of the Buddha on different doctrines should cohere, and only when there are inconsistencies between the views on different doctrines, certainly a doubt crops up regarding the genuineness of the Buddhist teachings. Under such circumstances views that do not cohere with the overall position may have to be discarded as alien to the Buddhist ideas.

Realising the difficulties involved in delineating the teachings of the Buddha from those of his subsequent followers, the present analysis relies on the contents of the *tipiṭakas* and immediate commentaries on them. Care has been taken to understand the Buddha on the basis of the over all teachings of the *tipiṭakas*. The *tipiṭakas* consists of three sections: *Vinaya, Sutta* and *Abhidhamma*. The *Vinaya piṭaka* consists of four texts: *Sutta Vibhaṅga, Mahāvagga, Culla-vagga* and *Parivārapāṭha,* dealing mainly with the question of discipline of monastic life. The *Sutta piṭaka* which consists of five *nikāyas (pañcanikāyas)*: *Dīgha, Majjhima, Saṃyutta, Aṅguttara,* and *Khuddakanikāya*[35] contains the observations of the Buddha on philosophical doctrines. The Buddha with the help of analogies and similies, has effectively communicated the essence of his teachings, that is *dhamma* to the common masses. The *Abhidhammapitka* consists of seven texts (*Sattaparana*): *Vibhaṅga, Dhātukatha, Puggala-paññatti Kathāvatthu, Yamaka, Dhammasaṅgaṇi* and *Paṭṭhana.* This section presents the philosophical doctrines in cryptic terminology.

The scriptural texts were orally transmitted through recitation by different groups of disciples known as *Bhanākas*[36] and were actually compiled and committed to writing not earlier than the last quarter of the First century B.C.[37] The language used in the *tipiṭakas* was *Pāli*, which was the dialect of the common masses of Magādha.[38] The Buddha opted for *Pāli,* for he felt that only the use of the language of the masses would form an effective means of communication. Apart from the *tipiṭakas,* the study and analysis of the early Buddhist conception of *dukkha* is incomplete without a study of the commentaries of the *tipiṭakas*. These commentaries (*bhāṣyas*) or compendium (*smgrahas*) are of utmost importance for the understanding of the doctrines embedded in the Buddhist scriptures. Apart from the usage of the important commentaries on the *tipiṭakas,* the *Vimuttamagga* (Way of emancipation) by Upatissa; the *Visuddhimagga* (Path of purification) by Buddhaghosa which is commonly referred to as the compendium of early Buddhism; *Milandapañha,* is one of the most important, as an exegesis of different early Buddhist doctrines, have been used in this study.

The study is presented in five chapters. The first chapter *'Duḥkha in Indian Philosophy': 'An Analysis'* is divided into two sections. The first section deals with the understanding and analysis of *duḥkha* in the non-Buddhist systems of Indian philosophy. The second section is exclusively devoted to the presentation of the *Early Buddhist conception of dukkha.* In the second chapter: *'The origin of dukkha'*, the constituents of human existence as carrying intrinsically the germs of suffering is brought out. The multifaceted aspects of *kamma* and causation that put such components of human existence to work is dealt with. The third chapter: *'means of deliverance'* is devoted to the study of the various components of the *Ariyo Aṭṭangiko Maggo* prescribed by the Buddha to overcome suffering (*dukkha*). The fourth chapter: *'Nibbāna': 'a state of deliverance'* is devoted to the study of the Buddhist conception of *Nibbāna* as a state of freedom from suffering. The various interpretations of *Nibbāna* have also been analysed. The concluding chapter presents the summary of the findings in other chapters in a succinct way.

REFERENCES

1. Radhakrishnan, S. *Indian Philosophy,* Vol. I, p. 364.
2. The English term 'suffering' is being used in the study as there is no exact term in English language, which can convey the full meaning and connotation of the term *duḥkha. Duḥkha* in the Indian philosophical tradition is a much more comprehensive concept.
3. Hiriyanna, M. *Outlines of Indian Philosophy,* p. 17.
4. *Ṛg. Veda,* II. 23.7.
5. *Ṛg. Veda.,* I. 17.8.
6. *Bhagavat Gītā.,* II. 20. Ref. *Hindu Scriptures,* Hymns from Ṛg Veda, Upaniṣads and Bhagavat Gītā (Ed.) N. Macnicol, London J.M. Dent Sons Ltd., New York, 1957, p. 231.
7. *Ibid.* II, 23-24.

8. *Chāndogya Upaniṣad:* VIII. 10. 1-4.

8a. *Chāndogya Upaniṣad:* VIII. 7, 3.

9. *Chāndogya Upaniṣad:* VII. 1.2.

10. *Chāndogya Upaniṣad:* VII. 1.3. I. Also in the *Bṛhadāraṇyaka Upaniṣad.* II. 4.3: Maithreyi implores Yajñāvalkya to give her the knowledge of the 'means' to attain immortality instead of material wealth. For material wealth cannot help one overcome suffering, permanently. It is self-knowledge that can lead one to *mokṣa.*

11. *Kaṭhoupaniṣad.* I. 1-6.

12. *Sāṅkhya Kārikā*—I duḥkha trayā 'bhighātāj jijñāsā tadabhighātake hetu. Trans & Ed. S.S.S. Shastri., p. 1.

13. *Yoga Sūtras* II. 15.

14. *Nyāya Sārāh* p. 59-60, 66.

15. Adi Śaṅkarācharya, *Siva Bhujangaṁ* (Ref. Śaṅkara: *The Missionary,* Central Chinmaya Mission Trust, Bombay, 1978) Verse, 31.

16. Adi Śankarācharya, *Bhaja Govindam,* Verse, 4 (Trns. & Comm., C. Rajagopalachari).

17. Sadhāna Pañchakaṁ–Introduction to Seekers Verse (Ref. Śānkara: *The Missionary*-P. 166).

18. *Bṛhadāraṇyaka Upaniṣad.* VI. 2.15.

19. *Prasno Upaniṣad.* 1.10.

20. "Punarbhavam Parigata Śatirātmabhuḥ" Abhijñāna Śākantala. Ed. Prof. R.M. Bose, p. 806. meter Ructirā-Ja bha sa Jaga.

20a. *Cullavagga,* IX, I., 4.

21. *Dīgha Nikāya,* II. 304.

22. Radhakrishnan, S., *Indian philosophy.,* Vol. I., p. 362.

23. The Buddhists belonging to all the sects and those of all countries wherein Buddhism is practised hold that there is no difference in accepting the Dhammacakkappavattana Sutta as the basic tent of Buddhas' teaching. Nalinakshi Dutt in his book *Aspects of Mahāyāna Buddhism* (p. 49) points to the fact that 'though the Hinayānists and the Mahāyānists did not agree regarding the conception of *Sunyata,* there is no disagreement among them in regard to the fact that Buddha preached the Four Truths and the Causal Law. But Scholars like A.J. Bahm have disputed this claim. Bahm opines in his book *'Philosophy of Buddha'* (p. 15) that the basic doctrine of Buddha is, "desire for what will not be attained ends in frustration, therefore, to avoid frustration, avoid desiring what will not be attained". He

contends that the Four Noble Truths are a later addition made by the disciples of Buddha, to make his teachings more easy and acceptable among themselves. The utterances of Buddha may have been cryptic, as was the fashion of philosophising in those days. Buddha was not averse to the idea that his staunch disciples such as Mahākassapa were at liberty to expound on the teachings, as long as they did not do away or do any violence to the teachings. In fact, in the *Petakopadesa* we find a passage, wherein such type of analysis is an accepted practice. To quote: "While the letters, the terms, the phrases, the moods, the language, and the demonstration of the Noble Truth of Dukkha are of ungauged measure" (Aug. ii. 182). "They are taught nevertheless by explaining, and describing, of that very meaning. And so of all the Truths". *Petakopedesa* p.5 (13). Further, Mrs. Rhys Davids provides reasons for doubting the present form of the First Sermon. She points out that as 'Titular Items' the Four Noble Truths do not appear in the Fourth Nipāta of the *Aṅguttara Nikāya,* or the *Sangiti Sutta* of the *Dīgha Nikāya.* (Ref. *What was the original gospel in Buddhism?* (p. 139). Professor Pande also supports it with the scriptural evidence from the *Dīgha Nikāya* Sutta 16.3.50 that 'the four noble truths do not form a part of the list of 37 Bodhipakhiya Dhammas which are supposed to have been the dying charge of the Master' (Ref. *Studies in the Origin of Buddhism,* p. 398).

Further, whether this particular formulation of duḥkha as cause, cessation and the path has been likened to the four-fold means of medical treatment. Though this formulation might have been borrowed from Medicine and given by Buddha's disciples, yet I feel that it does not do any injustice to Buddha's teaching of *dukkha.* It is a 'methodological' device' which might have been formulated, so as to render Buddha's doctrine more comprehensive and communicable to the common masses.

24. *Saṁyutta Nikāya,* Vol. I, fol. thai, as quoted by Oldenberg., *The Buddha, His life, His doctrine, His order,* p. 216.

24a. *Buddha Cākka.,* p. 7.

25. *Dhammapada.,* 277.

26. Radhakrishnan, S., *Indian philosophy,* 1983, Vol. I. p. 412. footnotes. (Caryle, Letter-days Pamphlets.).

27. R.O. Birnbaun-The *Healing Buddha,* pp. 13-14, London. 1976.

28. Vis. Maga. *The Path of Purification* (Trans) Bhikkhu N+ṭānamoli, Introduction page IX and Th. Stcherbaksky, *The Conception of Buddhist Nirvāna,* Introduction. p. 2.

29. *Tipiṭakas* literally means 'Three baskets', 'Tri' three and 'piṭaka'-basket. Just as in an excavation, wherein the earth dug out is transmitted to the top through a chain of workers in a basket in relay, similarly, the teachings, and doctrines of the Buddha were memorised and transmitted by the *Bhanākas.* Among the *Bhanākas* some are referred to as *Suttantikas*

(reciters of *Suttanatas*), some as *Dhammakathikas* (Preachers of the *Dhamma*) and some as *Vinayadharas* (experts in the *Discipline*) *Cullavagga* IV. 44.

30. Law, Bimala Churn, *A Manual of Buddhist Historical Traditions (Saddhamma Saṅgha)*, University of Calcutta, 1963, pp. 4., 23 to 56. The first three councils were held: 486 B.C. Rajagaha; 373 B.C. at Veśāli and 273 B.C. Aśokarama respectively. (Aśokarama is commonly known as Pataliputra).

31. *Ibid*. p. 25. There is mention of Upāli as being chosen by the Council of Elders to narrate the *Vinaya*. For he was considered to be well-versed and an expert on the *Vinaya* tests.

32. Ibid. p. 76. The text speaks of Ānanda, an expert in the discourses of Buddha being asked to narrate the Sutta Moreover, Ānanda being the personal attendant to the Master had the unique opportunity of listening to most of the discourses of the Master.

33. Ibid., cf. Geiger, *Dipavamsa and Mahāvaṁasa*, pp. 108 ff.

34. Grim George: *The Doctrine of the Buddha*., p. 24.

35. The texts under *Khuddaka Nikāya* are: *Khuddakapāṭha, Dhammapada, Udāna, Itivuttaka, Suttanipāta, Vimānavathu, Petavatthu, Theragāthaā, Therigāthā, Jātaka, Niddesa, Paṭisaṁbhidāmagga, Apadānas, Buddhavaṁsa* and *Cariyāpiṭaka*.

36. *Mahāvaṁsa:* Ch. XXXII., VV. 100, 102.

37. Law, B.C. *A Manual of Historical Tradition (Saddhammna-Saṁgha)* of. Dipavaṁsa, Ch. XX, 20-24: speaks that during the reign of the Lankan King Vattagāminī-ābhaya (433 years after the Buddha's parinibbāṇa), the Order of Monks felt the necessity of 'putting' down the *Tipiṭakas* and the *Atthakathas* in writing. For, they feared that with the decline of *Sāsana* (religion) and of the people, the entire sayings of the Buddha, comprised in the *Tipiṭakas* with the text and commentaries would be lost. Under the patronage of the King, the Order of monks selected many thousand learned Elders (experts in the Tipiṭakas, with advanced insight, able to refute the three-fold knowledge of the Vedas and other misleading interpretations and interpolations of Buddhist teachings) in order to hold the fifth council for the above purpose. Thera Mahākassapa, Thera Yasa, Thera Tima, Thera Mahīnda and other learned Elders after reciting the *Vinaya, Sutta* and *Abhidhamma Piṭakaś* had them committed in written form.

38. *Ibid*. p. xxxiii.

2

Duḥkha in Indian Philosophy

INTRODUCTION

Whether it be orthodox or heterodox systems, suffering (*duḥkha*) is the motivating factor for philosophical inquiry in Indian tradition. The analysis of *duḥkha*, in respect of its origin and annihilation figures prominently in all the systems of Indian Philosophy. Each system analyses and understands *duḥkha* within its ontological framework. The present chapter devoted to the analysis of *duḥkha* as found in non-Buddhist schools of Indian Philosophy. This analysis of *duḥkha* by the different non-Buddhist systems of Indian Philosophy can be brought under two categories namely, the materialistic and the non-materialistic interpretations. The former view is the of the Cārvākas whereas the latter is held by all other systems, orthodox and heterodox.

The Cārvāka View

The Cārvākas accept the fact of *duḥkha* arising out of a person's experience of objects through the senses.[1] An experience is termed as *duḥkha*, when it produces a feeling of pain, dislike, conflict and misery. *Duḥkha* is described as an experience in which the senses are not satisfied.[2] It is a feeling contradictory to one's liking. Disharmony, uneasiness and instability are the characters of *duḥkha*.

Suffering Pertains Only to the Body

In line with their materialistic outlook, the Cārvākas conceive of all things in the world, animate and inanimate, as originating from the different permutations and combinations of the four elements (*Mahābhūtas*), namely earth (*pṛthvi*), water (*āpo*), fire (*tejas*) and air (*vāyu*).[3] The physical body (*śarira*) is nothing but an aggregation of these *mahābhūtas* in a particular combination.[4] Consciousness (*Cetanā*) has no existence apart from these four elements. Just as the red colour is produced by pounding a combination of line, arecanut and betal leaf, similarly consciousness arises out of these elements when they are combined in a certain way. The self *(ātman)* is identical with the physical body.[5] There is no *ātman* over and above the perceptible body. It is this body which is the seat of all experiences, be it *sukha* or *duḥkha*. The *ātman* perishes along with the body's death.[6]

The world that we perceive and enjoy as the source of our tangible experience, is only the real world. *Mokṣa,*[7] in the sense of a state of freedom from pain implies a state of pure disembodied bliss being is only a mirage. The man striving for it is comparable to a weary, tired and thirsty traveller lost in the vast expanse of sand. He chases the mirage of an oasis, moving in a direction exactly opposite from the source. When all the good things and pleasures are imminent it would be futile to think, wonder and strive for the non-existent pleasures, of attaining *mokṣa*. All pleasant things could be enjoyed fully with the senses being adequately fed and satisfied.

Bṛhaspati observes the 'pleasure' which produces experiences of *sukha,* involves the proper understanding and avoidance of its deterrents like *duḥkha*.[8] He accepts that there is no hell other than mundane *duḥkha*.[9] These *duḥkha* are primarily products of purely mundane causes.[10] The causes are present within the object itself. All objects in this mundane world by *svabhāva* are full of *duḥkha*, for they are ingrained with the germs of decay and destruction. He further contends that there is no such thing as pure, absolute *sukha*. A feeling is termed as *sukha* or *duḥkha* depending upon the dominating factors of 'pleasure' or 'pain', in that particular experience. But this does not mean that man should totally avoid seeking or enjoying *sukha,* since it is never altogether free from *duḥkha*. Just as people do not stop cooking for the fear of beggars, just as people do not avoid going in for roses, because there are thorns. Man should use his rationality for avoiding the factors of *duḥkha* and enjoy the factors of *duḥkha*. Just as a person who wants to eat fish, carefully avoids the bones,[11] so also men should seek 'pleasure' and avoid 'pain'.

The Sāṅkhya-Yoga View

Among the orthodox schools of Indian philosophy, Sāṅkhya[12] and Yoga[13] give utmost importance to the analysis and discussion of *duḥkha*, the factors giving rise to it and the means of overcoming it. Īśvara Kṛṣṇa, in the very first *kārikā* of his *Sāṅkhya Kārikā* states that men are tormented by a three-fold pain.[14] He considers that the need for philosophical inquiry arises in the context of eliminating this three-fold pain. "Duḥkha-trayā-'bhighataj jijñāsā ṭadabhighātake hetu" "dṛṣte sā 'pārthṭā-cennai' kāntā-'tyanyato'-bhāvāt." *Sāṅkhya Kārikā* 1.1

Pātañjali, the founder of Yoga, speaks of the omnipresence of suffering in worldly existences.[15] Vyāsa refers to *duḥkha* as a necessity of all life, for it poses a challenge and stimulates man to transcend it.[16]

Duḥkha arises from man's attachment (*rāga*) and desire (*icchā*) for the objects of the phenomenal world[17] and aversion (*dveṣa*) for the unpleasant objects,[18] which are caused by ignorance (*avidyā*). Ignornace brings about the false identification of the real self (*ātman*) with the objective, unreal world and its objects of experience,[19] which causes pain.[20] The sense-object contact which results from this process of attachment and aversion, produces merit and demerit, which decide and produce experiences of *sukha* and *duḥkha.*[20]

Types of Duḥkha

Commenting on the three-fold pain that men are exposed to as stated by Īśvara, *Kṛṣṇa, in Sāṅkya Kārikā* Vācaspati Miśra in *Sāṅkhya Tattva Kaumadī* specifically mention them as *ādhyātmika, ādhibhautika* and *ādhidaivika.*[22]

1. *Ādhyātmika Duḥkha:* They are the pains caused by factors from within. They are of two kinds. Those that have their source in the body and those that originate from the mind.[23]

Bodily or physical pains are those caused by ailments such as cold, fever, headache and so on. Mental pains arise from factors which are purely psychological in nature. The *Sāṅkhya Tattva Kaumuadī* speaks of desire, wrath, avarice, affection, fear, envy, grief and non-perception of particular objects as sources of mental suffering.[24] Mental pains are more tormenting than bodily pains, for they leave behind a permanent scar on the mind, which man carries till his death. The bodily wounds, though painful, are temporary. They subside on receipt of medical attention. But the agony and torment which he suffers in mental pain lasts longer and is more tormenting.

2. *Ādhibhautika duḥkha:* They are those pains that are caused by external factors, such as birds, animals, fellow-beings and inanimate objects.[25] They produce two kinds of *duḥkha*, bodily (*S'ariraka ādhibhautika duḥkha*) and mental (*Manasika*

ādhibhautika duḥkha). For example, when a man gets beaten up, or collides with an inanimae object, he suffers from physical injury and resultant bodily *duḥkha*. Mental pains are those that man suffers when he is abused or discredited.

3. *Ādhidaivika duḥkha*: There are the pains that are caused by supernatural agencies such as evil spirits, planets, devils and such other superhuman agencies.[26] Floods, earthquakes, cyclones and other catastrophes, which result in manifold suffering are said to be caused by the influence of these supernatural forces. The suffering of this kind includes all those pains for which causes could not be identified within the realm of nature.

Yoga Sūtras[27] *speak of four different types of* duḥkha.

1. Duḥkha of change (Pariṇāma duḥkha)

Pariṇāma duḥkha is based on the principle that 'everything in this world is subject to the Universal law of change'. These changes fall under one of two kinds namely subjective and objective. Subjectively, there is no guarantee that a particular 'object' that has been a source of pleasure at a particular time should continue to be so at a later time. For instance, a certain person with whom one has friendly relations develops acquaintance with a bad person to whom we do not have liking: this knowledge brings a subjective change, because of which what had been a source of pleasure in the past now has become a source of pain. Objectively, it refers to the pain generated due to man's ignorance about the inherent change and decay to which all objects are bound. Man who thinks that there objects are permanent and the experiences produced thereof are also permanent, is bound to suffer, for the changed object may give a different kind of experience at a later date.

2. Duḥkha of anxiety (Tāpa duḥkha)

It arises from the feeling of misery and pain generated through man's attachment to (*rāga*) and aversion (*dveṣa*) for certain objects. Man, for instance, prays and works for possession of objects such as wealth, his own children and so on, for their presence produces within him an experience of pleasure. Again, he fervently strives to avoid contact with the objects of dislike such as disease, accidents and so on for they produce an experience of pain.

One might ask as to how attachment with the objects of pleasure would produce pain; it is a fact of our experience that man gets attached to those objects which are sources of pleasure. But he is constantly seized with the fear, that he is likely to be deprived of them, because these objects may be stolen, destroyed by fire, or get separated from him. This fear of deprivation torments him even when he enjoys them. It is this fear which produces the *duḥkha of anxiety*.

3. Duḥkha of habituation (Saṁskāra duḥkha)

Every experience of a certain object or a fact leaves behind an impression in our mind. For instance, our experience of eating sweets, leaves an impression of pleasure in our minds and man has a tendency to seek such objects which yielded pleasure in the past. Such impressions, which direct us towards objects of enjoyment, whether fulfilled or unfulfilled, invariably lead to misery. Being objects of pleasure, they lead to misery, when we are not able to experience them and also owing to excessive addiction to them, when fulfilled.

4. Duḥkha of qualities (Guṇa duḥkha)

It emanates from man's lack of discriminative knowledge about the true nature and functioning of the qualities. The physical body of man and objects of experience are nothing but the complexes of the three qualities: *sattva, rajas* and *tamas.*[28] Each of these three *guṇas* enjoins specific characteristics: *sattva*-illumination, *rajas*-energy and *tamas*-inertia, respectively. It is the joint functioning of these which produce an idea or experience, be it *sukha* or *duḥkha*.

When an experience is dominated by *sattva,* we have *sukha* whereas the domination of *rajas* and *tamas* leads to pain and misery, respectively. Lack of knowledge about the functioning of the *guṇas* lead to pain.[28a] For instance, Ravana, the great King of Lanka, whose actions were guided by *rajas* and *tamas,* inspite of his bravery, was subject to pain and misery. The wise, therefore should guard themselves against the delusions of the empirical world made of *sattva, rajas* and *tamas*. They should realise that this world is full of misery in its essence and should work for a way out.

Process of Duḥkha Generation (Guṇa Theory)

All *duḥkha* are confined to the physical body. The physical body, for them is made up of the three gunas of *prakṛti, sattva, rajas* and *tamas.*[29] *Sattva* is of the nature of pleasure (*Priti*)[30] It expresses itself as illumiantion.[31] It is buoyant and illumianting. *Rajas* is of the nature of pain (*aprīti*)[32], which expresses itself as activity. It is excited and mobile.[33] *Tamas* is of the nature of indifference (*Viṣāda*)[34], which expresses itself as delusion. It is heavy and eveloping.[35]

According to *Sāṅkhya* the three *guṇas* are mutually opposed.[36] They are in a state of armed neutrality (*Sāmyāvasthā*) at the beginning of evolution.[37] The process of products of evolution are determined by the victorious *guṇa*. When *sattva* dominates, *buddhi* is produced. From *buddhi ahaṁkāra* is produced. From *sattvic ahaṁkāra* the eleven organs[38] are produced. From *tamasic ahaṁkāra,* the five subtle elements[39] are produced. These elements produce the five gross elements.[40] Thus, *prakṛti* furnishes the entire universe through the three *guṇas.*[41]

Vācaspathi Miśra commenting on *Sāṅkhya kārikā* XIII speaks of all human experiences as being an admixture of these three *guṇas*. It is the proportion of each of these three *guṇas* in a given experience, which decides the final nature of an experience. When *sattva* dominates over *rajas* and *tamas,* we have an experience of *sukha.* When *rajas* and *tamas*[42] dominate in an experience, the final nature of the experience is *duḥkha*. The three *guṇas* operate through mutual suppression, support production and intercourse.

Freedom from Duḥkha

Pātañjali in the Yoga Sūtras[43] speaks of nine different obstalces, they are sickness (*vyadhi*), mental laziness (*styāna*) doubt (*saṁśaya*), lack of enthusiasm (*pramāda*), sloth (alasya), craving for pleasure (*avirati*), false perception (*bhrāniti*), despair caused by failure to concentrate (*darśāna ālabdhabhumi-katva*), and unsteadiness in concentration (*ānavāsthitatvā*) to gain knowledge about the true nature of the self. These obstacles produce mental modifications which result in experience of misery, loss of mental balance and certain physiological changes in the body.[44] These obstacles are products of affliction, which are five-fold, ignorance (*avidyā*), egoism (*ahaṁkāra*), attachment (*rāga*), aversion (*dveṣa*) and fear of death (*abhinivesa*).[45] These afflictions, in turn, are products of unreal cognitions. These cognitions arise from the deluded mind, covered with the cloud of ignorance. Therefore, Pātañjali concludes that *avidyā* is the root-cause of all suffering.[46] Vācaspati Miśra, commenting on Yoga Sutra II.4. feels that *avidyā* refers to the lack of knowledge about 'self'. Self-knowledge (*ātma-jñāna*) alone, he feels, can free the mind from the fetters of ignorance. The remedy prescribed is both physical and mental which takes the form of the eight limbs of yoga.[46a]

Īśvara kṛṣna also contends that the only remedial measure for overcoming the three-fold *duḥkha* is discriminative wisdom (*vivekajñāna*) of the *puruṣa* being different from *prakṛti* and its products. Philosophical inquiry helps man to acquire this discriminative wisdom.

"—— Vyaktā-ayakata-jña-vijñānat", *Śloka 2, Sā.ṇkhya kārikā."*

Vācaspati Miśra, commenting on śloka 2 of Sāṅkhya Kārikā in his Tattva Kaumudī,[48] explains the difference between the two metaphysical realities, *puruṣa* and *prakṛti*. *Prakṛti* is non-intelligence. It has evolved due to the work of the ultimate single cause, which though evolved, is not evolved. The purpose of this evolution relates to an intelligent being, *puruṣa*. *Puruṣa* is neither the cause, nor effect of the process of evolution, yet knows both. The knower (*puruṣa*), understanding this relationship, realises that the knowing, experiencing subject is other than and different in nature from the objects of experience. It is *prakṛti,* which produces these experiences of *sukha* and *duḥkha*. With the dawn of this wisdom that *duḥkha* is not of the subject (*puruṣa*) man is delivered from his *duḥkha*.[49]

3. The Nyāya-Vaiśeṣika view

The Nyāya sūtra defines *duḥkha* as obstructs or occasions a sense of constraints.[50] "Badhana lakṣanam duḥham iti". (*Nyāya Sūtras* I.1.21.)

It hinders or obstructs the soul (*ātman*) in realising its true nature.

Vātsyāyana, commenting on the Nyāya Sūtra I.1.21., terms *badhana* as annoyance.[51] Annoyance, primarily refers to pain.[52] Secondly, it refers to all factors, including body, which contribute to our experience of pain.[53] Vācaspathi Miśra, commenting on Nyāya Sūtra I.1.21., contends that *duḥkha* is not merely physical or ordinary suffering. It stands for a broader conception of 'unhappiness' and 'disharmony'.[54]

Praśastapāda, in his *bhāṣya,* defines *duḥkha* as a feeling of disharmony, unfavourableness and undesirableness.[55] It is of the nature of harm (*upaghāta*), whereby one is harmed (*upahanyate*)[56]. It is feeling of anger; and the idea of harm is its expression. This feeling essentially arises, when actions performed are contrary to the established '*dharma'*. *Dharma* is that, from which results the accomplishment of true knowledge of the categories (*padārthas*)[57] It also refers to the path of righteousness, which avoids the pitfalls of *duḥkha*.[58] Śaṅkāra Misra mentions it as that, which brings about the annihilation of the attributes of the soul including *duḥkha*.[59]

Types of Duḥkha

Bhāsarvajña in the *Nyāyasāra,* using the concept of *duḥkha* in a very broad sense, identifies twenty-one different types of *duḥkha*, which man has to undergo during his empirical existences.[60]

"Tatra heyam duḥkhaman agatam ekavimśati prakāram śarīram, ṣaḍindiriyāṁ saḍviṣayāh ṣaḍbuddhayaḥ sukha duḥkhe ceti" *Nyāyasāra.*

Broadly speaking, these *duḥkha* can be brought under three categorises; those pertaining to: 1. sense-organs, 2. body, and 3. pleasure and pain. We can discern three ways in which each of these sense-organs could be a source for *duḥkha*. Firstly, it may be due to a defect in the sense-organ. For instance, a person with a defective eye might not be able to see things properly, which can lead to his not being able to experience/ enjoy the beauty of nature and so on. Secondly, it may be due to wrong presentation of the objects under consideration by the sense-organ. For instance, a person in the dark perceives a statue to be a ghost. Thirdly, it may originate due to the wrong analysis and judgment by the intellect (*buddhi*) of the material supplied by the sense-organ. For instance, a person in dark mistakes a rope for a snake and suffers from fear of having seen a 'real' snake.

Bodily *duḥkha* refers to the physical and mental pains produced in the physical body. The physical body, resultant of *ātman's* past deeds,[61] is the vehicle of the sense-organs and objects. The sense-organs are benefited by their stay in the body and by whose injury, the body is injured. It is the body which is the receptacle, whenever the feeling of pleasure and pain caused by the contact between the body, sense-organs and objects appear. It is the body which suffers and is also a source of *duḥkha*.[62] Vātsyāyana contends that meditating on the body as suffering, helps one to attain liberation from *duḥkha*.[63]

Pleasure is also taken as pain, for there is no pleasure, which is free from the element of pain. Man suffers even when he is enjoying pleasure, for the fear that this pleasant experience will end is imminent. Further, man also suffers when the pleasure generated is not upto his expectations.[64]

World as Full of Suffering

Gautama observes that suffering starts from the moment of conception and exists till death. Man suffers from some sort of pain or the other during his existence.[65] The Naiyāyikas subscribe to the view that all the *bhuvanās*[66] of this universe and all forms of rebirth are invariably connected with *duḥkha*.[67] It is only in their intensities, that they differ. Vātsyāyana distinguishes three degrees of *duḥkha*: 1. mild (*hīnā*), 2. moderate (*madhyamā*), and 3. severe (*utkṛṣṭā*). He speaks of devas also being afflicted by *duḥkha*.[69] Thus, life of a being residing in any region of the universe is invariably connected with *duḥkha*.

Vātsyāyana, commenting on *Nyāya sūtras* IV. i. 55 & 56 in support of the statement that 'the world is full of *duḥkha*',[70] highlights certain basic facts. The cause for man's suffering is his longing (*paryesanā*), for the objects of pleasure. He visualises five situations, which though look apparently pleasureable ultimately end in pain:

1. A man attains the so called pleasurable experience, but it will not be a 'permanent' thing. With the passage of time, the pleasant experience may change or get destroyed.

2. He may not be able to attain the desired goal. This automatically produces in his a feeling of *duḥkha*

3. Though he may attain it, he feels that the experience of pleasure generated, falls short of this expectation. There is difference between the expected nature, form, intensity of pleasure and the actually obtained pleasure. This also produces an experience of *duḥkha*.

4. He may attain the goal of pleasure, but only after going through a number of difficulties, which involves a great deal of labour and pain. Thereby, he has to undergo *duḥkha*, in order to gain *sukha*.

5. Man is not easily satisfied with the fulfilment of a particular desire of pleasure. On the contrary, it acts as a stimulus for more craving, for these objects of pleasure. For example a poor man may think that one thousands rupees would make him 'wealthy'. But, on achieving it, finds that it does not satisfy his expectations and needs. This sets into motion the process of desire, willing and activity towards the direction of wealth-hunting. Even if he would have conquered the whole world of material comforts, he would be left desiring for something else.

It can be seen from the above analysis of Vātsyāyana that, each of the above five situations, though produces apparent pleasures, in its ultimate analysis, it produces *duḥkha*.

Factors Causing Duḥkha

Gautama[71] and Kaṇāda[72] speak of three main factors which cause activity, and resultant experience of suffering. They are (1) Desire (*Icchā*) 2. Aversion (*Dveṣa*) and 3. Ignorance (*Avidyā*).

1. **Desire (Icchā)**: It is the yearning 'for the unattained'. It is of two types: egoistic (*svārtha*) and altruistic (*Parārtha*). Egoistic yearning is a desire to attain

something for one's own self, which it does not possess. Altruistic yearning is a desire to attain something for others, which they do not possess.

Kaṇāda observes that, Man aspires for objects from which he derived pleasure in the past. He longs for attachment (*rāga*) with such objects.[73] Śaṅkara Misra, commenting on *Vaiśeṣika Sūtra* VI.2.13.,[74] speaks of every being as having desire corresponding to its distinct birth. For example, human beings have the desire for rice/wheat and so on, animals of the deer class, for grass and other vegitation. Desires could have originated from one of the several factors namely 1. sexual desire (*kāma*), 2. selfishness (*matsāra*), 3. enjoyment of worldly pleasures (*tṛṣṇa*), 4. longing for other's properties (*spṛha*) and 5. greed (*lobha*).[75] Desire is conditioned by three factors in its operation as mental actions. They are: 1. connection of the *ātman* with the mind (*mānas ātmamanah saṁyogah*); 2. experience of *sukha* and 3. recollection of *sukha* leading to the expectation of similar experience in future.[76] It initiates nine different kinds of mental modifications, namely sexual craving (*kāma*), appetite (*avilāsha*), passion (*rāga*), resovle (*saṅkālpa*), compassion (*karuṇyā*), Dispassion (*vairāgya*), Insincerity (*upadhā*) concealed desire (*bhāva* and desire for actions (*chikīrṣa*).[77] The body guided and conditioned by these mental modifications of the *manas* performs different *karmas.* The resultant experiences of these *karmas,* in the final analysis, are full of *duḥkha.*

2. *Aversion (Dveṣa):* It is a vindictive state of the mind, which is obssessed with the feeling that, the contact with a particular object will generate a feeling of pain. It is the repulsion towards those objects regarded as unfavourable, for the production of *sukha*, such as disease, thorns and so on. Man develops a feeling of dislike for certain objects, for he feels that contact with these would affect the harmony of the mind. With the disturbance of the mental balance, the mind is bound to generate a feeling of uneasiness, resulting in pain and misery. It produces a burning sensation in the subject (*Devesaḥ prajvalanātmakaḥ*)[78] Like desire, it has its cause in habituation, *adṛṣṭam* and racial distinctions.[79] It is conditioned by three factors namely, 1. contact of the self (*ātman*) with the *manas* (*ātma-manahsaṁyoga*), 2. experience of *duḥkha*, 3. recollections of the *duḥkha* leading to the apprehension of it in future.[80] *Dveṣa* originates from certain factors namely, 1. Anger (*krodha*) 2. Envy (*amarsha*), 3. Malice (*manyu*), 4. long to cause injury (*droha*) and 5. Intolerance (*akshamā*). These activate the body through the mind into performing *karmas* and produce resultant experiences of *duḥkha.*[82]

3. *Ignorance (avidyā): Avidyā* in the Vaiśeṣika sūtra IX.2.11. is defined as imperfect knowledge (*duṣta-jñānam*). It is a cognition which is unduly applied;

cognition that a thing is what is fact, 'it is not'. It is a cognition in which a thing is attributed with certain characteristics, which it does not possess. In it, the 'apparent' is mistaken for the 'real'; the non-self is taken for the 'self'.[83] The other two cease when *avidyā* is annihilated, by acquiring right knowledge.[85]

Freedom from Duḥkha

Vātsyāyana is pessimistic about ever overcoming *duḥkha*. He puts forward three arguments to substantiate his position. Firstly, an ordinary person is desirous about enjoyment of pleasure; he thinks that pleasure is the highest goal of life. He identifies living with pleasure seeking, due to which there is always a craving for pleasure. Craving for an object of pleasure, triggers the whole cycle of *karma* and resultant experiences of *sukha* and *duḥkha*. Man may conquer the world of material comforts, yet he will be craving for something more. Secondly, some people consider the various forms of suffering like old age, disease and so on, as part and parcel of the life cycle. Some even treat pain as a form of pleasure. Thirdly, that there is no pleasure free from pain thereby when man strives and gets pleasure, there is always the element of pain in it.[86] All these notions arise due to man's critical faculty being impaired by the concept that pleasure and pain are identical.[87] It arises due to the lack of insight, as the mind is rendered concrete by the evil of ignorance. Ignorance (*avidyā*) can be overcome by gaining right knowledge (*jñāna*) about the sixteen categories of *Nyāya*.[88] With the cessation of activity arising from ignorance, all experiences, their resultant *karma* and the cycle of birth and death are done with. All *duḥkha* comes to be annihilated.[89]

Kaṇāda in the *Vaiśeṣika Sūtra* stresses on the necessity for restraint of the mind, in overcoming *duḥkha*. The *manas* becomes steady, when it is endowed with the knowledge about the hollowness of the objects of enjoyment. At such a stage, there is non-production of volition and corresponding actions. Such a state is termed as 'Yoga'. In such a state, the intuitive knowledge about the *ātman* dawns.[90] This knowledge brings about the exhaustion of *adṛṣṭam;* with *adṛṣṭam's* extinction, the causal subtle body, the conuncetion with the gross body, the cycle of birth and death ceases. The *ātman* delinked with the minds, senses, body and objects remains completely cut-off from consciousness also. It is like a slab of stone, which is neither in a state of pain nor of pleasure. This state of the liberated *'ātman'* is termed as *Mokṣa*.[91]

The Purva Mīmāmṁsā view

Man is controlled by both the moral (*dharma*) and natural laws of the Universe. When his actions are consistent with both these laws, he enjoys harmony. Disharmony or conflict arises when he acts contrary to the established moral and natural laws, and produces *adharma.*[92] For instance, if a man commits an immoral deed, such as killing another person for wealth, he is bound to face the consequences of this deed. This feeling of 'disharmony' is termed as *duḥkha*. Sabara in his *Bhāṣya,* speaks of *duḥkha* as an experience characterised by a annoyance (*tāpa*).[93] He further opines that these experiences of *sukha* and *duḥkha*, which the soul (*ātman*) passes through, are purely private sensations.[94] The *ātman* experiences *sukha* and *duḥkha*, on account of its association with the physical body, sense-organs, mind and understanding. This association of the *ātman* is produced due to the merit and demerit (*dharmādharmau*) which inhere in *ātman* as *adṛṣṭa*[95] *Adṛṣṭa* controls, governs and decides the *ātman* birth in a particular garb, suffering, death and rebirth in the Universe.

The soul (*ātman*) gets connected with the physical, objective world through the medium of sense organs; it is through this medium of sense-organs, and their contact which produces judgment, and desire formations leading to the cyclic process of action and resultant production of *dharma* and *adharma.* Through the agency of *adṛṣṭa* this gets translated into experiences of pleasure and pain.[96] *Adṛṣṭa* produces *duḥkha* when the stock of *adharma* dominates over *dharma,* and vice-versa in the case of *sukha.* The role played by *adṛṣṭa* can be better understood by taking a suitable illustration of the operation of a bank account. It is *adṛṣṭa*, which controls the (*ātman's*) souls association, activaties and resultant experiences of *sukha* and *duḥkha*, arising out of bondage.

Bondage and Duḥkha Produced

Pārthasārathi Miśra, in his *Sāstra dīpikā,*[97] speaks of the self being bound in three ways in the state of bondage; The three-fold bonds are:

1. Physical body limtiations;
2. Sense-organs, and
3. Objective world.

In the state of bondage, the *ātman* is self-limited, on account of its association with the body and so on. This state is essentially one of pain and misery. Each of the above three bonds produces experience of pain in their final analysis.

1. **Experience of duḥkha arising from the limitations of the physical body:** (It refers to the pains and misery arising from bodily limittions). Man always wants to indulge in excesses of the pleasant experiences. This excess of pleasure, to a certain stage, produces *sukha*, but when it crosses the limit, that

is the tolerance limit, it produces pain. It can be better understood by an illustration. A person enjoys drinking wine; he likes it, for it produces in him an experience of pleasure. If that person indulges in excessive consumption of wine, to generate more pleasure, after a certain stage the alcoholic content crosses the alcoholic tolerance limit of the body, upsetting body's physiological rhythm. It may lead to vomiting, formation of ulcers, or damage the liver.. Thereby, it is clear that when a certain experience crosses the tolerance limit of the body, it results in pain and miwery.

2. **Duḥkha arising from sense-organs:** Man, getting himself addicted to the objects of the phenomenal world, aspires for attachment with them. For, he visualises the contact with such objects will produce within him an experience of *sukha*. These sense-object contacts are the basis for all human experiences. But does this mean that all types of sense-object contact generated by these contacts produce pleasures? No, there are several instances of sense object contact resulting in the production of pain. For example, the sight of a patient suffering from cancer, the sight of a crushed body and so on. Painful experience can also arise out of defects and malfunctioning of the sense-organs. For instance a person mistakes a statue for a ghost in a dark place, a rope for a snake, conch shell for silver, and other.

3. **Duḥkha arising from the objective world:** The objects of the phenomenal universe are no doubt a source of inspiration for man to perform various types of *karmas*. Man, taking these objects on their face value as permanent, ascribes to the notion that the object will produce an experience of joy, and will continue to do so at a later date but it is not the case. With change in them, space, time and casualty, there is every possibility of the very object becoming an object of ridicule and misery. For instance, man marries a beautiful woman with the hope that she will always remain beautiful. But, with advancement of age, her beauty diminishes, and wrinkles, folds make their appearance. He no longer finds her as an object of pleasure, but curses and wants to get rid of her. The 'very woman', who generated pleasure becomes an object of pain. Secondly, there are the objects of the world such as machines, aeroplanes, and so on which can produce an experience of horror, if involved in an accident. Man's notion, that these objects are eternal sources of pleasure, is a mistaken notion. This erring notion arises in the mind because it is deluded by ignorance (*avidyā*) which is the root-cause for all types of *duḥkha*.

The Mīmāṁsikas contend the wise realise the fact, that the pleasure of the world are always accomplished by some sort of pain. This realisation, they opine, gives them the correct perspective of worldly life as being full of suffering. It induces him to inquire into the causes and means to put an end to all suffering. They do not ascribe to an eternal cause of Man's suffering. All suffering is man's own creation. He alone is the master of his actions and resultant experiences. He is the agent and enjoyer. He alone can work his way out of this miserable existence. Both his mental and physical *karmas* are the causes, here. The mental cause can be overcome by acquiring *dharma-jñāna.* The governing factor of *adrṣṭa* can be cleared and exhausted by the performance of positive and neutral *karmas,* avoiding the negative *karmas* as enshrined in the Vedas. Further, by exhausting the accumulated stock of *'dharma-adharma'* and experiencing all the resultant of these *karmas,* results in disjuncture and non-birth of the *ātman* in any body. He can attain complete freedom from '*duḥkha*'.

5. The Advaita Vedānta view

Advaitins define *duḥkha* as that experience arising in the body out of its contact with an 'unfavourable' object.[98] Śaṅkara, in his *Vivekacūḍāmaṇi,* śloka 105,[99] clearly states that, when the sense object contact is favourable, it becomes *sukha* and *duḥkha* in contrary circumstances. He observes that, from the waking state till one's ultimate redemption (*mokṣa*), all expereinces of *sukha* and *duḥkha* are the creations of the *Jīva.*[100] These experiences are the characteristics of the mind and not the 'real self', just as a lady enjoys a different kind of relationship with different people. For one, she is a wife, for the other a friend, a mother to a son or a daughter, or a daughter-in-law and so on. The person remains the same, though the relationship changes.[101]

It is out of the mental modifications, arising from the different permutations and combinations of the three *guṇas* namely, *sattva, rajas* and *tamas* of the universe, that these experiences arise.[102] The *sattvic* modifications are detachment, fortitude, liberty and so on,[103] they produces *sukha*[104]. The *rajasic* mental modifications are desire, love for objects, attachment and greed,[105] which produce *duḥkha.*[10] The *tamasic* modifications are delusion, fear and so on,[107] which are 'base' and hence produce experiences of *duḥkha.*[108]

Process of Suffering: An Enumeration

Man, under the influence of ignornace (*avidyā*), perceives 'plurality' instead of 'unity', underneath. He identifies the *ātman*, the prue *sat-cit-ananda* with 'inert' matter. Śaṅkara contends that, this plurality is not real. It is unreal and apparent. it is unreal and apparent from the transcendental level, but as far as the empirical level is concerned, it is real. It forces the mind to perform *karmas*, which produce experiences of *sukha* and *duḥkha*. These expereinces, Śaṅkara observes, dominate worldly life (*saṁsāra*) and entangle him to the chain of repeated births and deaths.[109]

Man, who is full of qualities, unsteadiness and other forms, starts thinking that 'this is 'I' and 'that is mine', arising from the false identity between '*ātman*' and the '*body*'. This resutls in the binding of the infinite '*ātman*' with the finite '*ahaṁkāra*'. The influences and guides *jīva* to perform *karmas* leading to bondage and resultant suffering; the cause for which are *avidyā* and *adhyāsa*.[110] *Jīva*, under the influence of these two vicious principles, acts and experiences the world of plurality and the *duḥkha* within.

Types of Duḥkha

Śaṅkara observes that, the *duḥkha* that *jīva* undergoes in this world can be grouped into the following three heads: (1) Cognitive *duḥkha*, (2) Conative *duḥkha*, and (3) Emotive *duḥkha*.[111]

1. *Cognitive Duḥkha*: *Cognitive duḥkha* results from the superimposition of *adhyāsa* on the *jīva* of cognizership (*Pramātṛtvam*). Under the influence of *adhyāsa*, the *jīva* perceives the pure undifferentiated *Brahman* as a manifold objective reality. *Jīva*, under its influence, develops the false impression of being both the agent and the enjoyer; he conceives the notion of 'I' and 'mine'. This notion of 'I' and 'mine' is not confined to the self, but extends to the whole body, including the sense organs, and so on. Śaṅkāra opines that *adhyāsa*, which produces this superimposition, is the effect of the cause *avidyā*. *Avidyā*, he refers to, as the root-cause of all the mundane suffering.[112]

The *Jīva*, under the influence of *adhyāsa*, performs a number of *karmas*, which is guided by erroneous intellect. He experiences Brahman, the prue *sat-cit-ananda*, not as pure existence, nor pure consciousness and pure bliss, but as having an objective reference. For, all empirical judgements are mere propositions, involving a subejct-object relationship. There subject-object empirical experiences project the untrue, unreal nature of the object. Their true, real nature is hidden by the *avarana* function of *māyā*.[113]

Hence, the *Jīva* attaches himself to the unreal, untrue, temporal objects of the mundane world, which appear to him as pure existence, pure consciousness and pure bliss. This results in the *Jīva* undergoing untold suffering. For, these objects are non-permanent, undergoing change every moment. It is full of fleeting moments of bliss, which are essentially full of suffering in their ultimate analysis.

2. *Conative Duḥkha*

Conative *duḥkha*, like cognitive *duḥkha*, is caused by *adhyāsa*. The *jīva*, under the influence of *adhyāsa,* forms the wrong conception that 'I am this', 'this is mine', which are purely egocentric notions. With the birth of ego or *ahaṇkāra* of the form 'I' and 'mine', the *jīva* assumes itself as being both the agent and enjoyer of *saṁsāra*. Śaṅkara further contents that, *jīva* is made up of desire only.[114] It is these desires which determine the nature of *karmas,* he performs. It leads man to attaching to the mind, the sense organs, the body and so on. There are different kinds of desires like, the desire for wealth, desire for sons, desire for worldly pleasure, and others. There are as many *karmas,* as there are desires. He refers to the desires of life as the chief motivating factor for all other desires and their resultant activity. It is the experiences from these *karmas,* which produce pain and suffering. He refers to these desires of life, as one of the most important causes for man's *duḥkha* on this planet.[115]

It is these deluded cognitions of man that offer wrong objects of desire such as, wealth, sons and so on. To satisfy his desires, man does not hesitate to use any method or means. He gives up all his rational thinking about employing ethical means, for he is major concerned about attaining the ends. In the present day materialistic world, every man aspires to become rich, by hook or crook. In this venture, man may achieve success or failure. If he fails, he laments, grieves and undergoes untold suffering. While undergoing this experience of suffering, he plans evil means like killing, and other acts to gain his goal or destroy others' happiness. These sinful activities result in accumulation of *karmas;* he remains enmeshed in this tangle of *samāric* web,[116] or in other words the cycle or birth and death.

3. *Emotive Duḥkha*

Emotive *duḥkha* is interlinked with the two other kinds of *duḥkha*, which involve a process of 'knowing' and 'willing'. All these sufferings arise from the activities of the mind. All the three are mutually dependent on one another.[117]

Jīva, under the delusion of being both the agent and enjoyer, performs all the actions or *karmas* which are guided by the forces of *adhyāsa.* The motive for all these *karmas* is to gain *sukha*. But, being products of wrong cognitions and conceptions, it results in more confusion in the mind. The confusion is regarding the 'means' and the 'ends'. For instance, when one's son, wife or family members are ailing or rejoicing, one thinks that he is sick or happy. Man identifies himself and his feeling with the other worldly objects. It is due to this false identity that man is ready to adopt any means, bad or good, inhuman or human, ethical or unethical, to attain his goal. His prime concern is to attain the goal. This fact is all the more clearly perceptible in the present day materialistic world, where murder and deceit are matter of *decree.* The present day man has touched a rockbottom when ethical issues are taken for analysis.

The confusion of wrong 'ends' and 'means' produces experiences and feelings full of suffering. For, these experiences are full of dualities. The dualities of feeling being, attraction (*rāga*) and aversion (*devṣa*), pleasure (*sukha*) and pain (*duḥkha*) and so on. These dualities bind man emotionally and cause emotive suffering and resultant pain. It is also termed as the 'suffering of the heart'.[118]

Śaṅkara contends that, there are different types of emotive *duḥkha*, depending upon the degree and intensity of suffering each feeling generates. For instances, the *duḥkha* caused by the 'tamasic' impulses of the mind such as sex, cause more suffering than that *duḥkha* caused by rajasic 'impulses'. He further observes that, with the *jīva's* attachment to the object, he also develops a fear and anxiety that he may be deprived of them, that there may be impediments in his possessing these objects. The net-resultant of all such feelings is that, the *jīva* undergoes a chain of bondage, along with it a load of pain. It is mental *duḥkha*, which leads to physical *duḥkha*. Śaṅkara observes that, it is the man's desire for the pleasant sensual contact and the aversion for the unpleasant, which fuels the chain of feeling, resultant experiences being those of *sukha* and *duḥkha*.

The different types of *duḥkha* that Śaṅkāra speaks of, emanates from the false sense of identity, of pure consciousness (*ātman*) and inert matter (body).[119] This erroneous identity, a product of wrong cognition and conception, can be dispelled by acquiring right knowledge. Right knowledge about the true nature of the self and its relationship, that is *Brahmanjñāna* alone, can lift the screen of ignorance, which mystified by *māyā* is taking man for a ride into the abyss of endless births and suffering. Therefore, it is right knowledge, and right knowledge alone, that can help man free himself from the clutches of unending suffering of *saṁsāra.*

THE JAINA VIEW

Mahāvīra, the twenty-fourth Tīrthaṅkara, in his first discouse states that, the living world is afflicted and essentially full of *duḥkha.*[120] He draws man's attention to the fact that, considering the shortness of life, man should strive to gain knowledge about *duḥkha*, the *duḥkha* yet to come,[121] its causes, and work for is elimination. To quote the *Ācārāṅga Sūtra* I.1.2., "in this agonised world, see how the afflicted ones are causing pain, here and there, by various means".

The Jainas uphold the view that *duḥkha* is caused by the different *karmas* of the individual living beings.[122] These *karmas* are primarily aimed at seeking pleasure, honour and glory of life. Man, unmindful of his duty (*dharmas*) man desires for the qualities derived from the elements. He performs the various *karmas,* physical, mental and verbal, to satisfy these desires for the qualities.[123] These actions result in the formation of the eighty-two sins formed from the eighteen kinds of sinful acts.[124] It is due to the influx of these *karmans* that the *ātman* gets tied up to this miserable tangle of birth, death, and worldly career (*saṁsāra*). In the qualities of the external things, like the primary cause of *saṁsāra* and *duḥkha.*[125] It is due to delusion, that man desires these qualities. This delusion arises from ignornace (*avidyā*).[126] The Jainas use the term *mithyātva* to denote this notion of *avidyā.*[127] Many wrong notions and conceptions about the truth and reality arise due to *avidyā.* Under its influences, one accepts, and the unemancipated (*amutta*) as the emancipated (*mutta*) and vice versa.[128]

Factors Causing Duḥkha

The factors which bring about bondage and their resultant experiences of *duḥkha* can be brought under three categories namely, (i) *Mithyādarśana,* (ii) *Mithyājñāna* and (iii) *Mithyācārita.*[129]

Mithyādarśana

Man, under the influence of *mithyātva* about the true nature of *jīva*, world and so on, forms several misconceptions leading to misguided actions which produce *duḥkha.* They are guided by the forces of perversity of vision. The different types of *karman* and suffering produced, which man performs under this *mithyādarsāna*, are as follows:

(a) *Darśana āvaraṇa karman:*[130] A person due to this *karman* suffes from the lack of 'intuitive' knowledge. It results in the person suffering from sleep (*nidrā*). He cannot meditate or attend to his daily activities properly. This sleepy condition is of five types, depending upon the degree of one's sinful activities.

1. *Nidrā:*[131] The person in this state of sleep can be easily awakened. It is the mildest form, for the intensity of his *papakaram* is less. Herein, the person suffers from *duhkha*, due to non-attention.

2. *Nidrā-Nidrā*[132]: The person who performs a greater degree of *papa* suffers from slumber. When awakened, he finds himself in *duḥkha.* He wants to attend to his work but is overtaken by sleep.

3. *Pracala*[133]: The person who has committed grave sinful acts finds himself in a state wherein, even while standing or sitting he falls asleep. The lack of meditation and concentration results in the absence of mental peace, he suffers from *manasika duḥkha*.

4. *Pracalā-Pracalā*[134]: Grosser *papa* resutls in sleep overcoming a person even before movement. It seizes control over him even before he starts an act. It is a state of lack of control over sleep and produces *duḥkha*.

5. *Satyānardhi:*[134a] It results from the worst type of *papa*. In this state, man, though possessing plently of vigour, utilizes it in sinful activities. These produce experiences of *duḥkha*.

(b) *Cakṣurdarśana āvaraṇa karman:*[135] *Duḥkha* arises when the person, due to certain impediments, has lost both the spiritual and physical effects of perception. Depending on the intensity of his *papa,* it leads to *duḥkha*, ranging from night blindness to total blindness.

(c) *Acakṣurdarśana āvaraṇa karman:*[136] The persons eye-sight is obscured by this *karma.* He is not able to perceive things and activities taking place at a certain distance. He experiences a feeling of 'annoyance' on this account.

(e) *Kevaladarśana āvaraṇa karman:*[138] Persons also suffer pain through the lack of vision of the supernatural, which is possessed only by the omniscient.

Mithyājñana

When a person's intellect (*buddhi*) and mind (*manas*) is obscured by *avidyā,* the resultant knowledge that is produced out of the sense-organs and object contact, is false knowledge. This leads man to *papa karmans* which produce experiences of *duḥkha*.

(a) *Mithyājñāna karman:*[139] The *jīva* expereinces *duḥkha* due to impediments in the free usage of intellect (*buddhi*) due to this *karman.*

(b) *Srutijñāna āvaraṇa karman:*[140] Man, due to obscurity of the mind produced by this *Karman,* is not able to grasp the essence of the scriptural texts. He fails to draw distinction between the two meanings of a word, literal and implied. He misinterprets the scriptural texts' position regarding the *ātman*, *karman* and so on. This lack of correct knowledge about the true nature of atman, God and so on, makes the person involve himself in activities leading to the

entanglement of the *ātman* in the cycle of repeated births and death, in other words, of bondage. This state of bondage is essentially painful.

(c) *Avadhijñāna āvaraṇa karman:*[141] A person, due to impediments produced by this *karman,* is not able to use occult power. This failure resutls in his experiencing a feeling of *duḥkha.*

(d) *Manahparyayajñāna āvaraṇa karman:*[142] Suffering arises due to the accumulation of the *papas* of the previous births. These destroy the spiritual powers developed through austerities. Destruction is brought about by the working of his *karman.*

(e) *Kevalajñāna āvaraṇa karman:*[143] One faces *duḥkha* due tö the impediments in his attainment of omniscience, the highest knowledge of all, due to the accumulation of this *karman.*

Mithyācārita

Man, guided by the false knowledge about the self, gained through the deluded mind and its faculties, identifies it with the 'non-self', conducts himself in a manner so as to satisfy the needs of the 'non-self'. Taking the 'non-self' for the 'self' under this influence, he performs six types of sinful *karmans,* which produce experiences of *duḥkha.* They are:

(a) *Vedanīya karman:*[144] This *karman* produces feelings of happiness or pain. Happiness is treated as a form of pain, for these experiences are transitory. Even while enjoying pleasure, one is constantly tormented by the fear that, this pleasant feeling may change or end with the lapse of time. The feeling of pleasure is evanscent; he enjoys pleasure with anxiety and pain.

(b) *Mohanīya karman:*[145] Man's attachment for the objects of the phenomenal world is due to his deluded mind. He aspires for the 'transitory' objects, mistaking them for permanent objects. To gain contact with them, he performs different activities, both good and bad. When man is not satisfied with the (experience) object, as it falls short of his expectations, his greed increases. This sets forth the cycle of *karman* and the resultant feeling of *duḥkha.*

(c) *Āyuṣka karman:*[146] The type and intensity of suffering of a soul depends upon the form of existence and the time prescribed, that is, the age. The soul may be exposed to the harshest form of suffering in hell or it may be assigned to live for a particular length of time in the plant, animal, human or celestial worlds. But, all these are afflicted with suffering. Only the degree and intensity of suffering differs.

(d) *Nāma karman:*[147] A person also suffers on account of his birth in a particularly embodied form. For, this determines the environment in which he will stay, and the corresponding experiences of pain and pleasure. Depending upon the accumulated *karmaic* matter, he may be assigned the nomenclature and status of a particular creature in a particular garb in hell, plant, animal, human or celestial words.

(e) *Gotra karman:*[148] A person's birth in a 'low' economic class family is bound to be a difficult one. He may not be able to enjoy the pleasures of material comforts and has to sustain himself on the meagre 'means' available. Therefore, his suffering is determined by his birth. It is essentially an economic type of *duḥkha*.

(f) *Antarāya karman:*[149] This *karman* obstructs right conduct, resulting in suffering. This arises from four categories of action namely, (1) not being able to give gifts, (2) even though one is wealthy and wants to give, but is unable to do so; (3) not being able to run a profitable business; and (4) not being able to enjoy the available luxury besides not being able to use one's bodily strength as one desires.

In the *Tattvārthadigma Sūtra*[150] of Umasvati there is mention of twenty–five types of suffering arising from these karmans namely hunger, thirst, cold, heat, nakedness, insect bites, dissatisfaction, women, walking too much, sitting, sleeping, abuse, beating, begging, disease, failure to get alms, contact with thorny shrubs, discomfort from dust, respect or disrespect, lack of knowledge, conceit of knowledge and failure to attain supernatural powers.

The intenser the fortification of an inauspicious *karman,* the deeper is the suffering. In the *Karmagrantha,*[151] the gradation of intensity is conceived as falling into four groups, depending upon the degree of pain namely first group (*eka sthānika*), second group (*dvi-sthānika*), third group (*tri-sthānika*) and fourth group (*catuh sthānika*). The most virulent type of pain is generated in the fourth group.

Means of overcoming suffering

It is due to the joint working of the three *mithyātvas* that the inborn, inherent capacities of the *'ātman'* are obstructed by the different *karman* and their resultant experiences of *duḥkha*. These capacities of the '*ātman*' find expression in their mutilated and imperfect forms, resulting in worldly existence (*saṃsāra*), which is predomiently full of *duḥkha*. Many wrong notions and misconceptions about the truth and reality arise due to *avidyā*, under its influences one accepts of the *adharma as dharma, amagga* as *magga*, the *ajiīva* as *jīva* and the unemancipated (*amutta*) as the emancipated (*mutta*) vice-versa.[152]

Hence, the Jainas like other systems of Indian Philosophy accept *avidyā* as the root-cause of all human suffering. The method prescribed involves the triple principles of *samyak darśana* (right view), *samyak jñāna* (right knowledge) and *samyak cāritra* (right conduct).[153]

REFERENCES

1. *Sarva darśāna Saṁgraha* (S.D.S)., p. 3.
2. Yaśodhara Commentary on *Kāma sutras* I.2.46.
3. S.D.S., p. 2. tatra prthivyādini catvāri tattvāni tahhya eva dehakāraṇa pariṇatabhyaḥ kiṇavo dibhyo madaśaktivat caitanyamupajāyate
4. *S.D.S.*, p. 3. taccaitanyaviśiṣṭādeha evātmā.
5. *S.D.S.*, p. 3. dehatirikte ātmani pramānābhāvāt

   Because of their identification of *ātman* with the physical body, they are termed as *dehavādins'*. S.D.S. p. 6.

   dehātmavāde ca sthūloham kṛśohaṁ krsnohaṁityādi samadhikaranyopapattiḥ.
6. *S.D.S.* p. 6., dehātmavāde ca......
7. Unlike other systems of Indian Philosophy which consider moṣka as the highest ideal, here *kāma* (pleasure), the anti-thesis of pain, is regarded as the *summum bonum.* They opine that the moral virtues of dharma and *artha,* should be used as means to attain *kāma.* The supreme motto of life is "let us eat, drink and make merry, for tomorrow we die". Kāma eva puruṣarthiaḥ-*Advaita Brahma Siddhi,* p. 121.
8. *S.D.S.*, p. 3.
9. *S.D.S.*, p. 6.
10. *S.D.S.*, p. 13.
11. *S.D.S.*, p. 4: Maṭsyarthi sasalkan sakantakan maṭsyanupadatte sa yavadevam tavadadaya nivartate na hi bhikṣukaḥ santiti sthalyo nadhisriyante.

12. *Sāṇkhya Kārikā* I. 1

13. *Yoga Sūtras* (Y.S) Ii. 16. Hetuṁ duḥkhamanāgatham.

14. *Sāṅkhya Kārikā* (S.K.) I. 1.

15. *S.* II. 15 (Vyāsa comm. on Y.S. II. 15) Pariṇāmatāpa saṁskāra duḥkhhaiḥ guṇavṛtti virodhācca. duḥkkameva sarvaṁ vivēkinaḥ.

16. *S.D.S.*, p. 13.

17. *Y.S.* II. 7. Sukhānuśayī rāgaḥ.

18. *Y.S.* II. 8 Duḥkhānusayi dveṣaḥ.

19. *Y.S.* II. 17.

20. *Y.S.* II. 5 & 24.

21. *Y.S.* II. 14.

22. *Sāṅkhya tattva Kaumudī* (S.T.K.) 4 on Sāṅkhya Kārikā (S.K.) I., p. 3. tat khalu ādhyātmikam ādhibhautikam ādhidaivikam ca.

23. *S.T.K.* 4. p. 3. tatrādhyātmikam dividhham sāriram mānasam ca.

24. *S.T.K. 4,* p. 3., manasam kāma krodha lobha moha bhayairṣya viṣāda viṣaya viśeṣādarśana nibandhanam.

25. Tatrādhyātmikam mānuṣapaśu mṛgapakṣi sarīsṛpa sthāvara nimittam. S.T.K. p. 3.

26. Ādhidhaivikam tu yakṣarākṣasa vināyaka grahādyāveṣa nibandhanam. STK (4) 3

27. *Y.S.* II. 15.

28. *Y.S.* II. 18.

28a. Vyāsa Commentary on *Y.S.* II. 15.

29. Trīguṇam aviveki viṣayaḥ . . . *S.K.* 11.

30. Prītyātmakaḥ sattvaguṇah. *S.T.K.* 99, p. 61.

31. Sattvam laghu prakāśakam...*S.K.* 13, 12.

32. Aprītyātmako rajo guṇah. *S.T.K.* 99, p. 61.

33. Upaṣṭaṃbhakam calam ca rajaḥ. *S.K.* 13, 12.

34. .....guru varaṇakam eva tamaḥ *S.K.* 13.

35. Viṣādomohaḥ-viṣādātmako tamo guṇaḥ ityarthaḥ. *S.T.K.* 99, p. 61 and *S.T.K.*12.

36. Anyonyābhibhavāsraya janana-mithuna vṛttayaś ca guṇāh. *S.K.* p. 12; atra ca sukhaduḥkhamohāḥ paraspara-virodhinaḥ. *S.T.K.* p. 66.

37. Sattva rajastamasām sāmyāvasthā *S.T.K.* 14.

38. The eleven organs namely sense-organs (indiriyas) can be brought under two heads Jñānendriyas and Karmendriyas. The Jñānendriyas are manas, śrotha, tvak, cakṣu, rasana and ghrāṇa, whereas the karmendriyas are vāk, pāṇi, pāda, pāyu and upastha.

39. The five subtle elements (tanmātras) are śabda, sparsa, rūpa, rasa and gandha.

40. The five gross elemetns (Mahābhūtas) are ākāśa, vāyu, tejas, āpaḥ and pṛthivī.

41. mūla prakṛtiravikṛih mahadādyāḥ prakṛti vikṛitayaḥ sapta soḍaśakastu vikāro, na prakṛtirḥ na vikṛtiḥ puraṣah S.K. 3.

42. Tamas being of the nature of delusion produces unhappiness.

43. Y.S.I. 30. vyādhistyāna samśaya pramādālasya viratibhrānti darśanālabdha bhūmikatvānavasthitatvāni chittavikṣepāste antarāyaḥ.

44. *Ibid.*

45. *Y.S.* II. 3. avidyāsmitā rāgadveṣābhiniveśaḥ kleśāh.

46. *Y.S.* II. 29: Yama niyama āsana prāṇāyāma pratyāhāra dhāraṇa dhyāna samādhayo aṣṭvaṅgani

47. *S.K.* II.

48. *S.K.T.* on S.K. II; 14: p. 11.

49. *Ibid.*

50. *Nyāya sūtras* (N.S.) I. 1.21.

51. *Nyāya Bhāṣya* (*N. Bh.*) on N.S. I. 1.21.

52. *Nyāya sūtra* I. 1.21., Vol. I. trans. G. Jha, p, 282, 1984. footnotes tātparya.

53. *Nyāya vārtika on* N.S. I. 21.

etadevaśarīrāḍī bādhanānuṣangāt duḥkhamityucyate.

54. *Nyāya Bhāṣya* on N.S.I. 1.21. and *Nyāya tātaparyatīkā.*

55. *Praśastapāda Bhāṣya* text, p. 125.

56. Ibid. The effects of *duḥkha* are unfavourableness, and aversion towards the objects causing pain and paleness. Ref. S.K. Maitra, *The Ethics of the Hindus,* p. 187.

57. *Vaiśeṣika Sūtras* (V.S.) I.1.4 Dharma viśeṣa prasūtāt dravya guṇa karma sāmānya viśeṣa samavāyānām padārthānām.

58. *V.S.* I. 1.2, yataḥ abhyudaya niḥśreyasasiddiḥ saḥ dharmaḥ.

59. Śaṅkhāra Miśra on *V.S.* I. 1.2., p. 6.

60. *Nyāyasāra* p. 95 & 96; pp. 59-63 (Adyar). Part. II.

61. *Nyāya sūtras* II. 2.62-72.

62. Vātsyāyana opines that the body is not identical with suffering. It is said to be full of suffering in the sense that they are invariably attended with suffering.

63. *N.Bh.* on *N.S.* X. 1.51.

64. *Nyāya Bhāṣya* on *Nyāya sūtra* IV. 1.56.

65. *N.V. tātaparyatika* on N. Bh. on N.S.I. 1.21.

66. The fourteen *bhuvanās* consists of seven lower *lokas* namely *Atala, Vitala, Sutala, Rasātala, Tatatala, Mahātala, and Pātāla* whereas the seven upper lokas are *Bhūloka, Bhuvarloka, Suvarloka, Maharloka, Janaloka, Tapoloka and Satyaloka.....* Ref: Vāchaspayam (A comprehensive Saṅskrit Dictionary Compiled by Tārānātha Tarkavāchaspathi Vol. IV. The Chowkhamba Saṅkhāra Series Office, Varanasi, 1962, p. 2874-75.)

67. *N. Bh.* on *N.S.* IV. 1.54. dukkha saṁjñā vyavasthānāt sarvalokeṣu anabhiratisaṁjñā bhavati. Anabhisaṁjñāmupāśinasya sarva loka viṣāya tṛṣṇā vicchidyate tṛṣṇāprahāṇāt sarva dukkhāt vimucyate iti.

68. Ibid. Vividhā ca bādhanā h-īnā madhyamā utkṛṣṭā ceti.

69. Ibid. Utkṛṣṭā nārakiṇāṁ, tiraścāmtu madhyamā, manuṣyānam tu hīna, devānāṁ hīnatarā vītarāgāṇam ca.

70. *Nyāyamañjari* p. 47.

71. *N.S.* I. 1. 18, 20, and IV. i, 3-9.

72. *V.S.* VI. 2. 10. *Upāsakāra.*

73. *V.S.* VI. 2. 10, 11, 12 & 13.

74. *V.S.* VI. 2.13, Jāti-viśeṣāt ca.

75. *N.S.* VI. 1.3. (Vṛtti).

76. *Maitra*, S.K. *The Ethics of the Hindu.*, p. 196.

77. *Ibid.*, p. 198.

78. *Ibid.*, p. 199.

79. *V.S.*, VI. 2, 11, 12 and 13.

80. *Op.cit*, p. 200.

81. *Op. cit.*, 1.3. (Vṛtti)

82. *V.S.* IV. 2. 14 and 15.

83. *Upāsakāra* on V.S. IX 2.11 tat duṣṭa jñānaṃ.

84. *N.S.* IV. 1.3.-9.

85. *N.S.* I. 1.2.

86. *N.Bh.* on *N.S.* IV. 1.56.

87. *N.S.* IV. 1.57.

88. *N.S.* I. 1.1.

89. *N.S.* I. 1.1, 2.

90. *V.S.* V. 2.16. Tat anārambhah ātmasthe manasi śarirāsya duḥkha abhāvah sab yogaḥ.

91. *V.S.* V. 2. 17. Tat abhāvē saṁyōga abhāvaḥ apradinibhāvah ca mokṣaḥ.

92. *Śābara bhāṣya* (S. Bh) on *Mīmāmsā sūtra* (M.S.) 3/8/3/9. duhkhaphalabhōgya adharmaḥ sṛuyate.

93. *Ibid.* duḥkham hi tāpah.

94. *S.Bh.* on *M.S.* I. 1.5.

95. yaḥ khalu sāmsārikebhyo duḥkhebhyaḥ udivgnaḥ tadanuṣanga śabalebhyaśca sukhabhyopi gatasprho mokṣajottiṣṭhate sa tāvat bandhahetubhutebho niṣiddhebhyaḥ pratyavāyahetubhutebhyo abhyudaya sādhanabhyaśca nivarta mānah sannutpannapūvvau dharm-ādharmau bhogenakṛtvapi kṣayaṁ nayaṅ śammadama brahmacaryadi.. *Prakarṇa Pañcika,* p. 156-157.

96. Adṛṣṭāt dṛs.ṣṭakāryaḥ balīyaḥ. Ś. Bh on M.S. 10-1-9-23.

97. Tredhā hi prapañcaḥ puruṣam badhnāti bhogāyatanaṁ śarīram, bhogasādhanāni indirayāni, bhogyāḥ śabdādayo viṣayāh bhogetara sukhaduḥkhaviṣaya aparijnñāḥ ....tadasya trividhasyāpi bandhasya ātyantiko vilayōmokṣha. *Śāstra dipikā,* p. 125.

98. Ānukūlye harṣa dhīḥ syāt prātikūlye tu dukkha dhīḥ *Pañcadasi* XIII: 73, 1.

99. Viṣayāṇā mānukūlye sukhī dukkhīviparyaye, *Vivekacūḍāmani:* 105/1.

100. Jāgradādi vimokṣānataḥ: saṁsāro jīvakalpitaḥ, *Pañcadasi:* VI-213/2 and dhī-mayo jīva-bandha-kṛt, satyasmin sukha-duḥkhe stas tasminn asati na dvayam-*Pañcadasi.* IVI. 32.

101. Bhoktṛdhī vṛttinānātvāt tadbhogo bahudheṣyate: *Pañcadasi*: IV: 20.

Bhāryā snuṣā nanāndā ca yātā mātety anekadhā pratiyogi dhiyā yosid bhidyate na svarūpatah., *Pañcadasi*: IV. 23.

102. sāntā ghorās tathā mūḍhāh manaso vṛttayas tridhā.

Vairagyaṃ kṣāntiraudāryam ityādyah śānta-vṛttayaḥ.

Pañcadasi: XV. 3.

103. *Ibid.*

104. *Pāncadasi* XV: 13/2.

105. Tṛṣṇā sneho rāga lobhāvityādyā ghora vṛttayaḥ. *Pañcadasi*: XV: 4/1.

106. Ghoramūḍha dhiyor dukkham....

Pañcadasi: CV. 24/1.

107. Saṃmoho bhayam ityādyāḥ. kathitā mūḍha vṛttayaḥ.

Pañcadasi: XV. 4/2.

108 *Pañcadasi*: XV 24/1.

109. Pumānanātmānaṁ mohādahamiti śarīram kalayati: *Vivekacūḍāmani,* Śloka: 140/1.

110. *Adhyāsa* covers the total field of experiences, both objective and subjective. It starts from birth and continues till death, unless the *Jīva* attains true wisdom. The basic characteristic function of *adhyāsa* is to bring about the transfer of the subject and its qualities to the inert object and vice-versa. It brings about the mutual transfer of qualities between the subject and object. In this process, there is the association of consciousness namely, the subject 'I' with the inert matter, the object which is non-conscious. Both are totally opposed, as darkness is to light. Adhyāsa is nothing but a case of grand illusion, just as the rope-snake illusion.

111. *Brahma Sūtras:* II. 3, 17 and 18 and B. Gita XIII 22.

112. *Vivekacūḍa-mani Śloka* 145 and 146.

113. *Vivekacūḍa-mani Śloka* 113/1.

114. *Brh. Upaniṣad:* IV. 4, 5 and 6.

115. *Vivekacūḍāmani Śloka* 313.

vāsanāvṛdditah kāryam; kāryavṛddyā ca vāsanā

vardhate sarvatha puṃsah, saṁsāro na nivartate

116. *Vivekacūḍa-mani Śloka* 137.

atrānātmanyahamiti—avati viṣayaiḥ tanubhih kośakrdvat.

117. *Śaṅkara Bhāṣya* on *Brahma Sūtras* (BSS) p. 428.

ataścāvidyakṛto 'yaṁ tapyatāpakabhāvo na pāramārthika ityabhyapagantavyam.

118. *Brh. Upaniṣad* II. 45 and IV 5.6.

119. *Vivekacūḍāmaṇi Śloka* 137/1.

atrāṇātmanyahamti mathibhanḍa. . . . . .

119a. *Vivekacūḍāmani* 223.

The realisation of one's identity with Brahamn is the cause for liberation from the bonds of saṁsāra.

120. *Ācārāṅga Sūtra* I. 1. 3: 4.3. p. 5 & 6; . 9.

121. The *duḥkha* yet to come, refers to the future sufferings, which has not yet arisen.

122. *Ācārāṅga Sūtra* I. 1.4 & 5, p. 7-9.

123. Ibid., I. 1.4, p. 7.

124. Stevenson S, *The Heart of Jainism,* pp. 302-3.

125. *Ācārāṅga Sūtras* I. 1.5., p. 9.

126. Kundakunda's *Samayaprābhṛta* 25-27 with Comm.

127. Tatia, Nathmal, *Studies in Jaina Philosophy,* p. (SJP) 144,

128. *Stānāṅga Sūtra,* X. I. 734.

129. *Tattvārthaśloka vārttika (T.Sl.)* V, p. 72, *Tattvākrthasūtra (T.Su.)* I.1.

130. *Uttarādhyayamasūtra (U.A.S.)* 33-4 & 5.

131. Svāpo nidrā sukha-pratibodha-lakṣaṇā - T.Su.Bh. tia. Part II, p. 134 (S.J.P. 233).

132. Duḥkha—pratibodha-lakṣaṇā pracalā nidrā-nidrā. Ibid. p. 135.

133. ūrdhva śayana-lakṣaṇā pracalā-Ibid.

134. Caṅkramaṇam ācarataḥ śayanaṁ pracalā - pracalā - Ibid.

134a. Ibid. 135.

135. *U.A.S.* 33.6., *T.Su,* VIII, 7, (*S.J.P.P. 233*).

136. *Ibid.*

137. *Ibid.*

138. *Ibid.*

139. *U.A.S.* 33, *T.Su. VIII. 7.*

140. *U.A.S.* 33, *T.Su. VIII. 7.*

141. *U.A.S.* 33, *T.Su. VIII. 7.*

142. *U.A.S.* 33, *T.Su. VIII. 7.*

143. *U.A.S.* 33, *T.Su. VIII. 7.*

144. *U.A.S.* 33-7, *S.J.P.* p. 232.

145. *Ibid.* 33-8, 9, 10, 21. S.J.P. p. 232.

146. *U.A.S.* 33-22. (SJP p. 232).

147. *T.Su Bh.* VIII, 12. U.A.S. 33-23, S.J.P. p. 232.

148. *Ibid.*, VIII. 13.

149. *Ibid.*, VIII. 14.

150. Law, B.C. *Some Jaina Canonical Sutras,* p. 167.

151. Karmagatha (Kg) *Kg.* 2 pp. 64-67 (S.P.J. p. 237).

151a. *Kg* 2 p-67 (S.J.P. p. 237).

152. *Samayaprābhṛta* of Kundakunda 25-27.

153. *T.Su.* I.1.

3

Conception of Dukkha in Early Buddhism

INTRODUCTION

Although every Indian philosophical system starts its inquiry with an avowed intention to redeem man from pain, some of them got so much engrossed in metaphysical subtleties that their discussion looked not directly relevant to the elimination of man's suffering. It was the Buddha, who directly directed his attention to man's suffering and its elimination. Whatever the Buddha said or did, it was only in the context of man's suffering, its origin and elimination. The entire Buddhist philosophy is nothing but an attempt at understanding human suffering and redeeming man from the same. The Buddha says: just as waters of the ocean are impregnated with the sole taste of salt, so also his doctrine is impregnated with the problem of '*dukkha*'[1] and its elimination[2]. ("*Dukkham ca dukkhanirodham ca*"). He was averse to metaphysical questions that land us in interminable controversies and have no relevance to the deliverance of man from *dukkha*[3]. In the *Majjhima Nikāya*[4] there is a mention of Buddha's dislike for the discussion of metaphysical questions. A certain follower of the Budha by name Mālunkyāputta sought clarification for the questions:

Whether the 'world' is 'eternal' or non-eternal?

Whether the 'world' is 'finite' or 'infinite'?

Whether the 'soul' and 'body' are identical or separate?

Whether the 'saint' exists after death or does not exist after death?

He also threatened the Buddha that he would cease to be his disciple, if he failed to provide definite answers to these questions. In response to Māunkyāputta's questions, the Buddha asked him whether he had requested him to be his disciple, on the condition that he would answer all his questions. Mālṅkyāputta replied in the negative. The Buddha told him that it was futile to involve oneself in metaphysical discussions of this kind, which would lead man nowhere. Man should try to solve the problem of *dukkha* experienced by him in his daily life. Men, who involve themselves in such intellectual exercises will die even before they gain insight into these problems. Just like a man injured by a poisonous arrow should seek medical help to overcome the poison and save his life, rather than wanting to know the details of the person who shot the arrow, whether he is a Brahmin or a non-brahmin, dark in complexion or fair or tall or short, as precondition to receive any medical attention. So also we should address ourselves to the issues concerning the origin of suffering and its elimination rather than indulging in questions that have no bearing on man's suffering and its removal. The Buddha added that annihilation of *dukkha* does not depend upon such metaphysical questions whether the world is 'finite' or 'infinite' and so on. To him, it does not lead to the insight into the origin and cessation of *dukkha*. There would still remain birth, old-age, death, sorrow, lamentation, misery, grief and despair to torment man. Just as the leaves in the hand do not exhaust all the leaves in the Simsapa forest, so also the Buddha knows more than what he was teaching to his disciples. But, he was teaching only that which was absolutely necessary for the elimination of *dukkha*. The fact that Buddha's interest lay round 'knowing a person' and not 'knowing a fact'[6].

Buddha's conclusion that 'there is suffering every where' *sarvam dukkhaṁ* was not a product of mere 'apriori reasoning, but an outcome of his encounters with existential situation. Prince Siddhāttho[7], it is told one day expressed a desire to go to the Deer Park on his chariot. It was during this ride that he had his first glimpse of an 'old' man. It was a novel sight for him, for he had hitherto always seen only the healthy and the handsome, but not the weak, ugly and old. He enquired from his charioteer about the state of that 'man', who was 'old'. When he was informed that the same state was in store for everyone including himslef, he was taken aback, and he was agitated and perturbed with the suffering in store for him. He realised that he also would have to pass through this state of old age. A state in which the body is weak, trembling and bent, grey-haired, wherein the sense-organs are all burnt out; the old body is prone to all types of disease and decay due to ageing and the loss of resistance. He started to ponder over the problem of suffering *i.e., dukkha.*[8] The following day, he saw a sick man, thereafter a corpse and lastly an ascetic. The first two experiences troubled him further and set him thinking about the suffering underlying every stage of life. He was deeply moved by the suffering that human existence is subjected to[9]. He began to inquire into the origin and remedy of suffering. He repeatedly reflected on the issues of : why and how does this suffering originate? Is there any remedy, a way out of this dense forest of suffering[10]. It is at this stage that he was impressed with the sight of a monk. He ardently believed that the life of a monk, a seeker of truth, free from worldly bonds, would help him to gain freedom from the fetters of *dukkha*. He took it as his Ideal, to emulate[11].

It was at this stage that his father, king Suddhodano finding his son drifting away from worldly life into that of a recluse tried his best to avert him from it. He offered to abdicate the throne in his favour. His father had arrangements made at the palace with dance and music to entice prince Siddhāttho to the path of worldly life and prevent him from renunciation[12]. Prince Siddhāttho was unmoved by the offer and arrangements made by his father. He questioned king Suddhodano, his father: if his kingdom, riches and pleasures could free him from the fetters of pain and misery? In order that he would desist from the temptation of reunciation he wanted the king to ensure him that he would not be subjected to old age, disease, death and re-birth. He clearly perceived the ugliness, transitoriness and suffering underneath each of the so-called things of pleasure. To him the magnificent palace, the dancing girls, the beautiful damsels, the musicians and their instruments, appeared like a cemetery filled with dead bodies impaled and left to rot. He found misery in all things. He felt the ubiquity of suffering in saṁsāra.[13].

There were two forms of life prevailing prominently at Buddha's time namely self-indulgence (*Ucchedavādo*) and self-mortification (*Sassatavādo*) based on the belief of a non-eternal and eternal 'self', respectively. Buddha was convinced that the life given to self-indulgence will not lead us anywhere. He opted for the path of self-mortification expecting deliverence from suffering through it. He practised the path of self-mortification with the hope of gaining an insight into the truth of *dukkha*. He shed all his royal robes, got his head shaven, doned coarse clothes, equipped himself with the other requirements namely a bowl for alms, a razor, a needle, a belt and a water container needed for a monk.

Siddhāttho in his quest for the true knowledge about suffering sought the guidance of Ālārākālāma of Vaiśālī,[14] a follower of Sāṅkya[15]. With his strong will (Chanda), energy (Viriya), self-recollectedness (Sati), meditation (Samādhi) and intellect (paññā), he mastered the doctrines and attained the seventh stage of meditation —*Akincaññāyatana* (in which the mind seeks nothing). He still was not able to gain an insight into the truth of *dukkha*. He sought next the guidance of Uddaka Rāmaputa, an exponent of Vaiśesika, who highlighted the concept of kamma and transmigration of the 'self' to him. He was able to attain the eighth stage of meditation —*N'evasaññānāsaññāyatana* (in which the sense-perceptions are neither alive nor dead). But he felt that this stage of mediatation was not pure enough to give him an insight into *dukkha*. Thinking that by increasing the rigours of ascetism, he would be able to gain knowledge about *dukkha*, he began taking only one grain of corn for nourishment for a day and many a time not even that. He exerted his body severely, sweated even in extreme winter. His body was reduced to a bare skeleton. It was covered with a hard crust of earth, for he had not washed for it long. Inspite of all those forms of ascetic life of severe penance, control of senses, passions etc., he could not achieve the supreme knowledge. It soon dawned on him that penance only reduced the power of the mind and body, but could not help one gain an insight into *dukkha*.[16]

Thus, Siddāttho[17] realised the futility of self-mortification as a means of annihilating *dukkha*. He realised that the fundamental requirement for finding the right way was a continuing process of mental awareness[18]. He started a new course of reflection and self-examination employing his own reason to gain knowledge about the truth of *dukkha*. He meditated till he attained perfect insight into the mistaken means of liberation namely self-indulgence and self-mortification, for both produce *dukkha* instead of removing it[19].

This meditation revealed to him the insight into the causes of *dukkha* and also the path of deliverence from it, which took the form of the Four Noble Truths (*Cattāri ariyasaccāni*).

The Four Noble Truths (Cattāri Ariyasaccāni)[20]

Buddha gave his first discourse on the Four Noble Truths (Cattāri ariyasaccāni) to the Brahmanas[21] at the Deer Park called Isipattana (in Sāranāth). This fundamental teachings of the Buddha are found in the *Dhammacakkappavattana Sutta*.[22] The four noble truths read as follows:

The Noble Truth of Suffering (*dukkhaṁ ariyasaccaṃ*); The Noble Truth of the Origination of Suffering (*dukkhaṁ samudayao ariyasaccaṃ*); The Noble Truth of the Cessation of Suffering (*dukkhanirodho ariyasaccaṃ*); and The Noble Truth of the Path leading to the Cessation of Suffering (*dukkhanirodhagāminī paṭipāda ariyasaccaṃ*)[23]

First Noble Truth-The Noble Truth of suffering.

Birth is suffering; old age is suffering; death is suffering: sorrow, lamentation, grief and despair are suffering; separation from those one likes is suffering; not getting what one (desires) wishes is suffering; in summary, the five aggregates of attachment are suffering.[24]

Second Noble Truth-The Noble Truth of the Origin of suffering.

It is that craving which gives rise to fresh rebirth and, bound up with lust and greed, now here, now there, finds ever fresh delight. It is the sensual craving, the craving for existence, and (even) the craving for self-annihilation......

Wherever in the world there are the delightful and pleasurable forms, there this craving arises, there it takes its root.....[25]

Third Noble Truth-The-Noble Truth of the cessation of suffering.

The utter fading away and cessation of that very craving, leaving it, giving it up, the being delivered from, the doing away with it..[26]

Fourth Noble Truth The path leading to the cessation of suffering.

It is the Noble Eight-fold path of Right View, Right Thought, Right Speech, Right Action, Right Livelihood, Right Exertion, Right Mindfulness and Right Concentration.[27]

MEANING OF DUKKHA

'*Dukkha*' in Pali or '*dukkha*' in Sanskrit is a compound of two words 'du' and 'kha'. The prefix 'du' is used in the sense of 'vile' (kucchita). It signifies something 'bad', 'disagreeable', 'uncomfortable' or 'unfavourable'. The suffix 'kha' is used in the sense of 'empty' (tuccha). It signifies 'emptiness' or 'unreality'.[28] Therefore, *dukkha* stands for something that is 'vile' and 'imaginary'. Buddhaghosa is of the opinion that things that are impermanent, harmful and devoid of substantiality are characterised otherwise by ignorant people and this leads to pain and misery. Hence, these are called *dukkha*.[29]

In the ordinary sense, '*dukkha*' means suffeing, pain, misery or discomfort. It is something which is opposed to happiness, comfort or ease. *Dukkha*, according to the Buddha, does not merely refer to ordinary corporeal suffering of man. Rhys Davids[30] has rightly remarked that it is difficult to find one word which would embrace the whole concept of the term '*dukkha*' as used by Buddha in his teachings. 'The words in English are too specialised, limited and strong. The words such as ill, ill-ness, disease etc., are not exact but only half-synonyms in their connotation. *Dukkha* is equally mental and physical. Pain refers mainly to the physical plane; sorrow to the mental plane. But they have been used even in default wherein, more rendering was not possible. The words disease, ill, suffering, trouble, misery, distress, agony, affliction, woe etc., have been used in certain connections though they are never fully right.[31] Rahula is of the opinion that it would be better to leave it untranslated than to give an incomplete and wrong idea by conviently rendering it as pain or suffering.[32]

To limit the understanding of the Buddha's concept of '*dukkha*' as merely physical and mental is to get at a very inadequate view of the buddhist conception of *dukkha*. Inorder to have a comprehensive picture of buddhist *dukkha,* we have to add the philosophical dimension to it. Unless one understands *dukkha* from the three points of view viz., physical, mental, and philosophical, one misses to capture the significance of the Buddha's conception of *dukkha*.

Dukkha philosophically has an enormous and wider sense. To quote Christmas Humphery "*dukkha* covers all that we understand by pain, illness, disease-physical and mental-including such minor forms of discomfort, disharmony, limitations, frictions or in a philosophical sense, the awareness of incompleteness or insufficiency".[33]

Although, we do say that it is the perception of decay, disease and death that made him take a resolve to renounce, it is neither his own physical pain nor his own unfulfilled desire that compelled Siddāttho to take seriously to inquire into the cause of *dukkha*. But it is his ignorance concerning the true meaning of life that promoted him to philosophical inquiry, that which C. Humphery refers to as an 'insufficiency' or 'incompleteness.'[34] This ignorance is to be understood as suffering, for it refers to the absence of knowledge or wisdom, which is also a form of suffering.

Physical and mental suffering compelled the Buddha to inquire into the origin, existence and annihilation of *dukkha*. The physical and mental suffering that the Buddha was sensitive to finally led him to ponder over the deeper philosophical issues. To quote Prof. Pande "death, decay etc., while pointing to the limitation and uncertainties of life also gives one the feeling what my be termed as 'spiritual discontent'..It motivates one to seek what is beyond the body and mind *i.e.,* it motivaties for its transcendence".[35]

In the philosophical sense, *dukkha* points to our ignorance concerning the meaning of life. The suffering arising out of this type of ignorance is more intensive, acute and paralysing than the physical and mental suffering of man. In fact, one can find remedies (immediate or remote) for the pain arising out of the physical and mental factors. Fever can be cured, enemies can be vanquished and desires can be fulfilled. The pain caused by the absence of wisdom concerning the true significance of life is more frustrating and acute because it is very difficult to find easy ways of overcoming it.

Further, one should not get the impression that the Buddha is aiming at merely a collection of information on the meaning of life. He aims at illumination into the true significance of life embroiled with *dukkha* and repeated births. Absence of illumination into the meaning and significance of life causes *dukkha* and repeated births. But this pain is neither visualised nor experienced by one whose existence does not transcend the physical and mental level. Awareness of this kind of *dukkha* needs a sensitive mind that can penetrate beyond the physical and mental suffering of man.

Stcherbatsky[36] stressing the philosophical implications of *dukkha* observes that Buddha's statements like 'The vision is *dukkha*' or 'All the elements influenced by *rāgo doso* and *moho* are *dukkha*' can be properly understood, if their philosophical meaning is taken into consideration. The elements of the world influenced by passions are constantly in a state of flux (sāsravah). This agitated state of the elements have to be gradually appeased and finally extinguished from the influences of the passions. A state of uniform motion or rest of the elements (ānasravah) has to be attained.[37]

SOURCES OF DUKKHA

We understand the nature and sources of *dukkha* better if we analyse the contents of the First Noble Truth:

(a) Birth is Suffering (Jāti Pi Dukkha)

Birth (*jāti*) has been used in different senses in the Buddhist texts.[38]

Birth, in Buddhism, does not merely refer to human birth, it includes the birth of all living beings. It directly refers to the first manifestation of any aggregates in living beings, when they are born anywhere. It is the basis of suffering, for with it starts all the experiences of man which are essentially full of suffering.

Buddhaghosa elucidating the First Noble Truth brings forth the different categories of suffering connected with birth: They are 1. Suffering in the womb (*Gabbhokkantimūlaka dukkha*); 2. Suffering in gestation (*Gabbhaparihāraṇamūlaka dukkha*); 3. Suffering due to loss of pregnancy (*Gabbhavipattimūlaka dukkha*); 4. Suffering at the time of delivery (*Vijāyanamūlaka dukkha*); 5. Suffering on venturing outside the womb (*Bahinikkhamanamūlaka dukkha*); 6. Suffering due to self-violence (*Attūpakkamamulaka dukkha*) and 7. Suffering due to others actions (*Parūpakkamamūlaka dukkha*).

1. Gabbhokkantimulaka Dukkha

Birth in the womb is not a pleasant place like the interior of a lotus. It is living like a worm in a rotting fish. The position of conception is below the belly, between the stomach (undigested food) and rectum (digested food), between the belly-lining and back-bone. It is quite cramped, dark and pervaded by substances emitting a bad odour. The stay in such a place, for nine long months, is just like a pudding stuffed in an air-tight bag.[39]

2. Gabbhaparihāranamūlaka Dukkha

Suffering also results out of sudden movements of the mother. The embryo suffers by being dragged to and fro and being jolted up and down. He/she also suffers from the extremities of cold and heat, whenever the mother drinks cold or swallows hot food; acid or salty food stuff also produces pain.[40]

3. Gabbhavipattmūlaka Dukkha

Suffering is produced when the mother loses her pregnancy due to overstrain or bodily malfunctioning. The loss of pregnancy *i.e.,* abortion produces both mental and physical pain in the mother. For apart from the physical loss, the philological fear and anxiety whether she will be able to conceive again troubles the mind of the mother.[41]

4. Vijāyanamūlaka Dukkha

It refers to the pain in him/her when the mother gives birth. He/She is turned upside down and flung down the narrow and fearful passage through the mouth of the womb like an 'infernal chasm'. This painful experience is just like being pounded to pulp by colliding rocks.[42]

5. Bahinikkhamanamūlaka Dukkha

The moment he/she enters from the womb into the *saṁsara* his/her delicate, frail body is washed and rubbed, he/she is made to cry. This painful experience is comparable to the experience of being pricked with needles and being gashed with blades.[43]

6. Attūpakkamamūlaka Dukkha

With his entry into *saṁsāra* the person clings either to the belief, of a 'permanent self' or 'impermanent 'self'. Buddha, in his *Dhammacakkappavattana sutta* points out that the notion of 'self' as 'permanent' leads to the path of self-mortification, whereas the belief in 'impermanent self' takes to the other extreme of self-indulgence. Both these paths are unwise, ignoble and full of pain. The path of self-mortification involves in inflicting suffering on one's own self, wheareas in self-indulgence due to excesses committed by both the body and mind suffering results.[44].

7. Parūpakkamamamūlaka Dukkha

Apart from the self-inflicted suffering, man has also to undergo the suffering inflicted upon him by his fellow-creatures. The violent acts of others such as flogging, beating etc., and also the objects of the world which collide with man are also sources which produce pain.[45]

(b) Ageing is Suffering (Jarā Pi Dukkha)

Jarā is used in two connotations by the Buddhists. Firstly, it used as a characteristic of 'whatever is formed' and secondly, as 'oldness' of aggregates in a single becoming, 'brokenness' in the case of continuity.[46] The latter meaning is to be taken here. It characterises the ripening and maturing of the aggregates. It manifests as the vanishing of youth and the nearing of death and destruction. It is the basis of *dukkha* physical and mental. For, from it arises the conditions of 'leadenness' of the limbs, whereby the organs become prone to disease. Decline of the faculties, of strength, of attractiveness to others, loss of memory, of intelligence and the overall personality starts fading, all of which produce experience of suffering.

(c) Death is Suffering (Maranam Pi Dukkhaṃ)

Everything which is born has to die. Birth and death are two connected events in the chain of life. Death is a characteristic of the aggregates, it represents a fall. It is the serving of connection of the life faculty in a single becoming. It manifests as absence from destiny, in the case of re-birth.[47] Man lives with the constant fear of death.[48] It is the basis of *dukkha*, for it disjoins man from the people whom he loves, the treasured objects, property and other pleasant things.[49] In the story of kisa Gotami,[49a] who refuses to believe that her child is dead, Buddha asks her to get some mustard seeds from any house wherein death has never visited. It brings into light man's distaste for death apart from stressing on its universal occurance. The mental fear of re-birth based on deeds good and bad troubles man. The way in which it occurs also troubles him. For it may be by violence, by natural causes, failures of the senses, mind, poisoning and so on.

(d) Sorrow is Suffering (Sokam[50] Pi Dukkhaṃ)

It is the psychological pain, which arises in the mind due to painful experiences such as being separated from a treasured object, loss of friends, relatives etc.[51] The mind is set ablaze by this pain, for it has an inner consuming nature. It consumes the whole mind like a poisoned dart, which spread slowly and destroys the mind completely. It produces intrinsic suffering and manifests as continual suffering. The mind, which is consumed with this agitation does not remain in a state of equilibrium.[52] It devises ways of overcoming the pain by further deeds of violence resulting in future pains both physical and mental.[53]

(e) Lamentation is Suffering (Paridevanam[54] Pi Dukkhaṃ)

Sorrow is a mental experience of agony, whereas, lamentation refers to the verbal expression of this agony through crying. Crying results in the eye getting swollen, throat, lips and palate getting dried all leading to bodily suffering. Apart from the bodily discomfort the mental equilibrium of the person in also affected. His future acts arising from such a disturbed source will only bear more future suffering.[55]

(f) Bodily Pain is Suffering (Dukkha)

Dukkha herein refers to bodily suffeing *(kāyikam dukkham),* which arises due to the oppression of the body.[56] This causes mental agony in man, for his mind gets disturbed by the bodily pains. It has the potential to make the mind react in a violent manner resulting in more suffering.

(g) Grief is Suffering (Domansam[57] Pi Ḍukkhaṃ)

Grief refers to a state of mental pain. It stands for the conspicuous manifestation of suffering by such physical acts as tearing one's hairs, weeping, thumping their breasts, twist and writhe, swallow poison, hanging themselves with ropes, walking over fire and undergoing different types of suffering.[58]

(h) Despair is Suffering (Upāyāsam[59] Pi Dukkhaṃ)

It is the resultant of excessive mental suffering arising due to the loss of wealth, relatives and so on. It manifests as dejection. It burns and consumes the mind. The affected person bemoans. This results in the person's bodily systems getting impaired by fever, sickness etc.[60]

One is likely to be baffled by the distinction between sorrow (*soka*), lamentation (*parideva*) and despair (*upāyāsa*). One needs to have a clear perspective of these concepts, for apparently they look alike. Buddhaghosa being aware of this difficulty makes a clear distinction of the meaning conveyed by the three concepts by making use of the following anology. Sorrow is like cooking of oil over slow fire; lamentation is like the boiling over from the pot when cooking over quick fire; and despair is what remains in the pot after it has boiled over, and is unable to react anymore (cooking till the pot dries up).[61]

(i) Association with the Unloved is Suffering (Aapiyehi Sampaygo Pi Dukkhaṃ)

Suffering results when man comes into contact with disagreeable thoughts, speech and acts arising from disagreeable fellow-beings and inanimate things. This association affects the mind resulting in distress; he suffers from stress. This has the potency to get transformed into hatred (doso) making man to perform deeds bad, which form the seeds for future pains. Hence, it is the basis for suffering.[62]

(j) Separation From the Loved is Suffering (Piyehi Vippayago Pi Dukkhaṃ)

Man clamers for the association of things and persons that generate in him a feeling of pleasure. He strives for attachment with such beings and objects, but the fact is that many a time he is separated from them. This disassociation from the desirable *arouses* experiences of pain. He feels lost, that his existence has no meaning, for he considers, 'living' as being in association with these objects. It may lead him to the extent of ending his life. This suffering though initially psychological gets transformed into bodily suffering.[63]

(k) Not to Get what one Wants is Suffering (Yam P'Iccam Na Labhati Tam Pi Dukkhaṃ)

Man is a bundle of desires. He craves for association, possession and control of all pleasant things. But this proposition is practically impossible. There are many things which he fails to obtain. For instance, man wants to be immortal, non-changing (Vbh.101). He suffers from this feeling of wanting an unobtainable object. He seeks and strives for the impossible. This produces mental pain which manifests as disappointment.[64] This disappointment makes man devise 'means' of attaining the impossible. Trying for the unattainable, unobtainable object is nothing but inviting suffering on oneself.

1. Five Aggregates of Clinging is Suffering (Saṅkhittena Pañcāupādanakkhanda[65] Pi Dukkhaṃ)

Buddha expounding on the different types of suffering referred above, found that all of them be it, birth, death, ageing, etc., had their final bearing on the aggregates. He rightly arrived at the conclusion that these five aggregates (of clinging) form the basis of all suffering.[66]

Buddha in the Saṁyutta-nikāya[67] states that the five aggregates namely rūpa, vedanā, saññā, saṅkhāra and viññāṇa are all impermanent. They are produced by causes and conditions. They are 'conditioned', which is a characteristic of suffering. These five form the basis for craving and desire, and thus are enumerated as the five aggregates of suffering and attachment (*dukkhapañcopānakkhandah*). They are *sāsravah*—soiled with passions. They have birth as their initial suffering; ageing as their medieval suffering and death as their 'final' suffering; the suffering due to the burning of one (who) is a victim of pain, that which threatens death is sorrow. The crying out of one who is unable to bear the suffering is lamentation. The affliction of the body due to the contact with the undesirable, separation from the desired, not getting the wanted objects, is all pain.[68] Each of these five aggregates is the basis of each of the above suffering.

Buddha has enumerated a few kinds of suffering to show how these aggregates are the basis of all suffering be it mental or physical. Just as the taste of a drop of water from the ocean tells us the salty taste of all the water in the ocean.

TYPES OF DUKKHA

In the *Saṃyutta nikāya*[69] the different types of dukkha that man is exposed to are classified into three, 1. Suffering caused by pain (*dukkha-dukkhatā*); 2. Suffering caused by change (*Vipariṇāma dukkhatā*) and 3. Suffering caused by impressions (*Saṇkhāra dukkhatā*).

1. Suffering Caused by Pain (*Dukkha-Dukkhatā*)

It refers to the suffering caused by 'bodily pain' *i.e.,* the pain arising out of the body. Buddhaghosa[70] analyses the compound *dukkha-dukkhatā* as 'one misery follows another misery', in the sense that the body as an aggregate of the five 'khandhas' is firstly responsible for misery. It is with the birth (jāti) of the body that the manifold forms of suffering such as disease, grief, lamentation, sorrow, etc., get manifest. From the moment of birth the body undergoes change every second.[71] In the course of this change, he may fall a prey to the attack of certain diseases. Apart from the bodily suffering he also undergoes mental torture. He keeps on thinking and contemplating on problems such as 'why should one ever fall ill? 'When will I get cured'? 'Will it be complete or partial'? This form of thought is nothing but a form of 'unsatisfactoriness' of 'annoyance' with both the body and the mind. Any form of 'unsatisfactorinness' can never be an element of pleasure, but a form of suffering only.

The other forms of suffering that arise from the body such as those of lamentation, grief or sorrow, are essentially resultants of the body's attachment and craving for the objects of the world, little realising the suffering inherently present in clinging to these evanescent objects. In the words of the Buddha: 'Whoever seeks to acquire the worldly goods, the merchant...the crown must expose himself to the inconvenience of heat and cold to hunger and thirst'.[72]

2. Suffering caused by Change *(Vipariṇāma Dukkhatā)*

Literally, the word '*vipariṇāma*' stands for 'change'. When used with *dukkha* it refers to the suffering arising due to change. There is nothing in this world that does not undergo change even for a fraction of a second. There is only the process of 'becoming' without any 'being' underlying it. Becoming is a process, wherein the 'cause' becomes the 'effect' and the 'effect' the 'cause' for the next part of the chain. All things are governed by the law of impermanence. Being 'impermanent' and 'non-continuous' the experiences generated out of such a sense-object contact can never be one of permanence. At one time, an object may generate an experience of pleasure or pain. Man who attaches and identifies himself with these pleasant experiences is bound to suffer due to the inherent impermanence and essenceless nature of them. Hence, it is *sukkhavedanā*,[73] that is pleasure is also a form of suffering. Buddha opines that the pleasure generated out of sense-object contact should be understood by man objectively as they really are. Not only are these experienced unsatisfactory due to the fact of impermanence, but, because these experiences of pleasure and their consequent unsatisfactoriness do not provide a proper foundation for life. To quote the Buddha, "O Monks, if, objectively one understands in this way that enjoyment, that their unsatisfactoriness is unsatisfactoriness, that liberation from them is liberation, them it is possible that they themselves will certainly understand the desire for sense pleasure completely...[74]

Buddhaghosa however interprets the term 'vipariṇāma' not merely as 'change' but 'change for the worse'.[75] But, why should one believe that change is for the worse? That change is for the worse will become intelligible to us only when we have an insight into the momentary nature of things. When we observe the nature of the sentient beings, it involves a transition from birth, youth, adulthood, middle age, old age, which involve factors of pain. When we understand the insentient objects they are also under the grip of the law of impermanence *i.e.,* they are subject to decay and destruction. It is obviously for this reason that Buddhaghosa must have associated 'change' as a 'change for the worse'.

3. Suffering caused by Impressions *(Saṇkhāra Dukkhatā)*

The term *Saṇkhāra* in the buddhist texts[76] has been used in two senses. In the first sense, it refers to one among the five khandhas viz., *saṇkhāra khandha* (mental formations) and secondly to all conditioned things. In both senses, it is of the nature of *dukkha*.

In the first case, *saṇkhāra* as mental formations determines (1) How one views the world, and 2) How actively one is involved in it. The term *dukkha* when applied to it, herein, signifies a misdirected mode of existence. The entire mental and volitional aspect of one's own existence is bathed with false ideas such as belief in 'self' as an ontic entity.[77] Attachment to such ideas curbs the progress of one towards freedom from the fleeting pleasures. Attachment (*upādāna*) most severely affects this *khandha*. Mentally and volitionally one continues to seek meaning and draw his existence based on these fleeting things.

In the second sense, it signifies anything conditional. Herein, *dukkha* is identified with the actual process of one's existence. It signifies an 'unenlightened mode of existence'. It has a deeper claim to the effect that it bothers one's existence itself. It points to the fact that man's present mode of existence is nothing but a wastage of one's resources on fleeting pleasures of *saṁsāra*. Is one's existence meant for this pursuit? This deep sense arises, for one fails to see the objects as they really are. As one is attached and as one draws meaning and nourishment for one's attachment from the objects and false concepts, one's fails to see the truth namely, that everything in the world is characterised by impermanence (*anicca*), essencelessness (*anattā*) and suffering (*dukkha*). The point highlighted, here, is that one's whole mode of existence is misdirected and untrue.

In the Kathāvathu, the Theravādins claim that all conditioned things are dukkha is challenged by the Hetuvādins.[78] For them, *dukkha* is wholly bound up with the sentience and is not applicable to all things. Theravadins hold that both the sentient and non-sentient are' liable to *dukkha*.[79] Thus, we have two types of *dukkha* based on the above distinction namely (a) *dukkha* associated with life (*indriya*)-Senstient *dukkha* and (b) *dukkha* confined to the insentient-Insentient *dukkha*. The first refers to the ordinary suffering *i.e., dukkha-duhkkatā*, whereas the second refers to the insentient realm such as rocks, earth etc., for they also produce suffering through the law of impermanence[80] *i.e. vipariṇāma dukkha*. These insentient objects though can cause *dukkha* there is nothing intrinsic to the insentient conditioned objects that make them *dukkha*. It rather depends on how they affect the sentient world, our response to them, evaluation etc., which determines whether it is *dukkha* or not. Justifying the scriptural claim that 'all conditioned things as *dukkha*' the *kathāvathu* makes a significant distinction. The *dukkha*, which is associated with the insentient, no doubt is *dukkha*, but is not the Noble Truth of *dukkha* because it is not produced by *kamma* and defilements.[81] The Noble Truth has got to do with the sentient realm only and specifically with the actual process of one's existence. It relates to the 'being-in-the world'. *Dukkha* is associated with all conditioned things only in so far as they are 'liable to trouble' for sentient beings.

In addition to the three types of *dukkha* mentioned in the *Saṃyutta Nikāya* Buddhaghosa in the *Visuddhimagga* speaks of four kinds of *dukkha*. These provide us with more insight into the Buddhist conception of *dukkha*.

1. Concealed Suffering *(Paṭicchanna Dukkha)*

The physical and mental afflictions such as ear-ache, excessive bone growth, fever born out of lust, of hate etc., are termed as concealed suffering. Here, the misery is not openly evident. It can be known only by questioning the sufferer. It is also referred to as an 'unevident suffering.'[84]

2. Unconcealed Suffering (Appaṭicchanna Dukkha)

This type of suffering is caused through the bad *kammas*. Here, the suffering is openly evident, it is outwardly visible. It is also termed as 'exposed suffering's.[85]

3. Indirect Suffering (Pariyāya Dukkhaṃ)

Buddhaghosa uses indirect suffering, in the sense, that they are the basis for one kind of suffering or another. Indirect suffering includes all types of *dukkha* except intrinsic *dukkha i.e., dukkhavedanā,* starting from birth as expounded in the first noble truth under this category.

4. Direct Suffering (Nippariyāya Dukkhaṃ)

Buddhaghosa in this category brings intrinsic sufferings such as painful feeling (*dukkhavedanā*), which is referred to as *dukkha-dukkhatā*. Intrinsic suffering refers to those bodily and mental feelings which in their intrinsic nature, their name and in their individual essence are *dukkha*[89]

Buddhaghosa's distinction between direct and indirect suffering has profound significance. Direct suffering is obvious to everyone. Indirect suffering refers to the very nature of conditioned things with potentialities for generating pain. The unenlightened does not realise this intrinsic truth and finds pleasure in them not realising that at heart they are causative of pain and the so called pleasure that he experiences is not free from pain. But the enlightened is sensitive to this intrinsic truth and desists from his pursuit of finding pleasure in the conditioned things. The unenlightened being comparatively insensitive, fails to realise the indirect suffering of *vipariṇāma* and *saṅkhāra dukkha*. This is the crux of the Noble Truth.

PLEASURE AS A FORM OF PAIN

The feeling of pleasure, a state of harmony, agreeableness in the conscious stream, arises when the mind comes into contact with the 'objects of like' in the external and internal world. This contact is brought through the agency of the sense-organs. Buddha speaks of five types of sense pleasures depending upon the base sense-organ namely, agreeable material shapes, pleasant sound, pleasant smell, pleasant taste and agreeable tangible sensation. These pleasures are not pure pleasures for they inherently contain in them the germs of pain. Buddha supports this argument with an illustration. For instance: a man earns his living by doing some work in order to gain some pleasure. In his strife to gain pleasure he undergoes and withstands the attacks of cold, heat, diseases, hunger, thirst and so on, which are all experiences of pain. Secondly, even though he strives and exerts himself there is no guarantee that he will attain them. In case he fails, he is bound to be left in the midst of grief. Thirdly, if he succeeds and gains possession of the objects of his choice, his joy as short lived, for he is constantly haunted by the fear and anxiety that he is likely to lose them. Fourthly, it is in this quest for pleasure that friends, brothers, kings, parents and their children quarrel and are ready to inflict any type of suffering, physical or mental, on those whom they think are hindrances to gain their selfish objective of pleasure. Fifthly, if a person does not get possession of the objects of his choice, he adopts unjust means to gain them. For him the 'end' *i.e.,* the feeling of pleasure is more important and it alone matters and no the 'means' employed. When the means employed are bad such as killing, thieving etc., there is always the fear of being caught and punished. When he is arrested, he is bound to be punished. The punishment handed out may vary from lashing to beheading. Sixthly, a person leading a lustful life involves himself in the abuse of thought, word and deed, with the sole aim of gaining sensual pleasures. He is constantly haunted by the fear and dread of future life. He is tormented by the fact that due to his present wrong conduct he may be born in hell, which is mire of unending suffering.

The above analysis of the six situations arising due to the pursuit of pleasures clearly brings into light the fact that there is no such thing as pure pleasure and it is always mixed with the germs of pain.[92]

IS BUDDHISM PESSIMISTIC?

Buddha's analysis of existence (*saṃsāra*) as being full of *dukkha* has been questioned by the lay and the profound. They generally feel that this world with its immense quantity of pleasure, family life, wealth, power and position dominates the suffering present in them. They do accept the presence of *dukkha* in *sukha,* but it need not deter us from our pursuits of pleasure in our day to day life. Buddha being convinced that even the so called pleasure also being a form of pain on ultimate analysis adheres to the position that 'everything is full of suffering' (*sarvam dukkhaṁ*). The average man feels that Buddha has pained such a gloomy picture of man's life on this planet, that will make him shudder from the very thought of his existence. He believes that it will land man in distress and agony and will make him lose all charm in life. Threatened constantly by the miseries in existence, the impending suffering, he is liable to experience increased mental and physical suffering.

The average man's understanding of buddhist thought is likely to lead one to the impression that it is a philosophy of pessimism,[93] a life negating philosophy.

But a careful understanding of Buddhism discloses to us that pessimism in Buddhism is initial and not final, for, he suggests the way for the cessation of *dukkha*, leading to a state of freedom from *dukkha* namely *nibbāna*. In the view of Edward Holmes: 'So far was he from being a pessimist in the deeper and darker sense of the word, that at the heart of nature he could see nothing but light'.[94] To accuse Buddhism of pessimism would amount to the lack of imaginative sympathy for its insight into the suffering of others. Having an existence of identifying oneself with the fleeting pleasures of the world without an insight into the suffering within, is a shallow existence. If a system advocates that life is full of misery and there is no way out, man is born in misery, brought up in misery and dies in misery, them it is pessimism. But a system such as Buddhism that suggests a positive way out of suffering through the Noble Eightfold path (Arıya Aṭṭangıko Maggo) cannot be called pessimistic. It would, therefore, be appropriate to state that Buddhism encounters pessimism not to succumb to it, but to circumvent it.

The Buddha by his deep insight and reflection into philosophical issues has put forward the bare facts of man's existence. But people are not accustomed to hear or see the truth, for its is bitter and unpalatable. They prefer to live enjoying and identifying themselves with the fleeting pleasures. If stating the truth, calling a spade a spade is not palatable to some, they will still be what they are. If giving a correct insight into the facts of life is pessimism, then the critics are right.

Buddha's philosophy is a form of healthy realism. It presents a realistic understanding of all the problems and perils of existence and prescribes a way out. The Buddha feels that one who realises this truth namely *dukkha*, will have neither fear nor anxieties. He will always be calm, sure, and will not be upset or dismayed by a sudden change or calamity, for he can perceive things in a proper perspective. He will be able to mould and use his existence towards attaining a state of freedom from *dukkha-nibbāna*.

REFERENCES

1. *Dukkha* (Saṅskrit) whereas '*dukkha*' is Pāli. Pāli is the language in which the early Buddhist texts were composed.

2. *Cullavagga:* IX, 1.4.

3. Though there is no explicit ontology in Buddha's teaching, there is a good deal of it in an implicit form. There may be no ontological aim in what he taught, there certainly is an ontological view underlying it. Ref: Hiriyanna. M.*Outlines of Indian Philosophy,* p.13.

4. *Majjhima Nikāya Sutta* 63 II, ii Cūla-Māuṅkya sutta.

5. *Saṁyutta Nikāya* (S.N) V. 437. Woodward. Vol. V. p. 370.

6. The Theravādins contend that Buddha's prime concern is with personal experience. What it means to me personally to exist as a human being? It is a practical and experimental inquiry, not as a mere theoretical and metaphysical inquiry. There are two modes of inquiry, one concerned with 'Knowing a fact' and another with 'Knowing a person'. 'Knowing a person' alludes the way I know myself as a person. As a person I experience myself in a direct, immediate way. I have immediate access to my experience in a way that others do not have. The way one knows a fact differs from the direct way I 'know myself'. There is more of a distance in the knowing of facts, a greater separation between the 'knower' and the 'known' between the 'Subject' and 'object'. The *Points of controversy-Kathā-Vathu,* Book I Sec. I., p.9.

7. Price Soddhāttho was born to the Sākya Queen Mayādevi and King Śuddhodāno at Sālagrove of Lumbini, (So Boddhisātto.. Jāto sākyanām gāme janapade Lumbineye: khuddaka Nikāya, Vol. 1, p.37.cf: Dīgha Nikāya, II, p.48.

   "Khattiyojātiya .. khattiyakule udapādi...

   Gotamo gottena... assatthassamūle.... etarahi s'uddhodāno nāma rājā pitā ahosi,

   Mayānāma devi mātā ahosi, janetti, kapilavatthu nāma nagarm rājādhānī.'') which is marked by a pillar now called Rummindei (District Bhairhwa, Nepal Tarai) in the Janapada of Kapilavastu, a sākyam territory, His date of birth is now usually fixed at 563 B.C.

(Ref. Thomas, E. J. *The Life of Buddha* p. 27 fn. 1., Winternitz, *History of Indian Literature,* Vol. II, 1933, p. 597.)

The *Lalitha Vistāra* explains the meaning of 'Siddhāttho' as one whose aim is accomplished. This name was given by King Suddhodāno his father, for his long cherished desire of having a child was fulfilled by the birth of the boy. Rockhill, *(The life of the Buddha)* speaks of the prince's name as 'Srvārtha Siddha' on the basis of the Tibetan *Dulva* and the *Mahāvastu.*

8. Asvaghoṣa's *Buddhacarita,* Trans. E.H. Johnston, Motilal Banarasidass, Delhi, (1963), 1972: iii, 26-39, pp. 37-39.

9. To use Brewster's words, "Alas! This world has fallen upon trouble. There is getting born and growing old and dying and falling and arising, but there is not the knowing of an escape from suffering, from decay and death". Ref: Brewster, E. H. *The Life of Gotama, The Buddha,* p. 40.

10. His noble quest was to find the 'good'-the peerless way of desirable peace (kimkusalagavesi anuttaraṁ santvirarapadaṁ pariyesamano), *Majj. Nikāya* 161-163. Majj. Nikāya: 26.

11. Asvaghosā's *Buddhacarita,* III, 27, 40-54, pp. 39-43: *Nidānakathā*, LVI, Jātaka, I. P. 59.

Prince Siddhattho the Pali texts speak, went forth into the homeless state at the age of twenty-nine (Ref. Thomas, E. J. *The Life of Budha*, p. 60, fn. 1).

12. King Śiddhodāno feared that the prediction made by Sage Asita (or kāla Devala), wherein he had said by observing the birth marks of the child that he would either become a great Emperor or would become an ascetic by leaving household life affected by the four sights of old age, disease, a corpse and an ascetic, to gain knowledge to liberate man from suffering.

13. Buddha's rejection of worldly objects as being full of suffering is validity presented in Chap IV of Buddhacarita, pp: 44-88. For the Omnipresence of dukkha, see the story of Kisā Gotamī : Ref: Rhys Davids (Mrs), trans. *Psalms of the Early Buddhists—1.* pp. 106-110.

Cf; *Sutta Nipāta*, vagga 3, Sutta 8 (*Sallasutta*) 1, 5 74 animittaṁ aññataṁ ... maccānaṁ idha jīvataṁ Kasirañ caparittañca, tañ ca dukkhena saṁyutaṁ (Men cannot calculate, men cannot gauge, this life's brief troublous span, by woes beset).

14. *Majj. nikāya* 26, Ariyapariyesana & *Majj. Nikāya* 85, Bodhirājakumāra Suttas, it is pointed out that Ālārakālāma is different from Bharandu Kālāma, who is referred to as an old fellow student of Gotama.

15. Aśvaghosa in his *Buddhacarita* (Canto XII) ascribes Alārākālām doctrines to resemble that of Saṅkhya.

16. *Jat.* I. pp. 66-7

The austerities practised by 'Buddha' in the forests of Gaya are described vividly in: Majjhima Nikāya 4 (Bhavahherava Sutta); *Majj. nikāya.* 14. Cūla Dukkhakkhanada Sutta); *Majji. nika-ya* 36. (*Mahāsaccaka Sutta*); *Majji. nikāya,* 85, (Bodhi Rāj Kumāra Sutta). The following verse in the Daṇḍa-Vaggo of Dhammapada provides evidence of Buddha revised opinion about the futility of asceticism as a means for liberation. na naggacariyā na jaṭā, na paṅkā, nānāsakā thaṇdilasāyikāvā, Rajo ca jallaṁ ukkuṭikappadha-naṃ sodhenti maccaṃ avitiṇṇakaṅkhaṃ. *Dhp.* 141.

Not nakedness, no matted hair, not dirt, not fasting, not laying on the ground, not rubbing with ashes, not sitting motionless can purify a mortal who is not free from doubt. Dhp. 141.(Trans. Radhakrishnan, p. 105).

17. The Buddha is called *Gotama,* for it refers to his *gotra* meaning 'cow-stall', a clan whose members claim to have descended from the ancient brahmin Rsi Gotama. *Dīgha Nikāya* II, p. 48.

18. *Majj. nikāya I. 247.*

19. Extremes of self-mortification and self-indulgence appeared to śākyamuni Gotama as the faulty means. Self-mortification arises when one believes that he possesses a distinctive self, permanent and external, which he has to nourish and preserve, forever. His acts are based and guided by this false conception. He practices austerities, imposes conditions on his body. He inflicts upon himself both body and mind sufferings. Self-indulgence arises when one believes that the self perishes along with bodily death. They involve themselves in all kinds of acts, good or bad, ethical or unethical, to gain pleasure, For they have nothing to fear, the law of kamma and rebirth do not exist for them.

20. The Buddhists have suggested a number of criteria for Noble truths: (1) Noble truths are those truths that can be realised by the noble persons; (2) Noble truths are truths that belong to the enlightened ones; (3) The 'noble truths' are so-called because of the nobleness implied by their discovery. *Vis. Magga*, Chapter XVI, 495.

21. These five Brahmaṅas became the first converts. They were Aññāta-koṇḍañña, Bhaddiya, Vappa, Mahānāma and Assaji.

22. *Saṁ. Nikāya*, V. 421.

23. This particular dormulation of dukkha as cause, cessation and the path has been likened to the four-fold means of medical treatment. Though this formulation might have been borrowed from Medicine and given by Buddha's disciples, yet I feel that it does not do any injustice to Buddha's teaching of *dukkha*. It is a 'methodological' device, which might have been formulated, so as to render the Buddha's doctrine more comprehensive and cummunicable to the common masses.

24. *Dukkhaṁ ariyasaccaṁ*-jāti pi dukkhā, jarā pi dukkhā, maraṇaṁ pi dukkhaṁ, sokaparidevadukkhadomanassupāyāsā pi dukkhā, appiyehi sampayogo dukkho, piyehi vippayogo dukkho, yam p'icchaṃ na labhati tam pi dukkhaṃ sankhittena pañcaupādānakkhanadhā pi dukkhā. *Dīgha—nikāya* II, 304, *Vibhaṅga* 99.

25. *Dukkha-samudayam ariya-saccaṁ*: Yāyaṃ taṇhā ponobhavikā nandi-rāga-sahagatā tatra tatrābhinandinī, seyyathīdaṃ kāma - taṇhā bhava-taṇhā vibhava- taṇhā... yam loke piya-rūpam sāta-rūpam ... ettha nivisamānā V. 421; *Dīgha-nikāya* II. 308; *Vibhaṅga* 101-3.

26. Dukkha-nirodhaṃ ariya-saccaṃ; Yo tassa yeva taṇhāya asesa-virāga-nirodho cāgo patinissaggo mutti anālayo., *Dīgha-nikāya* II, 310-313.

27. Dukkha nirodha gamini paṭpāda ariya saccaṃ. Ayam eva ariyo aṭṭhaṅgiko maggo, seyyathīdam sammā diṭṭhi, sammā saṃkappo, sammā vācā, sammā kammanto sammā ājīvo sammā vāyāmo sammā sati sammā sati sammā samādhi. *Dīgha nikāya* II, 310-313.

28. *Vis. Magga,* 494.

30. Rhys Davids, *Buddhist Psychology*, pp. 83-86.

31. *Ibid.*

32. Rahula W., "Dukkha Satya", *Gotama Buddha 25th Centaniary* volume, Ed. N.N. Law, 1956, p. 141.

33. Humphery, C., *Buddhism*, Penguin books, Third ed., reprint, 1972, p.81.

34. This 'incompleteness' or 'insufficency' may pertain to knowledge or the pattern of life one leads or both. Ref: Humphery, C., *Buddhism*, Penguin Books, Third ed. Reprint, 1972, p. 81.

35. Pande G.C., *Studies in the origins of Buddhism,* p. 403.

36. Stcherbatsky, Th., *The Central conception of Buddhism.*, p.40.

37. *Abhidhammakośsa* I., 4-6

38. In *Dīgha Nikāya*, i.81, Birth (Jāti) is used in the sense of becoming. Vin.1.93., it is rebirth linking. For birth is due to the first consiousness arisen, the first congnition manifested, in the mothers' womb. In A.iii.152., it refers to clan, an event by which one is accepted into their family.

39. Ayaṁ hi satto mālukucchimhi nibhatta-māno na uppala paduma puṇḍarikadīsu nibbattatti, atha kho hetṭha āmāsayassa upari pakkāsayassa udarapaṭtla pitṭhi kantakānāṃ vemajjhe paranasambadhe libbanadhakāre nānā kuṇnapagandha-paribhāvita parama duggandha pavna vicarite...vicarite. *Vis. Magga*, XVI, p. 421 (B. B).

40. Yam pana so mātu sahasā upakkhalana gamana nisīdana - vuṭṭhana parivattanādīsu...yaṁ ca mātu sītūdakapānakāle aṅgāravutt./hi samparikṅño viya; *Vis. Magga* chap. XVI, 38, pp. 569-70 (Nanamoli), p. 422 (B.B).

41. Yam panassa mulhagabbhaya matuya millāmacca suhajjādihi pindassanā raho dukkhuppasiṭṭhāhc chedana phālanādihi dukkham upajjati: *Ibid*. P. 422. (B.B).

42. Yaṁ vijāyaman-/yamaluya kannmaje hi vātehi parivattctva narakapātaṃ viya atibhayānakaṃ patipātiyam-/nassa paramasambādhena yonimukhena tāl/.acchaggalena viya nikaddhiya mānassa mahānāgassa, naraka sattassa viya ca samghatapabbate hi vicunniyamānassa duhkham uppajjate, *Ibid*. p. (B. B).

43. yaṃ pana jātassa taruṇavaṇasadi sasukhumālasarīassa hatha gaha ṇa-sūcimukha khura dhārāhi vijjhana phālanasadisaṁ dukkham uppajjati idaṁ idaṁ mātukucchi to bahinikkhamana mūlakam dukkhaṁ. Ibid. p. 422. (B.B).

44. Yaṁ tato paraṁ pavatthiyaṁ attanā va atthānam vadhentassa, acelakavatā divasena ātāpana-paritāpanāuyogamanuyuttassa kodhavesena abhunjantassa ubbandhanatassa ca dukkham uppajjati idaṁ attūpakkamamūlakaṁ. Ibid. 422. (B.B).

45. Yam pana parato vadhabanadhanādīni anubhavantassa uppajjati, idaṁ parūpakkamamūlakaṁ ti. Ibid, p. 422. (B.B)

46. *Vis*. Magga. XVI, p. 423.

Majj. Nikāya iii. 249. Vis. Magga. chap. XVI (503,44, pp 571). In the Aug. Nikaya iii, 35.1. Ageing is referred to as one of three messengers of death. The two others being disease and death of others.

47. *Vis. Magga*. XVI. p. 424.

48. *Sutta Nipāta* (Sn.) 576.

49. *Sn*. 777 see how they are sticken in the thing they love, like fishes in the puddles of a failing stream.

50. Soka: Fr. 'Suc' means to gleam, grief. It is the 'flame of fire' later described as the 'burning grief'. Vis. magga, 503. (Ref. Pali. Dic. p. 724).

51. *Vis. Magga*. XVI p.424 (Buddha Bharati-BB); 504,

Sokādīsu sokonāma ñatibyasanādīhi phuṭthassa vacīpālapo cf. *Dh*. 15., *Peta*. 26 (5), 10.

He sorrows here, sorrows hereafter; In both wise sorrows the evil-doer, He sorrows and he mourns to see what he with his own acts defiled.

52. *Vis. Magga* XVI., p. 424 (B.B); 504,48.

Sattānaṁ hadayaṁ soko visasallaṁ va bujjati, aggitatto va nāraco bhusaṁ va dahate punaḥ.

53. *Sutta nipāta*, vagga 3, sutta 8 (Salla sutta) 11,584. No peace of mind comes not by grie and tears, which do but add to pain and bring men low. (Naruṇṇena sokena santiṁ

papoti cetaso, bhiyy 'ass' uppajjate dukkhaṁ papoti cetaso, bhiyy'ass' uppajjate dukkhaṁ sarīram upahaññati).

54a. *Parideva*. fr. 'pari' ā 'deva' of 'div', 'devati' means lamentation, Wailing, Ref. Pali. dic. p. 427.

55. *Vis. Magga* XVI, p.424 (B.B) & 504, 49 paridevo nāma ñatibyasanādīhi phuṭṭhassa vacīpalāpo Yaṁsokasallavihatoparidevamāno kaṇthoṭthatalutalasosaja-mappa sayham biyyadimattamadhigacchati yeva duḥkhaṃ duḥkhtitena bhavagā paridevamāhā ti. cf. Sn. 774.

56. *Vis. Magga*, XVI, p. 425 (B. B) & 504, 50 Duḥkhaṃ nāma kāikam duḥkham. Taṃ kāyapilanalakhaṇam.

57. Domanassaṃ : Skt. Daurmanasya, fr. 'duh'+'manas', means distress, dejectedness and grief. As mental pain opposed to physical pain (dukkha) Vis. Magga.505.

58. *Vis. Magga* XVI p.425 (B.B) domanassaṃ nāma mānasaṃ duḥkham ceto dukkha samappita hi kese pakiriya kondanti, urani paṭirpisanti ....aggīm pavisanti...

59. *Upāyāsa*: fr. upa + ayasa; a kind of trouble, turbulance, tribulation, unrest, distrubance, and an unsettled condition. *Vis. Magga*. 505 (Ref-*Pāli. Eng*. dic., p. 150).

60. *Vis. Magga* XVI. P. 425 (B.B) upāyāso nāma ñativyassanādīhi phuṭṭhassa adhimatta ceto dukkha ppabhāvito doso yeva.

61. *Vis. Magga* XVI. p. 426. (B.B) Ettha ca mandāgninā antobhājane pākoviya soko tikkhagninā paccamānassa bhājanato bhainiḥkha manaṁ viya paridevo.

62. *Vis. Magga*. chap. XVI. (505) 54, p. 574 (ñāmamoli) Appiyasampayogo nāma amanāpehi sattāsaṁkhārehi samodhānaṁtakaraṅaraso, anatthabhāva paccupaṭṭhāno.

63. *Vis. Magga* chap. XVI (506) 55, p.575 (ñ-ānamoli) piyavippayogo nāma manāpehi satta saṁkhārehi bināchāvo so iṭthavatthu viyogalakkhaṅo, sokuppādānaraso, vyasanapaccupaṭṭhāno cf. *Peta*. 32(11), p. 11. Just as a man on waking sees no more someone that he had met during a dream, so too no more the person loved he sees who passes onward when his time is up.*Sn.807*.

64. *Vis. Magga*, XVI, P. 426 (B.B) Sā alabbhaneyyavatthuicchanalakkhaṇā tappariyesanarasā, tesaṃ appatthipacchupaṭṭhānā.

65. The expression *pañcaupādānakkhandha* consists of three components. *pañca* + *upādāna* + *khandha*; *pañca* means five; upādāna clinging and khandha means aggregates, which are five in number in *rūpa*, *vedanā*, *sañña*, *viññāṇa*, and saṅkhāra that constitute the psycho-physical organism of man. The aggregates, when associated with upādāna causes suffering, when *upādāna* is eliminated there remains *pañcakkhandhas* intact but free from *dukkha*.

66. *Vis Magga*. chap. XVI. (506) 57, p. 575 (ñānmoli),*Vis. Magga*, XVI., p. 427 (B.B). jateppabhutikam duḥkkaṃ yam vuttamidha badina, avuttam yam ca tam sabbam vina na vijjati yam basma upādānakkhandha saṁkhepato ime, duḥkha pi vitta duḥkkhantadesakena mahesian

67. *Saṁ Nikāya* 21-2.

68. *Vis. Magga*, chap. XVI, 59, (506) p. 575.

69. *Saṁ. Nikāya* IV. 259.

70. *Vis. Magga* chap XVI. 35.

71. *Aṅguttara Nikāya* II (fol.thai) There are five things which no saṃsāra, nor Brahman nor God can bring about. That which is subject to old age should not grow old, to sickness, should not die, to decay, shouldnot decay, to be liable to pass away should not pass away.

72 *Majj. Nikāya*, I. ii, 13-Mahādukkhakkhanda sutta.

73. The pleasant experience which arises out of the contact of the indriyas with the external objects, is a result of its decoding in the mind. The mind and its images judge the experiences. these images and impedements change according to one's mood, will, feeling etc., conditioned by circumstances man lives. Mind is conditioned, anything conditioned is impermanent; anything impermanent will only produce suffering.

74. *Majj. Nikāya*. i.87.

75. *kathāvathu*. XVII. 4. Commentary - *Points of Controversy*, pp. 315-316, Ref. Pali-Eng. Dic. (1959), p. 626.

76. *Saṁ. Nikāya* IV. 259.

77. Refer chapter 4 for further details on the Buddhist concept of 'self'.

78. *Kathāvathu-Points of controversy*, PTS. p.315. ff.

79. Ibid.

80. Commentary to *Pañcappakāraṇna* of the *Abhidhamma piṭaka* (Sinhālese script) part I, ed. Rerukane Ariyanana Thera, the Tipiṭaka pub. Press, 1936, Colomboo., p.189. (udayabbaya patipīlanattena yadaniccaṁ taṁ dukkhanti saṅgahītattā dukkhaṁ).

81. Ibid. p.190 (kamma kilesehi pana anibbattattā).

82. Dutt.N. *Early Monastic Buddhism*, p.245.

83. *Vis. Magga*. XVI., 34, p.568 (N.M) and p.421 (B.B) Seyyathīdaṃ... paṭicchannadukkhaṁ, appaṭicchannadukkhaṃ, pariyāyadukkhaṁ, nippariyāyadukkhaṃ ti.......

84. kaṇṇasūla-dantasūla-rāgajaparilāha-dosajaparilādikāyika cetasiko abadho pucchitvā janitabbato upakkamassa ca apākaṭa-bhāvato paṭcchannadukkham nāma..*Vis. Magga* p. 421 (B.B).

85. dvattimsakammakaraṇādi samuṭṭhāno abādho apucchittā va janitabbato upakkamassa ca pākaṭabhāvato appaṭicchanna dukkham nāma *Vis. Magga.*, p.421. (B.B).

86. pariyāya. fr. pari+i, meaning revolution, lapse of time period. j.III. 460; V 367 (Pali.dic., p.432).

87. Āgatam jāti ādi sabbam pi tassa tassa dukkhassa vatthubhāvato pariyāya dukkham. *Vis.Magga.* (prakarana) p.421 (B.B).

88. Nippariyāya. fr.nis + pariyāya, meaning without distinction (Pali. Dic., p.360).

89. Duḥkkha duḥkhaṁ pana nippariyāya duḥkhaṁ ti vucchati. *Vis. Magga* (prakarana). p.421.

91. Prasaññāpāda on *Madhyamika kārikā*, Ed. P.L. Vaidya, Mithila Research Institute, 1960, p. 209.

92. *Majj. Nikāya* 186. Mahādukkhakkhaṇḍā sutta, P.T.S., P.110.

93 Pessimism is a philosophical doctrine, which subscribes to the view that the world is 'bad' and not a happy place, to dwell. It presents a depressing view of life, not making any attempt whatsoever to go beyond it.

94. Edward Holmes, *The Creed of Buddha*, the Bodly Head, London, 1957, p. 183.

4

Origin of Dukkha

INTRODUCTION

Indian philosophical systems trace duhkha to ignorance (*avidyā*), but they are not unanimous about the conception of *avidyā*. The concept of *avidyā* differs from system to system, for instance, the Cārvākas hold that *avidyā* refers to the false conception of the existence of a permanent 'self' apart from the impermanent body. Subscribing to annihilationism (*Ucchedavāda*)[1] the Cārvākas believes that the 'self' perishes along with bodily death. Contrary to the above, we come across systems, which subscribe to the conception of an 'immutable self'. They conjecture that there exists a 'self' over and above the perishable physical body. It is eternal, permanent and unchanging. It is the 'self', which is reborn in different bodies depending upon the *'karmas'* of the previous birth. This doctrine is called eternalism (*Sassatavāda*). It is the absence of discrimination between the perishable body and the imperishable self (*ātman*) that constitutes *avidyā*. 'Self' in its intrinsic nature is pure and perfect, but because of its association with body (non-self), which is impure, it wrongly appropriates its impurities, sufferings and resultant cycle of births and deaths. The six orthodox systems and *Jainism* among the heterodox systems of Indian Philosophy subscribe to this conception.

As against the above two conceptions of *avidyā*, we have a different conception of *avidyā*[3] in Buddhism. Buddha opines that it is precisely the notion of 'eternalism'[4] (*sassatavādo*) and 'annihilationism'[5] (*ucchedavādo*) that constitutes *avijja* leading to *dukkha*. Buddha rejects both the views that-body is the 'self' (*attā*) and that 'self' stands for an immutable reality that is, 'self' as existing over and above the body. Buddha holds that the 'self' stands for the psycho-physical complex (*nāma-rūpa*). The mental and physical constituents of this complex are known as *'khandhas'*.[6] There is no such thing as 'self' (*atta*), in the transcendental sense. This is the opinion gained from the teachings in the *nikāyas,* wherein, it is maintained that everything is substanceless or essenceless (*sarvamanattam*)[7] The term substanceless (*anattā*) in Buddhism implies two things namely, there is no such thing as a permanent substance over and above the transitional qualities in the realm of material objects and secondly, there is no such thing as an 'immutable self' over and above the five *khandhas.* 'Self' is the name given to the complex of mental and physical *khandhas.* It is based on this teaching of the *tipitakas* that Sage Nāgasena instructs King Milinda on the nature of the 'self'. The dialogue between King Milinda and Sage Nāgasena runs as follows:

When King Milinda claims to have come on a chariot, Sage Nāgasena asks King Milinda: "Your Majesty, if you came in a chariot, declare to me the chariot. Pray, your Majesty, is the pole the chariot?

"Nay, verily, bhante".

"Is the axle the chariot?"

"Nay, verily, bhante".

"Are the wheels the chariot?"

"Nay, verily bhante".....

"Pray, your Majesty, are pole, axle, wheels, chariot-body, banner-staff, yoke, reins, and goad unitely the chariot?" "Nay, verily, Bhante".

"Is it, then your Majesty, something else besides pole, axle, wheels, chariot-body, banner-staff, yoke, reins, and good which is the chariot?

"Nay, verily, bhante".

"Your Majesty, although I question you very closely, I fail to discover any chariot,"

"Verily, now, your Majesty, the word chariot is a mere empty sound..."

"The word "chariot' is but a way of counting terms, appellation, convenient designation, and name for pole, axle, wheels, chariot-body and banner-staff".

Just as the word 'chariot' is a mode of expression for axle, wheels, chariot-body, pole and other constituent members placed in a certain relation to each other, so also the word 'self' is nothing, but a name given to the psycho-physical complex (*nāma-rūpa*). Hence, the belief in an 'immutable self' is an instance of *avijjā*. A wise man does not believe in this doctrine of 'immutable self'. Since belief in an 'immutable self' being a product of *avijjā* leads to *dukkha*, it is necessary that we should go deep into the nature and origin of 'self'. Buddha observes that by analysing the contents of the 'self' one can see the alien nature of it, and can get a proper view of the underlying *dukkha*. To quote the Buddha "by analysis and understanding the 'self', the world and *dukkha* have nothing to do with me. I have to withdraw myself from them. I am still in the world, but no longer in the world. I have vanquished the world and am unspotted by the world."[9]

Self is the name given to the five khandha complex (Pañcakkhandha)

Buddha analyses the 'self' as being the name of the five aggregates complex namely, (1) *Rūpa khandha,* (2) *Vedanā khandha,* (3) *Saṅkhāra khandha,* (4) *Sañña khandha and* (5) *Viññāṅa khandha.*[10]

Rūpa Khandha

Rūpa means both 'colour' and 'form'. It is defined as that which changes or perishes (*rūppate bhijjati*).[12] It comprises all elements and their derivatives, which belong to the material such as elements constituting the body, sense-organs and the physical objects of sensation and perception. The *Visuddhimagga* speaks of *rūpa* being made up of the four primary elements (*bhūta*) and the twenty-four derived matter (*Upādāya rūpas*).[13] The four primary elements namely earth (*pathavī*), water (*āpo*), fire (*tejo*) and air (*vāyo*), are the fundamental units of matter. They are primary for the very origin of all constituents of material manifestations. It is by the combination of these four elements in different ways that derived matter comes into existence. Vasubandhu holds that each of these four elements are full-fledged '*dhammas*[14] having their own singular characteristic and function.[15] These specific characteristics provide the primodial foundation to the four basic states of material things namely solid, liquid, temperature and motion.

It is necessary to inquire into *Rūpa khandha* as a source of suffering. *Rūpa khandha* provides the outer form and contains the other four khandhas. It gives a label to the psycho-physical complex (*nāma-rūpa*), as beautiful, handsome or ugly, dark or fair and so on. From *rūpa* originates one's 'personality', one's separate 'identity' comes into being. A person based on which responds to his environment. Man attaches himself to these appearances and develops relationships taking them to be permanent, which arouses passions both in men and women. They are attracted to the resultant sensations, which lead to conceptions. These conceptions create impressions and the mind enjoys the feelings it generates and gets bound by them. Man, bound by them, develops attachment (*rāgo*) for these pleasant feelings and performs 'actions' to attain them. Due to the inherent insubstantiality, they are impermanent in nature, both the object as well as the 'individual' (subject) himself undergo change and the resultant experiences are painful.[16] (*Yadaṁ anattāṁ Yadaṁaniccaṁ taṁ dukkaṁ*).

Vedanā Khandha

One is likely to understand '*vedanā*' as standing for painful experiences. But Buddhism does not use it in this narrow sense. It has the characteristic of 'being felt'. *Vedanā,* herein, stands for feeling, which is of three kinds, pleasant feeling (*Kusula vedaṇā*), unpleasant feeling (*Akusula vedanā*) and indetermiante feeling (*Kusula-akusula vedanā*) depending upon its association with a particualr consicousness. These feelings are resultants of the contact between the six sense-organs and their corresponding sensory matter (*viṣayas*).[19] There is no guarantee that a particular feeling of pleasure generated at a particular time could recur, for the 'subject', 'object' and other conditions producing the resultant feeling are undergoing change. The mind is troubled with this thought that is going to lose it, or it is not going to occur the next moment. The idea that it would slip away from one or again have the same pleasant feeling produces suffering. Therefore, *Vedanā khandha* is suffering.

Saññā[20] Khandha

Saññа stands for an abstract 'sign' given to the worldly (sensual) experiences. The tangible sensuous experiences are transformed into abstract 'signs' as in the case of a man, who discloses the experience of a physical cow by means of an abstract sign namely the word 'cow'. It has the characteristic of 'perceiving'.[21] It establishes the cognitive apprehension and synthesis of the full-fledged material objects. It has a triple function to perform:

1. To make an object known through its characters just as the carpenter determines the quality of wood.
2. To make the characteristic engage the attention of the person as a bright colour engages the attention of a person.
3. To draw the attention to the immediate function of the object for instance, a human being cannot resist eating a tasty morsel of food.[22]

Saññā is of three kinds, on the basis of the consciousness it associates itself derives its nomenclature and nature, pleasant 'perception' (*kusula saññā*), unpleasant 'perception' (*akusula saññā*), and indeterminate 'perception' (*kusula-akusula saññā*).

Saññākkhandha is also a source of *dukkha,* for the abstractions formed by man are also impermanent. Man formulates his action on the basis of these abstract 'signs' that they are permanent, when in reality, they are impermanent. The idea that they are impermanent and ever-changing leads to the idea of dissatisfaction, which is painful. Thus, *Saññākkhandha* is suffering.

In the *Abhidhammakośa, Vedanā* and *Saññā khandhas* have been identified as being mainly responsible for disputes among men. Further, repeated existences (*saṁsāra hetu*) are resultant due to their attachment to desires and wrong views. One gets attached to desire because one enjoys the senses, whereas one becomes attached to wrong views due to erroneous notions. *Vedanā* is regarded as food (*āhāra*), whereas *Saññā* makes its tasteful.[28]

Saṅkhāra[24] Khandha

Literally, *Saṅkhāra* refers to the former impressions, but here as *khandha* it stands for the 'Composition' aggregate. It has the characteristic of 'forming' or 'agglomerating.'[25] It stands for the mental state (*cetanā*)[26] and the mental formation groups. Its function is to accumulate-bringing together two or more mental activities. It provides the necessary stimulus for the mind to go into action which produces experiences.[27] It is caused by the joint action of three *khandhas namely, Vedanā, Saññā* and *Viññāṇa.* It represents the resultant mental state brought about by the joint effect of these three *khandhas.*[28]

Saṅkhāra is of three kinds, on the basis of its association with a particular type of consciousness namely profitable formation (*kusala saṅkhāra*), Uprofitable (*akusala saṅkhāra*) and indeterminate formation (*kusala-akusala saṅkhāra*).[29]

The Buddhists draw a distinction between the functions of *saṅkhāra* as a *khandha* and *saṅkhāra* as a *nidāna* in the *Paṭiccasamuppāda.* Saṅkhāra as a *khandha* comprehends only the operation of the two forces, active forces (will) and reactive function (propensities) whereas, the third, passive potentials, which determines future birth (rebirth), is performed by saṅkhāra as a *nidāna* of the causal chain.

Saṅkhārakkhandha is also a source of dukkha. These formations of the mental state are impermanent and are dependent upon the other three khandhas. Man's actions are based on such formation assumed as permanent, whereas in reality they are impermanent. The idea of impermanence leads to dissatisfaction producing pain. (yadaṁ aniccam tam dukkham). Thus, *Saṅkhara khandha* is suffering.

Viññāṅa Khandha

Viññāṇa is the basic and most important *khandha* as it is actively engaged in the processes of living and rebirth.[31] It is towards *Viññāṇas* purification that the whole path is directed. It is the essential ground without which no *Vedanā* and *Saññā* can take place; *Saṅkhāra* cannot function in the absence of *viññāṇa;* Rupa would have no cosmolgical role in the absence of viññāṇa.[32]

Viññāṇa has the characteristics of 'cognising'.[33] Vasubandhu explains it as the relative impression gained on the apprehension of each object.[34] It is identified as a stream of consciousness, constantly undergoing a change, and as holding together memory, images, feelings, desires and perceptions. It is built upon *vedanā* and *saññā* and this relationship is as follows: 'Whatever one feels, that one perceives whatever one perceives, that, one is conscious of'.[35] The individual perceives the world not as it may exist, but projects and externalises his own notion regarding the state of existence. It is *viññāṇa,* which provides substance to the entire process of sense contact and resultant experience. In its absence the psycho-physical complex (*nāma-rūpa*) one cannot distinguish between the feelings or impressions profitable, unprofitable or indeterminate.

Viññāṇa is three-fold, depending upon the kind of resultant consciousness namely, profitable consciousness (*kusala viññāṇa*)[36], unprofitable consciousness (*akusala viññāṇa*).[37] and indeterminate conseiousness *(Kusala-akusala viññāna)*[38]. These give rise to eighty-nine types of consciousness, which operate in fourteen different modes of rebirth-linking, life-continuum, advertising, seeing, hearing, smelling, tasting, touching, receiving, investigating, determining, impulsion, registration and death.[40] The rebirth linking consciousness (*Paṭisandhi viññāṇa*) causes rebirth according to one's *kamma.* The span of life is limited by the two *viññāṇas* of rebirth-linking and death consciousness, based on which the other twelve function.[41] With birth appears the life-continuum consciousness (bhavaṅga *viññāṇa*), the resultant of one's past *kammas* (*kammassa vipikabhutam*). The *bhavaṅga viññāṇa* becomes inactive when the organs of sense become strong enough to function in their respective spheres, the function of the mind is to receive the objects seen, sound heard, and so on, and to make the organs of sense function actively, when the mind ceases to function, *bhavaṅga viññāṇa* renews its activity, ceasing at death, when it is followed by death consciousness (*cuti viññāṇa*), which in turn gives rise to the rebirth consciousness (*paṭisandhi viññāṇa*). In this way the *cittas* continuity is maintained and the cycle of existence continues.[42]

Viññāṅa and Dukkha

The role of consciousness in the process of *dukkha* is important. Devoid of consciousness, none of the other four *khandhas* can function. Moreover, without the production of the rebirth consciousness (*Paṭisandhi viññāṇa*) the psycho-physical complex (*nāma-rūpa*), the seat of suffering cannot come into existence. The psycho-physical complex (*nāma-rūpa*) derives the meaning of its existence from the contact with the object of the external world through the medium of the senses, which operate only through consciousness. It is in consciousness, the congizing character of consciousness, wherein the impressions are recorded and transmitted. The whole process of self-awareness of the external objects and the feeling (*vedanā*), the craving (*taṇhā*) for attachment with the 'pleasent object', the resultant *kamma* and the experiences generated of *dukkha* or *sukha*, are all dependent upon consciousness. Thereby, it is referred to as the life process or 'life-continuant'.

Consciousness cannot be conceived devoid of an object. Consciousness without an object is impossible, the two are inseparable. It is only in verbal expression that we speak or talk of them as being separate. It is defined as 'the knowing that cannot know itself without an intermediatory and that cannot function an experience except negatively'.[43] Its function is comparable to the projection of an object in light. Light projected on the object casts a shadow, which is a characteristic of light. The cast shadow represents the 'unknown'. It is 'unknown', in the sense, where the traces of knowledge are not distinguishable. It does not project things 'as they really are', but gives us the 'shadow' or 'apparitions' of the 'real', which represents false knowledge. This false knowledge is a source of fear and is the cause of suffering apart from itself being one of suffering.

SELF AND SUFFERING

Self is nothing, but a mere name given to the five-fold aggregate (*nāma-rūpa*). Some people tend to identify the 'self' with one of these five aggregates, the *rupa, vedanā, saṅkhāra, saññā* and *viññāṇa*. In the *Paṭisambhidāmagga*[43a] it has been shown how these misconceptions arise. Firstly, the 'self' is the same as *'rūpa'* or ... *'viññāṇa'*. It arises due to the identification of the subject with the object, just as the flame and colour are identified though they are separate. (*yā acci so vaṇṇo yo vaṇṇo sa accīti*). Secondly, the 'self' possesses the faculty of '*rupa. . . . Viññāna,* is born out of mistaken identification like a tree and its shadow (*rukkho imāya chāyāya chāyāvā).* Thirdly, the *khandhas* exist in the 'self', (*attani rūpaṃ passati*) in relationship of one existing in the other, just as we say that the smell and the flower are identical. Fourthly, the khandhas contain the 'self', the relationship between them is one of the 'container' and the 'contained'. Thus, the invalidity of these conceptions is proved. If '*rūpa*' is the 'self,' then it should be permanent, in the sense of the indestructible having no rise or fall.

Further it should be independent, not being subject to destruction, but the truth is that '*rūpa*' has opposite characteristics. *Rūpa* is impermanent, destructible, changing, subject to rise and fall, to fading away, to cessation, it does not have any core of a 'self', to be conceived as a 'self', an abider, a doer or an experiencer. Applying the same method, Buddha has shown that in *vedanā, sañña, saṅññā, saṅkhāra* and *viññāṇa* the absence of any core of 'self', ought not to be conceived as a 'self'. *Paṭisambhidāmagga*[44] speaks of forty ways in which these aggregates become sources of suffering. The five aggregates are sources of suffering as impermanent, as painful, as a disease, a boil, a dort, a calamity, an afflication . . . . . . a disaster, a terror . . . as fickle, as perishable. . . . .

In the *Maājjhima nikāya*[45], Buddha, expounding the doctrine of *Anattā,* points to the fact, that if *'rūpa* . . . . . '*viññāṇa*' is self, one should be able to master control over its origin and development just as a king possesses power over the functioning and destiny of his kingdom. Anything over which one has no control cannot be one's own. To identity oneself with that which does not belong to oneself is ignorance, which is nothing but suffering.

EVERYTHING IS CAUSED/NOTHING HAPPENS BY CHANCE

We have shown that each of the five khandhas is a generator of suffering. At this juncture, it would be appropriate to examine the origins, sources and causes of these *khandhas.*

The Buddha firmly believed that nothing happens by chance, everything arises out of 'causes'. In fact, the universe is one eternal process, a continuous vibration and an infinite growth, bound by the iron chain of causation. The Buddhists speak of five causal laws: *Pañca Niyāma Dhamma*[46] which operate the universe. They are:

1. *Utu Niyāma:* This law governs the formation of seasons, change in temperature and other physical conditions. It governs the conditions related to floods, storms, epidemics, famines, harvests and so on.

2. *Bīja Niyāma:* This law governs the reproduction of species, such as 'man' giving birth to 'man' or a mango tree producing only mangoes.

3. *Citta Niyāma:* This law governs the psychic phenomena or the mental process. The function of a particular type of consciousness, in a particular way, in conjunction with its concomitment (*cetasika*) factors, is governed by this law. For instance, the *kusala, akusala, vipāka* and *kiriya* types of *citta* are functioning together with their cetasika in a regulated manner.

4 *Dhamma*[47] *Niyāma:* This is the cosmic law, which operates in rare and special circumstances, causing unusual and miraculous manifestations. When for instance, Perfected Beings like the Buddha appears, all changes that are witnessed during such events, like unprecedented prosperity and other miracles, come under the purview of this law.

5. *Kamma Niyāma:* This law governs the order of actions. It is the psycho-ethical law of cause and effect known as moral causation. It relates a cause to an effect on the basis of certain conditions, such as bad and delusory actions producing painful and disagreeable results.

Therefore, every occurance in the universe comes under the purview of these *pañcaniyāmas*. Since, we are concerned with the suffering, we propose to limit our inquiry to the discovery of causes of suffering and its manifestations in the present chapter. Since, suffering is linked with human action (*kamma*), we propose to analyse the nature of *kamma* in the pages that follow.

Kamma

Kamma, in Buddhism as referred to in other systems of Indian Philosophy, has two meanings. Firstly, it refers to the 'deed' or 'act' itself, secondly, it refers to the 'fruits' accruing of these 'deeds', which modify and determine the future of the 'doer'. This subjective effect continues even after death into the next birth, determining rebirth. *Kamma,* thus embraces both the past and present 'deeds'. We are the result of what we are.'[48]

Not all the 'acts' performed by man during his life span are *kamma,* it is only those 'acts' which are 'willed', or voluntary actions of man, that become *Kamma.* Here, *kamma* is primarily and fundamentally to be understood as human action. It is an act, which is performed by man with the consent of the 'will' cetana. Cetana, here, is designated as the 'free', mentally and intentionally, grounded exercise of the 'will'.[49] Cetana formally constitutes the essence of *kamma.*

Types of Kamma

Kamma manifests in three ways depending upon the outlet namely thought, word and deed. Based on the outlet through which a *kamma* presents itself, it derives its nomenclature as being, *Mano-kamma* (when it is purely mental), *Vācākamma* (when presented through the organ of speech) and *Kāya-kamma* (when it manifests as physical action).[50] These kammas performed by man, dependent upon the citta, associated with derive their nomenclature as *kusala kamma, akusula kamma* and *kusala-akusala kamma.*

(a) Meritorious acts (*Kusala kamma*): Those moral actions, which are brought about by the reasoning forces of self-sacrifice (*alobha*),[51] love (*adosa*)[52] and insight (*amoha*)[53] are known as meritorious acts. There are twenty-one *kusala kammas.*[54] These involve the acts of giving away gifts (*dāna*) and observance of the norms of morality. These acts ensure progress, generate merit and are conducive to development and purity. They uproot the mental defilements and help in attaining liberation.

(b) *Demeritorious 'acts' (Akusala Kamma)*: Those immoral actions which are brought about by the reasons forces of greed (*loba*), hatred (*dosa*) and delusion (*moha*) are known as demeritorious acts. There are twelve *akusala kammas.*[55] They consist of 'acts' like causing harm to other creatures, such as killing, stealing and so on. These acts keep beings bound to the cycle of birth and death, and repeated existences just as the silkworm which spins a cocoon, only to bring its own bondage and death. These acts cause rebirth in Hell (*niraya*)[56]

(c) *Neutral 'acts'* (*Kusala-akusala kamma*): These 'acts are indeterminate deeds, which are devoid of ethical substance. They result in rebirth, in the *Arūpaloka.*

WORKING OF KAMMA

In the *Abhidhamma,* Buddha has explained the operation of *kamma,* making use of four *Samaṅgis,*[57] which constitute the parts of the kamma cycle: 1. Volition equipment (*Cetanā samaṅgi*), (2) Karmic force equipment (*Kamma samaṅgi*), (3) Opportunity equipment (*Upaṭṭhāa samaṅgi*) and (4) Resultant equipment (*Vipāka samaṅgi*).

1. *Volitional equipment (Cetanā samaṅgi*): Volition, which refers to the 'willed' actions of man arise from *cetana.* It is the *cetana samaṅgi* which forms the generator of *kamma.* It sets into motion a willed action-volition.

2. *Kammic force equipment* (*kamma samaṅgi*): Until the resultant *kamma* matures, it remains as a potent force. *Kamma samaṅgi* maintains the potent kammic force, flowing along with the life-flux, awaiting an occasion to fructify and mainfest.

3. *Opportunity equipment* (*Upatthāna samaṅgi*): It plays an important role by providing the occasion or the mode of life, that helps the *kammic* energy to mature and produce results.

4. *Resultant equipment* (*Vipāka samaṅgi*): It refers to the resultant equipment, which brings about the resultants of the kammic energy into manifestations, either in the form of rebirth or life sitautions such as health, beauty, ugliness, and so on.

EFFECTS OF KAMMA

It is the '*kamma*' that causes 'rebirth'. Rebirth, according to Buddha, does not refer to the transmigration of a permanent principle of consciousness. Herein, rebirth pertains only to the transmigration and rebirth of the '*kamma*' of the individual. For instance, our knowledge of our friend is derived from that which our senses tell us of his body. We observe this from the deeds he performs. It is the person's deeds, which mould and shape his 'character'. It is this character, which survives death and gets reborn. It causes the emergence of the psycho-physical organism (*nāma-rūpa*) in the form of the five-fold aggregate. In the *Jātaka* texts, there is mention of the previous births of the Buddha before his present birth, wherein he stresses the aspect that 'character' alone is responsible for the birth of an individual in a particular form. Rebirth takes place within the three lokas of *kāma, rūpa* and *arūpa* of the universe, depending upon *kamma*.

Saṁsāra consists of five realms namely 1. *Niraya,* 2. *Pettivisaya,* 3. *Tirechānayoni,* 4. *Manusā* and 5. *Devaloka.* These five realms of existence are characterised according to the degree of dukkha one experiences during one's stay in them.[58]

1. *Niraya*: This realm is compared to hell, which resembles a pit of hot charcoal. Here existence is more dreadful than life in a concentration camp. It is a state of untold misery. The inhabitants of hell are 'ripped apart, mangled, devoured by titanic, maggots, spiked a thousand times and tortured in myriad ways'. There is unmitigated torment in hell, without an interval, which continues till all the kammas of sheer wickedness, diabolic depravity and satanic savagery are exhausated.

2. *Pettivisaya:* It is the realm of animal existence. It is equally gory with mutual killings and swallowing. It is rooted in violence and aggression. There is constant fear with no recompense.

3. *Tirechānayoni:* This realm is inhabited by titans and demons. Here, beings are constantly struggling and warring, as they are filled with violent passion for power and other psychic abilities. They lead a most wretched life of hunger, thirst, and discomfort of various kinds. They have bloated bellies and mouths

no bigger than the eye of a needle, and have extremely slender neck. They find the moon hot in summer, the sun cold in winter, 'rivers turning dry, athirst', as they look at them. Whatever little food they manage to get, turns into swords, knives and splinters in their bellies and all these are because of the avarice and greed, indulged in earlier existences.

4. *Manusā Loka:* The realm of human existence has a still lesser degree of *dukkha* than the former. It is like coming under a shady tree. The beings here are endowed with a measure of merit and can find protection on their own. It provides one with a medium for gaining liberation, but human beings might also fail to make proper use of it. The Buddha represents it as a gem-studded golden bowl, which man can fill with vomit, urine and dung meaning bad kammas leading to lower forms of rebirth, or can make it more beautiful with good *kammas*, resulting in higher rebirth, or leading to nibbāna.

5. *Deva Loka:* The world of gods,[59] does have within it some *dukkha*, but is lesser than that of *Manusā loka.* It is comparable to a beautiful Palace.

The rūpaloka is inhabited by *Brahmas* with a subtle form. It is a place where there is *dukkha* of a small intensity. The *arūpaloka* is inhabited by Brahmas who do not have a subtle form. But they are also not completely free from the fetters of *dukkha*, but the *dukkha* experienced here is of a much lesser intensity than that one suffers in the *rūpaloka.*

Birth, in the first four realms of *kāmaloka,* represents a state of extreme woe (*duggati*). The begins are born here to expiate the evils done in their previous existences. The realms of *Manusa* and *Devaloka,* all the realms of *rūpa* and *arūpalokas* are referred to as sugati-happy or meritorious existences. Rebirth in any *loka* is an unsatisfactory existence, only varying in the degree of suffering, experienced. But, the fact remains that complete freedom from *dukkha* is not yet attained, it can be attained only when one transcends all these three *kokas* and attains *nibbāna.*

PATICCASAMUPPADA

It the preceding section, we have shown how *kamma* is at the root of the origination of the psycho-physical organism (*nāma rūpa*), the conglomeration of the five *khandhas* and rebirth. The Buddha next addresses himself to the logic of the cycle of births, of this psycho-physical organism. He seeks to explain this through the doctrine of dependent origination-*Paticcasamuppāda.* It is demonstrative of the process of *kamma.* It refers to the moral aspect of causation. It establishes the fact that the suffering of a 'being', subject to repeated existences, depends upon certain factors like 'cause' (*hetu*) and 'condition' (*paccaya*).[61] Further, that there is nothing like a self independent entity. Everything comes into being depending upon the other. When one exists, there is the possibility of existence of other, when one does not exist, the possibility of existence of other is also not seen.

In the *paṭiccasamuppāda*, the earlier or preceding link in the causal chain gives rise to the subsequent. In other words, the preceding one is considered to be the cause of the succeeding one. Both the 'cause' and 'effect' here are used in a broader sense. For 'cause', herein, refers to a complex of factors or conditions (*paccayas*) that go on to produce the 'effect'. Although, we speak of 'cause' as one and 'effect' as one, each stands for the many. For instance, we speak of 'seed' as the 'cause' for the 'effect', 'sprout'. The seed alone is not the 'cause', the soil, temperature, moisture, light along with the condition of the seed, all these factors constitute the 'cause'. Similarly, the 'effect', 'sprout', is not one but a complex of form, odour, weight and such conditions. There is no single or multiple effect from a single cause, nor a single effect from multiple 'causes', but only multiple effects from multiple causes. But in common usage, we speak of one representative 'cause' and 'effect' as a methodical device, but this does not exhaust the ontological analysis. The Budha, similarly, used one representative 'cause' and 'effect' when for instance he speaks of ignorance (*avijjā*) as the cause for dispositions (*saṅkhāra*), altough there are other causal conditions, the representative 'cause' 'ignorance', will be sufficient to make the disciple understand the logic of the doctrine of dependent origination. The twelve links (*nidānas*) of the *paṭiccasamuppāda* are:

1. Ignorance (*avijjā*), 2. cognative dispositions (*saṅkhāra*), 3. Resultant consciousness (*viññāṇa*), 4. Mind body complex (*nāmarūpa*), 5. Six sense-organs (*salāyatana*), 6. Contact (*phasso*), 7. Feeling (*vedanā*), 8. Craving (*taṇhā*), 9. Attachment (*upādāna*), 10. Becoming (*bhava*), 11. Birth (*jāti*) and 12. Ageing and death (*jarā-maraṇa*).[62]

There are four ways in which the *paṭccasamuppāda* can be analysed; (1) starting from the beginning to the end *i.e.,* from *'Avijjā'* to *'Jarā-maraṇa'*, (2) starting from the middle upto the end from *Vedanā* to '*Jarā-maraṇa*', (3) from middle down to the beginning from *Taṇhā* to ignorance *Avijjā,* and (4) from the end to the beginning *Jarā-maraṇa* to *Avijjā.* The present analysis, here, is from the end to the beginning, (inverse order) that is from *Jarā-maraṇa* to *Avijjā.* The purpose is to show that this world is full of *dukkha.* Further, it also goes to show an individual's 'evolution' and the various forms of suffering he faces, starting from the twin factors of ageing and death (*jarā-maraṇa*) upto its prime cause, *avijjā.*[63]

Ageing-death (Jarā-Maraṇa)

In this present life man is a creature of the past and an agent of the future.[64] The thread, which joins this is 'moral will' working together with intellect, deluded by ignorance. The *khandhas*, due to this process, come into an aggregation known as the psycho-physical organism (*nāma-rūpa)*. The psycho-physical organism is identified as a 'personality'. For Buddha, *saṃsāra* or worldly career is an endless chain of these singular personalities strung one to the other. It is the immediate cause of *dukkha*. It ages and withers; it becomes worn out, grey and wrinkled. Its vitality disappears and the senses become dull and get dampened. To quote the *Saṃyutta Nikāya* 'whatever is born, or becomes old, or dies or perishes or originates—that is the corporeal organism together with consciouness.[65] Hence, there are two fundamental features of the pyscho-physical organism, ageing (*jarā)* and death (*maraṇa*). These two features make up the whole process of life transitory and full of *dukkha*. Ageing does not stop even for a second. Right from birth, this process of ageing starts and continues till death. Ageing, especially old age and death are the most commonly recognised forms of mundane *dukkha*. In the Tibetan texts old age and death are depicted by an old man carrying a corpse.[65a]

Birth (Jāti)

Buddha observes that ageing and death (*Jarā-maraṇa*) are the effects of the 'cause', birth (*jāti*).[66] Birth (*Jāti*) is the *upanissaya-paccaya of Jarā-maraṇa*.[67] In the absence of *Jāti*, *Jarā-maraṇa* and its companion miseries like sorrow (*soka*), lamentation (*parideva)*, pain *(dukkha)*, grief (*domanassa*) and other which is experienced by the psycho-physical organism, are impossible.

Jāti is defined as the process of the arising of the body endowed with consciousness, taking place within the material womb.[68] It starts from the moment of conception and ends with the extrusion of the foetus from the womb. The Buddha further defines it as the germination, the conception, the appearance of the groups, and the grasping of the realms of senses.[69] In the implied sense, it refers to the first appearance of the mental and material aggregates constituting the seat of suffering. The psycho-physical organism apart from itself being a seat of *dukkha*, also forms the source of all other *dukkha*. Birth as a 'form' and 'source' of *dukkha* has been discussed in Chapter I. Birth, in the Tibetan texts is depicted by the picture of child birth, a painful and utterly helpless process[69a].

Becoming (Bhava)

Buddha contemplating on the immediate cause of birth (*Jāti*) comprehended the process of 'becoming born'. He opines that it is an internal part of yet another universal process, termed as 'becoming' *(Bhava)*. 'Bhava' is universal process, yet it is unique process within the whole world. There is only 'Becoming' but 'no Being'. Becoming alone is 'real', Being is 'apparent'. There is no 'Being' behind the process of 'becoming', 'Becoming' is the 'Reality'.

Becoming is a two-fold process, consisting of (a) *kamma bhava*-the volitions and (b) *Upapatti-bhavai* or the resultant of these volitions. *kamma-bhava* is performance of volitions in the present life, which determines the future life. These volutions are of three kinds, meritorious (*puñña)*, demeritorious (*apuñña*) and steadfast (*anenja*). These volitions are due to the impressions (*saṅhāra*) left on the mind by ignorance (*avijjā*).[70] *Upapatti* bhava consists in existence constituted by the mental and material aggregates resulting from volitions (*kamma*). It is *kamma-bhava* alone that constitutes the causal condition for *jāti* and not *Upapatti-bhava*. *kamma-bhava* acts as a *kamma-paccaya* and *upanissaya paccaya* to *jāti*.[71]

In the Tibetan texts in is represented by the simile of a pregnant women[72].

Attachment (upādāna)[73]

Becoming (*Bhava*) is caused by the factor of attachment *(Upādāna)*.[74] Just as a young man who harbours some ambition to shape into a professional, grasps the thought arising within him, of becoming an army officer, a scholar or an artist. This thought he cherishes, cultivates and clings on. As a result of this thought, he translates his actions in accordance with this thought, 'becoming' sets in and remains in action till the person has actually become an army officer, a scholar or an artist. It is in consequence of this grasping (attachment), he becomes that which he has grasped. If there was no such attachment within him, he would not have become any of 'these'. Therefore, 'becoming' involves some expectations, and when this expectation is not fulfilled it lands him in disappointment leading to misery. Even, if one 'becomes' leading to the desired objects, it is a painful experience, since the 'object', the 'contact' and the 'subject' are impermanent. The idea, that we are likely to be deprived of what one has 'become' also is a source of suffering, leading to pain.

Attachment (*Upādāna*) is of four kinds namely *kāmaupādāna*, *diṭṭiupādāna*, *sīlabhatupādāna* and *attāvādupādāna*. 1. *Kāmaupādāna* involves cliniging to the objects of sensual enjoyment, 2. *Diṭṭhiupādhāna* consists of clinging to false notions or things, 3. *Sīlabhatupādāna* consists of holding belief in rituals and disciplines and 4. *Attāvādupādāna* involves clinging to the false notions about the 'self'.

The Buddha opined that *Attāvādupādāna* is the source of all *upādānas*. One believes that there is a 'self' either permanent or impermanent. He develops a purely ego-centreic attitude in all forms of deeds, be it physical, verbal or mental. He falls prey to the false notions of 'eternalism' and 'annihilationism', which constitutes *diṭṭiupādāna*. The notion of 'eternalism' is founded on the belief that there is a 'self', which is eternal. This leads to the invention of false rituals and mortification, for the purification of the 'self'. These acts produce more suffering than purifying the 'self'.

The notion of annihilationism, is founded on the belief that there will be complete destruction of the 'self' at the time of bodily death. The 'self' is there, but it is non-eternal. It leads man to crave for the sensual objects of the world. Man is constantly attracted by sensual objects and cannot be separated from these pleasure, for he is aware that they cease with his death. It leads to *kāmaupādāna*.

The Buddha observes that these four kinds of *upādānas* form a major source of human suffering, leading man into the blind alleys of 'eternalism' and 'annihilationsim'. Attachment, in the Tibetan texts, is symbolised by a man feverishly plucking fruits from a tree and trying to fill a basket that is already full. Attachment, thus represents an intensification and multiplication of craving.

Craving (taṇhā)

The Buddha, examining the factors which cause and govern 'attachment' (*Upādāna*) enjoined that craving (*taṇhā*) was the cause.

Taṇhā is craving[77] after the sensual objects of saṁsāra, whose contract would produce sukha. *Taṇhā* is six-fold, for the object it craves falls within six different classes namely 1. visible form (*rūpa*), 2. Sound (*sadda*), 3. odour (*gandha*), 4. taste (*rasa*), 5. tangible object (*phoṭṭabbha*) and 6. cognizable object (*dhamma*).[78] Each of these six kinds of *taṇhā* is further classified, for the objects of each class can be motivated by three different instincts, *kama*, *bhava*, and *vibhava*.[79] *kāma taṇha* creates a craving for the objects of sensual pleasures, of *rūpa*, *sadda* and so on. It refers to the thirst, which is associated with sensual objects. *kama* '*tanha* is related to *kamma upādāna* by way of *upanissaya paccaya*

Bhava-taṇhā is the thirst, which is associated with belief in eternalism. It results in attachment for future existence, rebirth within *saṃsāra*, which is full of *dukkha*. *Vibhava-taṇhā* is the thirst, which is associated with the belief that there is no after life. It makes man seek attachment and enjoy all the objects employing all 'means' possible, good or bad. It leads to the path of self-indulgence, which is full of pain and misery. In the

Tibetan texts, craving is symbolised by a boozer lost in a drinking bout and a woman supplying the drinks.[81] Buddhist texts refer to it as a skeleton, of much pain... a torch of dry grass... a pot of glowing embers..a slaughter house...a snake's head.[82]

Feeling (Vedanā)

Feeling (*vedanā*) is the cause of craving (*taṇhā*). The Buddha refers to it as the fountain head of all *taṇhā*. *Vedanā* acts as *upanissaya paccaya*,[83] for it is the driving power, conditioning *taṇhā*. *Vedanā* is of three kinds, pleasurable *(Ksukha)*, pain (*dukkha*) and indifference (*upekkha*). It is painful feeling that generates in man an aversion *(doso)* for pain and arouses the desire for pleasure, a form of *taṇhā*. The feeling of indifference is borne out of imperfection and not out of enlightenment, hernce it is a state of pain, to be avoided. It also leads to the craving for pleasure. Man wants attachment only with the states of pleasure. Man expects these states, but they may or may not be produced. Even if produced, they are not permanent and evanscent; anything impermanent is painful.

Vedanā, when associated with the firmly rooted latent bases of sensual passions *(kāma rāga)*, lust for life (*bhava rāga*), aversion (*paṭigha*), pride (*māno*), error (*diṭṭi*), perplexity (*vicikicchā*) and ignorance (*avijjā*), produce *taṇhā*. It is *taṇhhā*, which forces man to act and generate unsatisfactory experiences. In the Tibetan texts, it is depicted by an arrow piercing the eye of a person.[84]

Contact (phasso)[85]

The Buddha observes that the cause for the arising of feeling (*vedanā*) is contact (*phasso*).[86] *Phasso*, opines Buddha, is the contact of a sense-organ (*āyatana*) with its object. The contact is not physical but sensual and it is termed as sense-impression.[87] These sense impressions are of six kinds, depending on the sense-organ from which they arise. It is the sense-impressions gained by man namely the beautiful, the ugly, and so on which start the cyble of *taṇhā* leading to attachment, 'becoming' and getting translated into *kammas* and resultant experiences of pain. In the Tibetan texts '*phasso*' is depicted as a man and woman in embrace.[88]

Six sense organs (salāyatana)

Contact (*phasso*) is the effect of the working of the sense-organs (*salāyatana*). For they are the doors for contact. (*phasso*). The sense-organs numbering six are visual, olfactory, auditory, gustatory, tactitle and mental, termed as 'salāyátana'. The Buddha contended that it is through the agency of five sense-organs that man's mind comes into contact with the 'objects' of *saṁsāra*. With this contact (*phasso*) arises the *taṇhā*, leading to attachment (*upādāna*), the process of 'becoming' and the performance of *kamma*, and the resultant experiences of suffering follow. The *salāyatana* is depicted in the Tibetan text as a house with six-windows.[89]

Psycho-physical Complex (Nāma-rāpa)

Nāma-rūpa, regards the Buddha is the cause for the origin and existence of the salāyatana.[90] *Nāma-rūpa* or the psycho-physical complex is an aggregation of the five *khandhas: rūpa*, *vedanā*, *sañña*, *saṅkhāra* and *viññāṇa*. The term '*nāma*' stands for the four *khandhas* namely. *vedanā*, *saññā*, *saṅkhāra* and *viññāṇa,* while the term '*rūpa*' stands for the four primary material elements (*mahābhūtas*) earth, water, air and fire. '*Rūpa*' forms the container for the four *khandhas* and shapes the 'appearance' of the psycho-physical complex. It is the joint working of the remaining four *khandhas,* which provides the working principle for the psycho-physical organism. *Nāma* has no power of its own to perform and activity. *Rūpa* also is without power or acitivity, on individually. It is only when both of them are joined together and mutually support each other, that it forms the psycho-physical organism, just as a blind person cannot see but can walk, whereas a crippled though possessing vision cannot move about. If, both the blind and the crippled mutually support each other they can go around using their complemented organs for mutual benefit. The Buddha refers to *nāma-rūpa* as the seat of suffering. As a result of it the whole cycle of existence, starting from desire leading to *kamma* and the resultant suffering is enacted. In the Tibetan texts, *nāma-rūpa* is depicted as a boat full of holes, being rowed by a boatman with a few passengers across the swift currents

Resultant Consciousness (Viññāṇa)[92]

The cause for the *nāma-rūpa* is rebirth consciousness *(paṭisandhi-viññāna)*. Rebirth-consciousness is formed and governed by the past *kamma* for the individual. The rebirth-consciousness sets into motion the process of aggregation of the five-*khandhas* into a psycho-physical organism'-*Nāma-rūpa*.

The resultant rebirth linking consciouusness, a vipaka, is depicted as a monkey leaping from one fruit bearing tree to another. It devours the fruits and 'enjoys' the experiences as a consequences of past *kamma.*

Cognitive Dispositions (Saṅkhāra)[93]

These *viññāṇas* are psychic aggregates or moulds of *saṅkhāras*. *Saṅkhāras* are the cause for the origin and existence of all *viññans*, contends Buddha. *Saṅkhāras* refer to the traces or impressions left in the mind.

The function of *saṅkhāra* of the previous existence is to produce the thought *(citta)* with which a 'being' is reborn, or in other terms, rebirth consciousness *(paṭi-sandhi viññāṇa)*. The mind and its mental states that follow rebirth consciousness *(paṭi-sandhi viññāṇa)* are also dependent on the '*kammas*' of the past life. Therefore, it represents the pre-natal forces which cause the *viññāṇa* and resultant birth of the psycho-physical complex in *saṁsāra*. In the Tibetan texts, volition *(saṅkhāra)* is represented as a potter engaged in making of a variety of products, some beautiful *(kusala kamma)* while others ugly *(akusala kamma)*.[93a]

Ignorance (Avijjā)[94]

For the Buddha, these impressions of the mind *(citta)* are produced as a result of wrong views (*diṭṭhi bhava*) of objects. These wrong views constitute *avijjā*. Therefore, *avijjā* is the cause for the origin and existence of all *saṅkhāra*.

The Buddha defines *avijjā* as that, which makes a person learn 'what should not be learnt', and 'not learn what should be learnt'. It deludes the mind from taking a true and proper perspective of things in the universe. It consists of mistaking *dukkha* for *sukha*, an everchanging aggregate of feeling *(vedanā)*, consciousness *(viññāṇa)*, co-efficient of consciousness (*saññā*), predispositions *(saṅkhāra)* for an abiding ego (*ahaṅkāro*), a perpetual flow of energies for unchanging staticity, impermance for permanence.

The nikāyas, refer to *avijjā* as the non-comprehension of the four Noble Truths.[95] It also means the non-comprehension of the world beginning (*pubbanta*) and the world ending (*aparanta*), eternalism (*sassata*) and annihilation (*uccheda*)[96] and this conditioned nature of objects (*idappaccayāta*).[97] *Avijjā* is responsible for the mind being unsteady and wavering. It is such a mind, which influences and governs man's life. Under its control man performs '*kammas*' with the hope of enjoying the resultant experience of *sukha*. But it produces experiences which appear to be *sukha*, but are in reality *dukkha*. For there is no such thing as pure '*sukha*' devoid of '*dukkha*'. Even the so called experiences of '*sukha*' bound to the factors of change and decay produces *dukkha*. Moreover, man desires and identifies himself with the 'worldly objects', which are characterised with *anicca*, *anattā* and *dukkha*. *Avijjā*, thus becomes the root-cause of the whole chain of suffering. The Buddha is firm that the five-fold aggregate (*Nāma-rūpa*) does not arise from desire, or from time, or from nature (*prakṛti*), from themselves (*ārabhavat*) from a Lord (*īśvara*), yet they are not without cause (*paccaya*) they arise from ignorance (*avijjā*). All our misfortunes in *saṁsāra* have their roots in ignorance (*avijjā*). In the Tibetan texts, *Avijjā* is represented as a blind man, old and infirm, supported by a stick, gropping about. He is led by a boy. Mental blindhess is symbolised by the blind man. *Avijjā* does not go alone, it is always accompanied by *bhavataṇhā* that seeks the continuity of existence, which is represented by a boy leading the old man.

The Buddha observes that though *avijjā* is beginningless, it is not uncaused. It is dynamic, conditioned by affliction and is eradicable. It can be annihilated by cultivation of right knowledge, thought and deed.

The Buddha believes that both ignorance (*avijjā*) and craving (*taṇhā*) are the fountain-head of the world process, the wheel of existence (*saṁsāra*). 'The chain of suffering is headed by avijjā'. It lies dominant at the root and is conditioned by *taṇhā*. The dominant determines the weak and as such can be regarded as a condition of the latter. Therefore, '*avijjā*' determines '*taṇhā*', which is born as a condition of the latter's profilement. One is essentially associated with the other, and the two can never be separated. The two can be distinguished only in respect of function. '*Avijjā*' is a specific condition of such volitions, as one responsible for bad form of life, whereas *taṇhā* is a specific condition of volition leading to a 'good form of life', *avijjā* being perverted belief is an aspect of knowing, while '*taṇhā*' being a kind of 'craving', is a place of 'willing. Both 'knowing' and 'willing', though distinct, are inseparable functions of the mind. When *avijjā* reigns supreme, the mind becomes a slave of circumstances and has no control over its own development. This results in hapazard 'growth' and activities of the mind. *Avijjā* forces the mind to perform '*kammas*' based on wrong beliefs. These *kammas* produce resultant experiences, which are full of *dukkha*.

People generally speak of *avijjā* and *taṇhā* as the two starting points of the wheel of existence. This conception is based on wrong knowledge. It leads to the conception of two separate self-sufficient rounds of existence, eternalism and annihilationism. The first round starting from *avijjā* to vedanā constitutes a self-sufficent round of existence. It is conceived by those whose psyche is dominated by speculative confusion about the 'self'. They believe that there is a permanent and unchanging 'self', (eternalism). It is the self which is reborn in different existences; the rebirth of which is influenced and controlled by the *kammas* performed in the past. They perform actions guided by this belief of eternalism. This leads to the path of self-mortification, which the Buddha opines is ignoble, unwise and full of *dukkha*.

The second round, starting from *taṇhā* to *jarā-maraṇa* also constitutes a self-sufficient cycle of existence. It is conceived by those whose psyche is influenced and governed by the wrong conception about the 'self'. The 'self' exists for them, but is not permanent. It perishes with bodily death (annihilationism). Man, under the influence of this conception of annihilationism, identifies the physical body with the self. He performs actions to satisfy the desires of the physical body, for him it is the 'self'. He pays no attention to the *means* employed, for the believes that he has to make the maximum out of his present existence as he is not going to be reborn or experience the fruits of his 'deeds'. This leads one to the path of self-indulgence. The Buddha opines that self-indulgence is a path, which is ignoble, unwise and full of *dukkha*.

Having understood the nature of the psycho-physical organism (*nāma-rūpa*) to be constraint and one of suffering, man would like to transcent beyond this body-mind limitations. The Buddha has prescribed for this transcendence the *ariyo-aṭṭaṅgiki maggo*, himself having practised this technique of transcendence to attain *nibbāna*.

REFERENCES

1. In the *Saṁyutta Nikāya* Buddha there is mention of seven kinds of *Ucchedavādins* (Annihilationists). All of them susbcribe to the view that the 'self' becomes extinct after death.

   (a) The soul has a form and is made up of the combination of the four great elements. It is similar in composition to the human beings.

   (b) The soul is heavenly and has a form. It remains in the *kāmāvacara* sphere, and is nourished by material elements.

   (c) The soul though heavenly, has a form and substance just like the mind. It is equipped with a physical body and all the sense-organs.

   (d) The soul is made up of the same substance as beings of the *ākāsāññañcāyatana* (*Arūpāvacara gods*—4th class)

   (e) The soul is of the same nature as the beings of the *viññāṇānañcāyatana* (3rd clas of *Arūpāvacara* gods).

   (f) The soul is similar to the beings of the akincaññayatana (*Arūpāvacara* gods-2nd class).

   (g) The soul is similar to the beings of the nevasaññasaññayatana (*Arūpāvacara* gods-1st class). *Saṁyutta Nikāya*, IV, p. 401. cf. *Brahmajāla Sutta*. *Dīgha Nikāya*. I.1.

2. The eternalist (*Sassatavāda*) holds that both the the self and the world exist eternally. Rf. *Saṁ. Nikāya* IV.p.40. *Majjhmika Nikāya*. (I pp.98, 182) mentions that they ascribe to the notion that one of the five khandhas is the 'self' or something apart from them, which is eternal and immutable. This 'self', for them is the performer and enjoyer of all action and its fruits, good or bad. It is permanent (*nicca*), fixed (*dhuva*), eternal (*sassata*), Unchangeable (*avipariṇāma-dhamma*) and is steadfast. *Majj. Nikāya* .I.P 8, *Papañcasūdani*

I.p.71. The eternalists are divided into four classes. The basis for the division for the first three classes is the number of previous births remembered by them (some ascectics develop the power of remembring their former births upto a certain limit). The fourth class includes those eternalists, who base their conclusion about the eternality of soul and world by means of logic and reasoning. Dīgha. Nikāya. III, p.109-110.

3. *Avijjā* (pāli) and *Avidyā* (Sanskrit) [fr. a+vid], means Ignorance. *Saṁ. Nikāya*. II. 6, 9, 12.

4. Eternalism (*Sassatavādo*): They believe in the conception of 'self' as a permanent, unchanging and static entity. The body undergoes all the changes and the resultant sufferings. It is the 'self' as a permanent, unchanging and static sufferings. It is the 'self' which undergoes rebirith depending upon the *karmas* performed in previous existences. This leads man to the path of 'self-mortification', which is ignoble, unwise and full of suffering. In the *kassapasīhānada Sutta* (*Dīgha. Nikāya.* I.161) Buddha argues with the naked ascetic kassapa and successfully builds a case against self-mortification. "Not nakedness, not platted hair, not diet, not fasting, or lying on the earth, not rubbing with dust, not sitting motionless can purify a mortal who has not overcome desires'. *Dhammapada.*141.

5. Annihilationism (*Uccedavādo*): They believe that the 'self' perishes along with bodily death. They involve themselves in all kinds of acts with the sole purpose of pleasure. It leads man to the other extreme of self-indulgence, which is ignoble, unwise and full of suffering.

6. *Skandha* (*saṅskrit*) *khandha* (pāli) is translated as aggregate. It also connotes the interactive co-ordination among the 'heaps' of qualitatively different dharmic elements, as these offer the basis for sensation and perception. they are referred to as saṁghata, for they make-up the perceptible compounds of materiality which associates with the subjective factor of consciousness (*viññāṇa*) and other mental functions accompanying such elements. Thus, khandha denotes the results of the classifying of different dharmas depending upon their specific characteristics (*laksaṇas*).

7. *Sarvaṁ anattāṁ* is a logical outcome of *sarvaṁ aniccam,* whereby there is no object which is permanent. Everything in this world is under flux: change or impermanence is the essence of things. There are numerous passages, in the Pali texts which refer to the fact of impermanence. Buddha in the *Saṁ. Nikāya* I.109 points that 'as the waters of the river ever hasten and flow away and once gone never return, such is the life of man, that which is gone knows not any return'. Buddhists speak of two types of impermanence namely.

1. Impermanence of the life period and 2. Momentary impermanence. The first is that which is experienced. We generally regard the 'same man' as living between the period of his birth and death, where birth is, death inevitably follows, a particular variety of continuity

or booming is recognised. Here, we have a relative duration and not 'permanence' a duration, such an impermanence is self-evident. The second momentary impermanence refers to the fact that 'everything is undergoing change every moment or a thing is an aggregate of such a change'. The first one refers to the change in the 'micro', whereas the second stands for change of time *i.e.*, 'macro' such a distinction is essential so as to avoid confusion over the nature of physical things. The first gives us an immediate experience of 'duration', whereas the second denotes the experience of 'flow'. Buddhism explains both, but, is essentially concerned with the law of becoming, in the micro level. Impermanence, in the first sense, upholds the commonsensical belief, spoken as that there is a permanent'-relatively permanent bodies, which also undergo change.

8. In the *Saṁ Nikāya* I. 135, Nun Vajirā when asked by Māra about 'person' replies that this is nothing but a lot of processes, no 'person' is found here'. Just as the word 'Carriage is used when the parts are combined, so the word 'person' is commonly used when the factors are present. Ref. *Milindapañha* (25) Trans. Warren H. C., Buddhist Discourses, pp.128-33.

9. *Aṅguttara Nikāya*: as quoted by Oldengerg. H., *The Buddha*, *His life*, *His doctrine*, *His order*, pp.249-50.

10. *Saṁyutta Nikāya* — I. 135: *Order of enumeration of the khandhas*: Vasubandhuuu opines that the five *khandhas* are arranged on the basis of their grossness. *Rūpa* is the grossest: *Vedanā*, *Saññā*, *Saṅkhāra* and *Viññāṅa* are less grosser.

    Secondly, they are arranged in accordance with the process of attractions. Men and women are passionately attracted towards each other first by *rūpa,* then they get attached by sensation *(vedanā)*. This leads to wrong conception, wherein 'unhappy' is taken as 'happy'. These misconception creates impressions (*Saṅkhāra*) and the mind (*viññāṇa*) enjoys the results and gets tainted with them. Thirdly, Rūpa is the container (*Bhājana*), Vedanā-food (*Bhājana*), Sañña makes it tasteful, the combination of the three leads to impression (*Saṅkhāra*) while *Viññāṇa* is the enjoyer (*Bhokta*). *Abhidhammakośa* (ABK) p. 82., *ABK Vrtti*- p. 48.

11. *Pāli Eng. Dic.* P. 574.

12. *Vis. Magga* XVI, 34, p. 489.

13. *Ibid*, XVI, (444), 34, 35, 36 p. 489 cf Dhs. 585.24. The twenty-four derivatives (*Upādāya (Rūpa)* are: (a) *pasādarūpa*:- The five sensitive material qualities of eye (*cakkhu*), ear (*sota*), nose (*ghāna*), tongue (*īvhā*) and body (*kāya*); (b) *Visayarūpa*: The five material qualities of sense fields of form (*rūpa*), sound (*sadda*), smell (*gandha*), taste (*rasa*) and tangible object (*phoṭṭhabba*); (c) *Bhāvārūpa*: the two material qualities of sex : Feminity (*itthindriya*) and mascuulinity *(purisindriya)* (d) *Hadayarūpa*: The one physical basis of mind-the heart base *(hadayavatthu)*. (e) *Jīvitarūpa*: The vital force or life principle in

matter, the faculty of life (*jīvitindriya*) (f)*āhārarūpa*: The one material quality of nutrition edible food (*kavaliṅkārāhāra*): (g) *paricchedarūpa* : The one material quality of delimination space element (*ākāsadhātu*); (h) *Viññattirūpa*: The two material qualities of communication, Bodily intimation (*kāyaviññ'atti*) and verbal intimation (*Vacīviññatti*), (i) *Vikārarūpa*: The five material qualities of plasticity or flexibility, lightness of form (*Rūpassa lahutā*), the pliancy of form (*Rūpassa mudutā*), adaptability of form (*Rūpassa kamaññtā*) and 4 & 5 same as *Viññattirūpa*; (j) *lakkhaṇarūpa*: The four material qualities of salient features growth (*Rūpassa Upaccaya*), continuity of form *(Rūpassa Santati*), decay of form (*Rūpassa Jaratā*) and Impermanence of form (*Rūpassa Aniccatā*). In the *Abhidhammattha saṅgaha* two more forms of rupa are referrred to namely the karmically grasped materiality (*Upādinnakarūpa*) and the karmically ungrasped materiality (*Anupādinnakarūpa*). cf: *Dīgha Nikāya* p. 214.

14. 'Dhamma' derived from the Saṅskrit word '*dharma*', where the root 'dhr' means 'to hold' or 'to carry' designates the basic primordial constituents of the conscious stream of individual being. They are considered as the subject of world conscious experience. These elemental factors intervene in bringing about the four-fold aspects of the total world experiential dhammas are divided into two classes based upon the characteristics of their manifestations, *saṁskṛtā* and *asaṁskṛtā* dhammas. *Saṁskṛtā Dhammas*: The manifestations here are relative and interdependent upon each other. They are constituents *kṣaṇika saṁsarga* and are goverened by the law of causation that is, they are momentary and conditional. The manifestations which are eternally unchangeable, ever-present and indestructable, free from the laws of causation and destruction, these are known as *asaṁskṛtādhamma*. They are *nibbāna*, *ākāsa*, *prati-sankhyanirodha* and *apratisaṅkhya nirodha*. Ref. *Abhidhamma Kośa*. I.

15. *Vis. Magga*. XIV, 36, p.489., *Dhs*. 596.

17. *Vedanā* (fr.Ved) meaning feeling, sensation. *Digha Nikāya* 11.58, *Vis. Magga*. 460sq, *Majj. Nikāya* 1, 302.

18. *Majj. nikāya*. 1, 293.f.

19. Eye-contact (*cakkhu-Samphassajā Vedanā*)

Ear-contact (*Sota-Samphassajā Vedanā*)

Nose-contact (*Ghana-Samphassajā Vedanā*)

Body-contact (*kāya-Samphassajā Vedanā*)

Tongue-contact (*Jīvahā-samphassajā Vedanā*)

Mind-contact (*Mano-samphassajā Vedanā*)

Saṁ. Nikāya-IV, P.232.

20. *Saññā* (fr. san+jñā) literally it stands for sense perception, recognition, assimilation of sensations, awareness. *Majj. Nikāya.* 1, 293; it differs from *viññāṇa* and *paññā* as a child's 'perceiving' differs from (a) an adults (*Viññāṇa*) and (b) an expert's (*paññā*): Ref. *Vis. Magga*. 436.

21. Majj. Nikāya. 1, 293.

22. Dutt. N. *Early Monastic buddhism*, p. 200.

23. *Abhidhammakośa* (ABK) p. 78.

24. *Saṅkhāra* (fr. San+kr) not vedic, but as *saṁskāra* in Epic & classical saṅskrit meaning 'preparation' and 'sacrament' also in philosophical literature 'former impression, dispositions, composition aggregate. *Saṁ. Nikāya* II.60., *Pāli. Dic*. p.664.

25. *Saṁ. Nikāya*. III. 87., Pm. 484.

26. *Vibaṅga*, p. 7.

27. *Abhidhammakosa Vrṭṭi* V.29 4, *Saṁ. Nikāya*.III. 87.

28. *Saṁ. Nikāya.* III. p.60. katamā ca saṅkhāra? chayime cetanākāyā; rūpasañcetanā, saddsa—, gandhasa—, rasasa—, phoṭṭhabhasa-, dhammasancetanā. cf. *Vibhaṅga*. 144; *Sumaṅgalavilāsinī*, p.64.

29. *Vis. Magga*. Chap. XIV. 132, p. 521

29a. *Majj. Nikāya* I. 435.

30. (fr. vi+jñā) Vedic *Vijñana*: cognition, a mental quality or a constituent of individuality, the bearer of (individual) life. *Dīgha Nikāya*. III.233. In fuundamental application it may be characterised as the sensory and perceptive activity, commonly expressed, by "mind". In *Saṁ. Nikāya*. II. 95.,it is used as synonym of '*citta*' and '*mano*', in appopriate; *kāya* refers to the body: *Pāli. Dic*. P. 618.

31. *Saṁ. Nikāya*. I. 122, III. 54, d: 11.68, *Majj. Nikāya* I. 259.

32. *Digha Nikāya* 15. *Mahāniddana sutta* (Warren's Trans. p. 207-208).

33. *Majjhima Nikāya* (M.N.) 1.292; *Dīgha Nikāya*. III. 243.

34. *Abhidhammakośa*., p.79. visayam visayam prati.

35. *Majj. Nikāya.* 1.293 *Mahāvedalla sutta*. yaṁ vedeti taṃ sañjānati, yaṃ sañjānati taṃ vijānāti.

36. Profitable in the sense of health, faultless and pleasant result. It the sense of health, faultless and pleasant result. It is of 21 types operating in the four spheres of sense, fine material, immaterial and supramundane.

37. Unprofitable consciousness is of one kind for they belong to the sense-sphere. But it is of three kinds depending upon the root namely greed, hate and delusion. The total of unprofitable consciousness arising from these three roots are twelve.

38. It is indeterminate in the sense that it cannot be described either as profitable or unprofitable. It is of two kinds; resultant (36) and functional (20). The resultant operates in all the four spheres, whereas the indeterminate does not operate in the supramundne sphere. The total number of indeterminate consciousness are 56 (for a complete and detailed study regarding the 89 types of consciousness, refer to *Visuddhi magga*, Chapter XIV, 82-110, pp.506-514).

39. profitable consciousness....... 21

Unprofitable consciousness......... 12

indeterminate consciousness........ 56

Total 89

40. *Vis. Magga*. XIV, III to 124. pp.514 to 518.

41. *Ibid*. For detailed explaination about the 14 modes of operation refer to *Vis. Magga*. XIV pp. 514 to 518 (*ñāamoli*).

42. *Ibid*.

42a. *Sutta Nipāta* verses 734, 735 whatever suffering arises it is all because of consciousness. "Yaṃ kinci dukkhaṃ saṁbhoti, sabbaṁ viññāṇapaccaya".

43. Patisaṁbidāmagga, (Ps) I. pp. 146-150.

44. Ps.ii. 238, the five aggregates are sources of suffering as impermanent, as painful, as a disease, a boil, a dart, a calamity, an affliction —— a disaster, a terror,...as fickle, as perishable...

45. *Majj. Nikāya*, 35, i. 231, *Cūlasaccāka Sutta*.

46a. *Digha Nikāya Aṭṭakatha* on *Dīgha Nikāya*. II. II, Dhs. A. 272 (trns. 360)

46. *Saṁyutta Nikāya* I. 134.

47. *Dhamma* has been used in various senses in the Buddhist texts. Buddhaghosa in the *Dhammasangaṅi atṭṭhakatha*. 38, I.22., has given some of the meanings in which it is used: 1) applied to good conduct: 2) to preaching or moral instructions: 3) to the nine-fold collection of Buddhist Scriptures: 4) to the cosmic law; 5) doctrine formulated: 6) condition or causal antecedent; 7) mind quality. (*Pāli-Eng. Dic*. p. 335).

48. *Aṅguttāra Nikāya*, I. 122.

48a. *Th. A*. 270; *Majj. nikāya*. 11. 104 cf. *Dhammapada*. 80.

49 *Ang. Nikāya.* III. 415; *Vis. Magga.* 469.

50. The Buddhists speak of a relationship between the three types of kammas performed by man. It is *mano-kamma* (mental action) when human actions are confined to mere mental intention. When the mental intention is externally manifested, otherwise through the act of speach *vācāviññāatthi* then, it is known as *vācākamma*. When such an intention is physically excuted through the agency of motive organs, the mental intention has reached its end through an act of *kāya-kamma*; *kāya-kamma* is the last act which completes the process, whereby a morally imputable action is posited.

51. *Alobha*: Though it is a negative term, meaning absence of greed; it positively means charity, generosity and renunciations.

52. *Adosa*: It does not merely mean the absence of hatred, but it represents a positive quality of goodwill and friendliness. It also means universal love.

53. *Amoha*: It means non-delusion; it represents knowledge, insight or wisdom, which permeates the reality of things. supramundane (*lokuttara*) and seventeen mundane (*lokiya*). The *lokiya* belong to the three spheres of existence, kāma, rūpa, *arupalokas*. Whereas the lokuttara does not belong to any particular loka, but are attainable from any of the three lokas. These are ñānas or insights. The lokiyas are subdivided into eight *kāmāvacara kusala kammas*, belonging to the sensual sphere; five *rūpāvacara kusala kamma* belonging to the sphere of subtle matter; and four *arūpāvacara kusala kamma* belonging to the immaterial sphere. Among the eight *kāmāvacara kusala kammas*, four are duhetuka rooted in *aloba* and *adosa* only; the remaining four and the nine *rūpa* and *arūpa kusala kammas* are *trihetukas* rooted in all the three *kusala* roots namely *aloba*, *adosa* and *amoha*, of the twelve *akusala kammas* (*akusala cittas*) eight are rooted in greed (*lobhamūlaka*), two in *hatred* (*dosamūlaka*), and two in delusion (*mohamūlaka*). They occur in all the three spheres of existence.

55. Of these twelve *akusala kammas* eight are rooted in greed (*lobamūlaka*), two in hatred (dosamūlaka) and two in delusion (*mohamūlaka*). They occur in all the three spheres of existence.

56. *Dhammapada*. 306.

57. *samaṅgi* (fr. Saṁ+aṅgin) means endowed with, possessing. It refers to something with which one is equipped, which propels the life-flux. *Pug.* 13, 14, *J.*1.303, *Vin.* 342., *Vbh.A.* 438. Refer *Pāli dic.*, p. 681-82.

57a. *Dīgha Nikāya*—30: *Abhidhammakośa* IIi pp,148-169 (Lavallee Poussion Brussels, 1971) The *Abhidhammatto Saṅagho* speaks of these three *lokas* as being further divided into thirty-one realms. *kāmaloka* has two sub-divisions namely *apāyabhume* and *kāmasugati*. *Apāyabumi* consists of four realms of Niraya, tiracchāna, pettivisaya and *Asuraloka*. *kāma-*

sugati consists of two realms *manusa-loka* and *Devoloka*; *Devaloka* has six-spheres. *Rūpaloka* consists of sixteens realms inhabited by higher gods known as Rūpi Brahma. Arūpaloka consists of four realms (*Abhidhammoatto Saṅgaho*, Chap. V. 2-6, 10).

58. *Majj Nikāya*. 12-*Mahāsihānada sutta*. *Majj*. *Nikāya* i. 74-77.

59. The concept of God here is different from that of the Advaitins conception of Brahman. He is neither 'Omniscient' nor 'Omnipresent', he is just a 'higher being', who due to his *kusala kamma* has attained birth in this form. He is not fully purified, not fully realised; He is yet to attain *nibbāna*. Ref. *The message of Buddha*, Jayathilleka, p. 114.

60. The term '*Paṭiccasamuppāda*' is made up of two words *paticca* + *Samuppada*. The word '*paṭicca* (Skt.*pratitya*) is derived from the root 'i' with the prefix '*paṭi*' (Skt. *prati*) plus the suffix *ya*' meaning reaching, depending on, resting on, falling back upon. '*Samuppāda*' is derived from *Sam*+*pād*+*a* (Skt.*Samutpāda*) meaning, 'Origin'. Joining the two words together we get 'dependent origination'. It means, depending on a preceding cause, happening by way of a cause, causal geneis. The causal formula being; This being, that becomes; from the arising of this, that arises; this not becoming, that does not become: from the ceasing of this, that ceases (*Majj*. *Nikāya*. II. 32: *Saṁ*. *Nikāya*. II.28). Buddhaghosa in the *Visuddhi Magga* uses that the word 'paticca' in the sense that a thing does not originate by itself (*ekekato*) nor without a cause (*napiahetuto*). It originates depending upon certain other things (*paccayasamaggim paticca*) as a fruition (*phalaroharena*). Therefore, *paṭiccasamuppāda* means that a 'cause' leads to an effect unalterably and the cause and 'effect' are mutually dependent and their dependence is unalterably fixed. (*Vis*. *Magga*. XVII, .522).

61. 'Hetu' and '*paccaya*' are almost identical as synomyous, yet differentiated (*Dīgha Nikāya*. I. 53). 'paccaya' came to be distinguished from '*hetu*' as 'genus' of which '*hetu*' has the typical chief species implies that paccaya becomes synomyous with 'relation' understood in a causal sense; 'hetu' meaning condition, causal antecedent, and the other 23 relations being added as special modes of causality. *Ps*. II.116, 59, (*Dic*. of *Pali-End*. p.733). *Hetu* and *paccaya* are synomyous. D. I. 53-"attha hetu attha *paccaya*". In the *Visuddhi Migga*. a fact which is conceived to be indispensable for the origination and continuance of another is regarded as the '*Paccaya*' of the latter. Hence, a *paccaya* is a causal condition in the absence the 'effect' cannot be brought into existence. Thereby a 'paṭicca' can be taken as 'cause' in the widest sense of the term (Chap. XVII, 68, (533) pp. 611-12.)

62. *Sam*. *Nikaya* XII. 35 (Warren) p. 166-69.

63. *Vis*. *Magga*. Chap. XVII., 31, p. 601 (ñānamoli).

64. *Sam*. *Nikaya* XII, 35

65. *Sam*. *Nikaya* XII, 2.

66. *Sam*. *Nikaya*, XXII, cf. (Warren) p. 165-66.

67. *Vis. Magga*. Chap XVII 272, p. 666

Upanisaya paccaya—A state by virtue of its intrinsic power renders service to other states. *Vis. Magga*. XVII. 80.

78. *Vis. Magga*. XVI, 37, (501) P. 569.

69. *Saṁ. Nik-/ya*. XII.2.

70. *Saṅkhāra* and *bhava* are not the same. *Saṅkhāra* refers to volitions of a past life, leading to the present one, while bhava consists in volition of the present life, leading to the origin of a life hereafter.

71. *Vis. Magga*. XVII, 270, P.665.

72. The child, though is not born, has nevertheless arrived. It is only a matter of time when the partnutition brings it into the world. Similarly once craving arises, and kamma is committed, the resultant is already wrought. It is only a matter of time when its actualisation will be accomplished. Ref.91

73. Attachment (*Upādāna). Upādāna*. fr. *Upa* + *ā*, + *dā*, literally the (material) substratum by means of which an active process is kept alive or going, fuel, supply, provisions: *Saṁ. Nikāya*. I. 69. Ref. *pali-Dic*. p. 149,

74. *Saṁ. Nikāya*. XXII. 90.

75. Saṅskrit, tṛṣṇa-thirst, for craving, hunger for, the fever of unsatisfied longing, greed for. *Saṁ. Nikāya*. V. 420, *Pāli. Eng. Dic*., p.294.

76. *Saṁ. Nikāya* XXII, 90.

77. In this context of defining tanha as 'craving', there is need to understand that it is different from 'mere desire', craving refers to 'excessive desire' which stands for 'greed', wherein man aspires for things more than the required. This distintion between 'need' and 'greed' is significant, especially in the present context, wherein resources are limited and people are many. Man has to use his rationality to utilise the available resources in a manner in which the entire humanity can be benefited. Man should be able to rise from satisfaction of his individual desire to universal desires.

78. *Saṁ. Nikāya* II.3. Chayime...taṇhākāya: rūpataṇhā saddataṇhā gandha taṇhā rāsataṇhā phoṭṭhabbataṇhā dhammataṇhā.

79. Buddha observes that each of these 18 taṇhās may either refer to an internal (subjective) or an external (objective) object of craving. They may also refer to the three temporal determinations of the past, the present and the future. Therefore, there are 108 types of taṇhā which cause attachment and produce suffering.

80. *Vis. Magga*. XVII 248, p. 660.

81 The booser symbolises the instability and thirst that characterise action (kamma). Craving is an active volitional action and is supported by ignorance, just as a boozer is supplied with drinks by a woman. Ref. 91.

82. *Majj. nikāya*. I. 130.

83. *Vis. Magga*. Chap. XVII. 233, P.655.

84. This illustration stresses on the immediate and sharp impact that it imparts to the personality. It is an emotional response to the contact between the sense and its object. Ref.91.

85. *Phassa*: Vedic, *sparśa*-means contact, touch. It is the fundamental fact in a sense-impression and consists of the combination of the sense, the object and perception. *Majj. Nikāya*. 1.III; Pāli. Dic. p.478.

86 *Vis. Magga*. XIV, 134.

87. It stresses on what is called 'made for each other'. The arising of a consciousness comes though the agency of contact. It is 'contact' which 'brings in' the external object.

88. *Vis. Magga*. XVII, 227, P.654 (ñānamoli).

89. Ibid.

90. *Saṁ. Nikāya*, XXII, 90.

91. The boat represents the *nāma-rūpa*, the boatman and passengers represent the mind which is a compound of *Vedanā*, *Saññā saṅkhāra* and *Viññāṇa*. *Viññāṇa* is the boatman, whereas the swift currents represent perilous and unstable saṁsāra through which life has to be lead. The twelve links of the causal chain in the Tibetan tradition is symbolically represented. Ref. Hphags-pa-rten-cin-hbrel-bar-hbyun sher-bya-va-theg-palchen-poi-mdo Sutta No 878 Vol. 34 (Bkah-Hgyur) for details see: Saṅgharakshita, Bhikkhu, *The Three Jewels*, pp. 76-79. Cf. Conze, Edward, *Buddhist Meditation*, p.157.

92. *Viññāna* (fr. *vi +jñā*) It forms a factor for rebirth *upādhi* S:ii, 41. It is likened to the seed in the field of action. A.I. 223. It is an ahāra or through which rebirth comes. Ref. *Pāli. Dic*. p.618.

93. *Saṅkhāra* is the purposive, aspiring state of mind to induce a specific rebirth, Ref. Pāli Dic., p.665.

94. *Avijjā*: Skt. *Avidyā* fr. *ā+vid* means ignorance, the main root of evil and of continual rebirth. Ref. pali Eng. Dic. p.85.

95. *Dīgha Nikāya* II.p.306, Majj. Nikāya, II, p. 249.f.

96. *Saṁyutta Nikāya*, IV, p. 40.

97. *Dhammasangaṅi*, 1162.

5

Means of Deliverance from Dukkha

INTRODUCTION

Suffering (*dukkha*) arises out of 'craving' (*taṇhā*) with 'ignorance' (*avijjā*) as the base. Therefore, ignorance is the root cause of all sufferings. It is the ignorance of the true nature of things that they are impermanent (*anicca*), essenceless (*anattā*) and full of suffering (*dukkha*). The ignorant takes them as permanent (*nicca*), full of essence (*attā*) and as the nature of pleasure (*sukha*). This leads to 'craving' (*taṇhā*) for attachment with the objects. But as they are impermanent and lack an essence, the resultant experience is one of suffering.

The nerve centre of these false experiences of objects as permanent, full of essence and pleasure is the 'mind'. 'Mind' is the master power that moulds and casts 'thoughts'. In the mind, if, there are evil thoughts, then the words are evil, the deeds are evil, and sorrow which results from sin follows that man as the chariot wheel follows the 'drawer' who drags it[1].

The mind subjected to ignorance is conditioned by the five-fold defilements (*nīvaraṇas*). Hence, the essential process of deliverance from suffering consists of getting the mind completely purified from the defiling factors, which hinder the proper perception of objects. One attains liberation when one perceives things 'as they really are' and not 'and they appear to be'.

The Five Defilements (Nīvaraṇas)

Buddha, in the *Sāmmaññaāphala Sutta*[2] speaks of the five defilements, (1) Sensual desires (*kāmacchanda*); (2) Malevolence (*vyāpāda*); (3) Inactivity and drowsiness (*thīnamidda*); (4) Worry and flurry (*Uddhaccakukkucca*) and (5) Doubt and wavering (*vicikicchā*), which have to be overcome on the path of deliverance.

(i) Sensual Desires (Kāmacchanda)

Man strives to satisfy the sensual desires arising out of sense-object contact. When sensual desires prey upon a man (*mind*) he happens to acquire the psyche of a debtor, who has failed to pay back the borrowed loan[3]. There is similarity between the behaviour of the two, the 'debtor' and the 'lustful being'. Both possess the capacity 'to endure'. The debtor endures all forms of humiliation he faces from the creditor. The man overpowered by sensual desires endures all difficulties and injuries inflicted upon him in the course of seeking the object of gratification[4]. His behaviour and nature of these sensual desires have been aptly depicted by the Buddha in the *Potaliya Sutta*[5] as follows: 'A butcher throws before a dog, tormented by hunger, a bare and fleshless bone. Such a bone cannot satisfy the hunger of the famished dog. Sensual desires and resultant pleasures are like 'a bare bone' that would never yield any genuine happiness. It is like a beautiful dream vision, which vanishes when one awakes. It is a borrowed treasure, a changing phenomenon, which is envied by those who do not 'perceive' its borrowed, impermanent nature; its true nature as distinct from its appearance[6]. It is like a sugar-coated pill, which internally is full of bitter content.

(ii) Malevolence (Vyāpāda)[7]

Vyāpāda consists in wishing evil, rejoicing at other's suffering and being ill-disposed towards others. When gripped by this 'malevolent' mind man loses the light of reason and is overtaken by emotion. Such a person having lost the sense of discrimination between good and evil is not sensitive to the consequences of his actions. All that he wants is pleasure, even at the cost of inflicting pain on others. Buddhaghosa likens him to a 'sick person'[8].

(iii) Inactivity and Drowsiness (Thīnamidda)[9]

Buddha speaks of inactivity and drowsiness as a state of mind emanating from a state of 'carelessness'. The mind herein, is completely inactive and confused. This state is comparable to a person in prison, due to his careless behaviour and thus is incapacitated to participate in the festivities of life. Man, by this careless attitude, fails to enjoy, the fruits of 'dhamma'.

(iv) Flurry and Worry (Uddhaccakukkucca)[10]

Man, when he finds that he has not been able to achieve or change things as desired by him, starts worrying and gets desperate. Buddhaghosa compares 'this mind' to that of a slave. It is only an unruffled mind that is capable of understanding things in the right perspective, that paves the way to realisation. On the other hand, a mind bound by worry and flurry can never lead to right knowledge and hence, like a slave who is not in a position to repay the amount by which he was purchased, has to ever remain a slave; the man whose mind is under the influence of worry and flurry can never get out of this state of bondage.

(v) Doubt and Wavering (Vicikicchā)[11]

The state of the mind overpowered with doubt and wavering resembles a man, who has lost his way. The man so lost, is surrounded by the danger of uncertainty and suffers mental agony . Similarly, the 'lost mind' is gripped by the danger of doubt and uncertainty. Such a mind is not conducive to 'knowledge' for attaining *Nibbāna*.

Buddha observes that to attain freedom from *dukkha*, one has to overcome the five-fold defilements (*nīvaraṇas*), which have made the mind conditioned and unstable. In the *Vatthūpama Sutta*,[12] the Buddha compares the defiled mind to a 'dirty cloth'. The 'dirty cloth' when dyed, would be 'dyed bad' and would not be bright in colour. But a clean cloth when dyed, would be bright on dyeing. Similarly, good results can be expected only when the mind is unsustained. The final effort is the purity of mind. The purity of mind can be achieved only by the practice of the Noble Eight-fold path *(Ariyo Aṭṭaṅgiko Maggo)*.

Ariyo Aṭṭaṅgiko Maggo

Buddha refers to the two forms of life prevalent during his period, namely the path of 'self-indulgence' and the path of 'self-mortification'[13]. Buddha contends that both these forms of life are unsuitable to help man from misery. To quote the *Dhammacakkappavattana Sutta*: 'one should avoid the 'two extremes', one being the life of a worldly man, (remaining immersed in pleasure) self-indulgence; and the other, the life of a recluse given to self-mortification'. For both these paths are ignoble, unwise and full of suffering[14]. He speaks of what he calls the middle path' avoiding the two extemes of 'self-mortification' and 'self-indulgence', the *Ariyo-Aṭṭaṅgiko Maggo*[15]. This path is like the 'golden mean' of Aristotle. It is founded, firstly on Buddha's belief that an 'Universal Dhamma' operates on this mundane earth as a norm. This path is an admixture of ethical life, clubbed with the '*dhamma*'. Suffering, according to him, is nothing but a sign of deviation from the '*dhamma*'. Secondly, it is based on the knowledge of the causes and conditions which are responsible for suffering. The ideals in the path are purely based on facts of life.

Before accepting the '*Ariyo-aṭṭaṅgiko maggo* the Buddha expects the aspirant to critically analyse and reflect over it. He warns against the acceptance of it, by blind faith or reverence. Only after the doctrine is reflected and tested upon, can the aspirant gain confidence and faith, which are essential prerequisites for attaining freedom from suffering. Just as the goldsmith tests the purity of gold by rubbing it on his touch-stone, declares it as genuine gold, only his rational thinking can man decide upon the usefulness of this path as 'mean' for attaining freedom.

There is no supreme power which manifests, controls and preserves the Universe. No supreme power will come and help one in attaining freedom from *dukkha*. Man alone is responsible for his deeds, and he is alone in his pursuit for freedom; it cannot be got by proxy. Man has to work out his freedom all by himself. This point is well-illustrated in the advice given to Ananda by the Buddha, before his death.

"O Ananda do not grieve for the Master in dying,
work out for your freedom, follow the Noble Eight fold
path, work out your salvation by diligence[16]".

The *Ariyo aṭṭaṅgiko maggo* as stated by the Buddha in his famous *Sarnath Sermon* consists of the following eight limbs or stages.

1. Right views (*Sammā diṭṭhi*),
2. Right resolve (*Sammā saṅkappo*),
3. Right speech (*Sammā vācō*),
4. Right conduct (*Sammā kammanto*),
5. Right livelihood (*Sammā ājīvo*),
6. Right effort (*Sammā vāyāmo*),
7. Right contemplation (*Sammā sati*) and
8. Right concentration (*Samma samādhi*)[17]

The above eight limbs can be brought under a three-fold conceptual scheme namely *Sīla, Samādhi and Paññā* based on their main functions[18]. *Sīla* includes those steps dealing with ethical perfection. It consists of the three steps-Right speech, Right conduct and Right livelihood of the eight-fold path. *Samādhi* includes those steps dealing with critical reflection—Right effort, Right contemplation and Right concentration. *Paññā*, includes those steps dealing with the epistemic perfection - Right views and Right resolve. *Paññā*, stands for wisdom, the knowledge about the 'truth of *dukkha*'. The above three-fold classification is comparable to the Jaina means of liberation namely Right knowledge (*Samyakjñāna*), Right attitude (*Samyakdarśana*) and Right conduct (*Samyakcāritrani*).

Sīla is to be practised and mastered, first to ascent to the stages of *Samādhi* and *paññā*. For, the avoidance of the extreme of 'self-indulgence' in sense-desires is shown by *Sīla*; the avoidance of the other extreme of 'self-mortification' is shown by *Samādhi* and the cultivation of the 'middle way' is shown by *Pañña*. The means for purification from defilement is given in *Sīla*. The means of overcoming the element of sense-desires, the suppression of, prevention and purification from the defilement of craving is given in *Samādhi*. The means of overcoming all 'becoming,' the cutting off, the prevention and purification from the defilement of false views is given in *Paññā*[19].

The primacy accorded to *Sīla* over *Samādhi* and *Paññā* is not incidental, but essential. Only when the aspirant has trained his body and senses for self-control, then he enters into cleansing the mind from its defilements and gains a true understanding of the truth of *dukkha*, thereby attaining *Nibbāna*. There is no short-cut to *Nibbāna*. But there are also exceptions to this established rule. To quote from the *Mahāvagga*- Yasa[20] a son of a rich merchant, and a lay-follower, who while attending to the instructions of the Buddha, suddenly, happened to realise *Nibbāna*. However, *Sīla* is an essential pre-condition, for it provides the base or foundation[21] essential for the sustenance of the stage of *Samādhi*, leading finally to *Nibbāna*. The Buddha opines that in practice, these are inter-dependent and function simultaneously, when fully evoked. He has characterised the interplay, resulting in the liberation, actually practising it in the following manner: 'When noble conduct (*Sīla*) is realised and known, when noble meditation (*Samādhi*) is realised and known, when noble wisdom (*Paññā*) is realised and known, then the craving for existence is destroyed and there is no more birth'[22].

Sīla: Its Meaning and Function

Sīla, in general, means behaviour, habit, nature and character[23]. In particular, it denotes good conduct, moral practice or a code of morality. In Pāli Buddhism, '*Sīla*' is synonymous with 'virture' standing for the precepts, the *Pañca Sīla*, *Aṭṭaṅga sila* and *Dasa sīla*. It is important stage in the path of deliverance, for its provides the 'base' for the aspirant's onward progress into the stages of *Samādhi* and *Paññā*.

Its function is similar to 'karmayoga' the preparatory stage for liberation, wherein stress is laid on the development of a sound moral base. The aspirant, herein, is not only advised to refrain from committing physical, mental or verbal misdeeds[25], but is also instructed to perform certain physical, mental and verbal moral acts[26]. *Sīla* has both the positive and negative elements, which helps clearing the mind from the defiling factors and prepares the mind to be receptive to the knowledge leading to *Nibbāna*.

Sīla can be better understood, when we analyse each precept.

(i) Pañca Sīla

The five percepts (*Pañca-sīla*) form the base of *Sīla*.

1. I undertake the vow to abstain from the taking of life. (*pāntipāta veramaṇī sikkhāpadaṁ samādiyāmi*).

Pāṇa (*Skt-Prāṇa*) refers to the life-driving power; it is synonymous with a 'living being'. Killing, a volitional activity, signifies the depriving of the life-driving force, wherein a living being is deprived of its existence knowingly or intentionaly. It is an extreme form of the manifestation of anger. The mind, which is overpowered with anger makes one perform such an 'immoral act' of killing.

The Buddha observes that 'everyone fears violence, everyone likes life; comparing oneself with others one would never slay or cause to slay"[27]. It is for this reason that the Buddha argues against animal sacrifice, apart from the evil effects of 'decay' and 'impurity' in such 'means'. He is against the act of killing oneself or committing suicide, or motivating others to suicide. Even, killing in self-defence is forbidden. To quote the Buddha, 'If villainous bandits were to carve your limb from limb with a two handled saw, even then the man that should give way to anger would not be obeying my teaching'[28].

The followers of Budhism have to follow this precept of non-killing strictly[29]. The Bhikkhus are supposed to filter drinking water to avoid swallowing the microbes in the water.

Non-killing, apart from stressing on cultivation of control over the passion of anger, has also a positive import-the import of Universal love '(*metta*)'. It involves in the mind being brought under control and the development of patience. For killing is an expression of anger, a state of turbulence. The mind which has developed patience, possesses the capacity of clearly understanding the relationship between all living things and can devote itself to develop universal love amongst all creatures[30].

2. I undertake the vow, not to take which is not given. (*Adinnādāṇa veramaṇī sikkhāpadaṁ samādiyāmi*)

The kammic effect of theiving results in great suffering in the next birth for a long period, or rebirth as a person devoid of any possessions. To quote the *Telakaṭāhagāthā*: 'If man in order to benefit himself is guilty of stealing the property of others, in his next birth he becomes a contemptible beggar clad in dirty rags, with a broken vessel in hand, he ever begs his daily bread at the doors of his enemies, while suffering a hundred insults'[31].

The Buddha observes that abstinence from stealing helps one gain control over the desire for material possessions. There is nothing wrong with material possessions as such, only that one should refrain from clinging to them. The Buddha, while instructing Sigala, observes that the virtuous man amasses wealth like a roving bee and parts with it in the rightful manner[32]. In the broad sense, this precept is aimed at developing control over all forms of dishonest activity. The kammic effect of practising this precept is rebirth endowed with the qualities such as possessing noble wealth, position and peaceful living[33].

This precept is similar in import to Right livelihood. For, it makes man realise that one must make one's earning not by involving in trades, which involve trickery and deceit such as astrology and palmistry.

3. I undertake the vow to abstain from misconduct in sexual action (*Kāmesu micchācārā veramaṇī sikkhāpadaṁ samādiyāmi)*

Kāma means lustful attachment to males or females. '*Micchā*' means wrong and '*Ācārā*' - is doing; the compound therefore refers to the committing of sexual misdeeds. Sexuality is the strongest instinct of living beings. Man, being more sensitive to sexual stimulation, spends most of vital energies in such 'unchaste' activities. The 'unchaste mind' is comparable to a ill-thatched house, which allows rain water in[34]. Lust enters and deludes the 'unchaste mind' away from meditation, and thereby from gaining knowledge leading to *Nibbāna*. To quote from the *Dhammapada,* "The harm that an enemy will do to an enemy or a foe to a foe is not so great as that, which a wrongly directed mind will do to oneself'[35]. The kammic effects of such immoral activities will result in rebirth in a lower realm, or rebirth in the human realm, with plenty of suffering[36].

Further, this precept refers to abstinence from all indulgences in the five-sensual objects: visible, auditory, olfactory, gastatory and tactile objects. It implies abstinence from evil conduct with regard to the five sensual organs. This precept has its positive import in celibacy and chastity. Buddhism advocates strict practice of celibacy by all, except lay followers, who are also required to observe it during *Uposatha* days[37]. It is not mere intercourse that is forbidden, to relish even the feeling of a woman or the thought of the opposite sex is forbidden. Chastity is prescribed for the lay followers. It involves seeking satisfaction in one's own wife and not aspiring, sharing or exchange of wives. The Buddha exhorts: 'Refrain from all unchastity, just as wise men avoid stepping into a burning charcoal pit'. If one cannot exercise control over sexual desires completely, one can atleast avoid transgressing its limits by not seeking satisfaction with another man's wife[38].

Observance of celibacy and chastity helps one to meditate properly with all energy. The practice of this precept helps one overcome evil desires and enables one to cultivate Right conduct. He derives benefits such as respect, honour, not having enemies and so on[39].

The first three precepts cover the stage of 'Right conduct' (*Sammā kammanta*) of the *Ariyo Aṭṭangiko maggo.*

4. *I undertake the vow to abstain from false-hood* (*Musāvādā veramaṇṇī sikkhāpadaṁ samādiyāṁ*)

Musāvādā refers to lieing or falsehood. Lieing is a willed immoral activity, wherein a person convincingly presents the falsehood as 'truth'. It implies the acceptance of 'truth', in one's mind, as that which one knows to be 'untrue' or 'false'. The act of lying consists of four conditions: 1) falsehood itself, 2) intention to deceive 3) effort so involved and 4) act of communicating the falsehood[40]. In the absence of any one of the above four conditions, the 'act' cannot be termed as lieing. Lieing expresses itself in various forms like hypocrisy, perjury, conditions for 'untruth' or false-hood, whereas 'truth' in only to be discovered. Thus, lieing involves a wast of ones vital energies in formulating and making a false statement appear to be true. Such a mind which is ill-directed and drained of its energy can never lead one to *nibbāna*. It cannot see the true nature of things, life and existence as being plagued with the three ills of impermanence, essencelesseness and suffering.

The effects of lieing start with the person losing credibility among his fellow people. He will have no friends to help him in distress. He will be reborn in hell or in the animal world. If he is reborn in human realm, he will suffer from false accusations. The practice of this precept positively is speaking truth, it will result in a person's endowment with qualities such as having a radiant appearance, sweet and faultless speech, and so on[41]. This precept's content and import correspond to 'Right speech' (*Sammā vācō*)

5. I undertake the to vow to abstain from liquor that causes intoxication and indolence: (*Surā-meraya-majja-pamādaṭṭhānā veramanī sikkhāpadaṁ samādiyāmī*)

The consumption of liquor and other fermented drinks affects the mind and the mental processes of thinking, speaking and acting. It distorts the mental vision and is deterimental for one who wants to maintain sanity and vigilance necessary for acquiring freedom from *dukkha*. Buddha strictly forbids all forms of drinking[42] but allows its use only as a medicine[43]. The danger lies only when sober drinking turns into a habitual drunkenness followed by immoral activities. Such a person, apart from polluting himself and the social environment, makes it difficult for others to abstain from intoxication.

The kammic effects of intoxication can result in his rebirth in a lower realm. He will be inflicted with insanity, if reborn in the human relam[44]. Practice of the precept of non-intoxication is endowed with qualities such gratefulness, mindfulness, generosity and so on[45].

(ii) Aṭṭaṅga Sīla

The Buddha prescribes three additional precepts for the monks and the lay followers from *pañca-sīla*, thereby making it eight. The lay-followers observe these precepts on '*Uposatha*' days, whereas Bhikkhus have to strictly adhere to these precepts on all days. The three precepts are: Abstinence from taking untimely meals; Abstinence from all forms of entertainment and ornaments; and Abstinence from use of high seats.

6. I undertake the vow to abstain from taking untimely meals. *(Vikālalabhajanā veramaṇī sikkhāpadaṁ samādiyāmī)*

This precept stresses on developing control over the habit of eating and diet regulation. When appetite is controlled, the mind streamlines its energy and activities only in the direction of meditating on the 'truth' - the truth of *dukkha*. On *Uposatha* days all Buddhists take only one main meal at mid-day and abstain from taking anything during the rest of the day.

7. I undertake the vow to abstain from dancing, singing, music, from using garlands, perfumes, cosmetics and ornaments. (*Nacca-gīta-vādita-visūkadassana*

mālāgandha-vilepana-dhārṇa maṇḍana- vibhūsanaṭṭhānā veramaṇī sikkhāpadaṁ samādiyāmī)

This precept consists in abstinence from dancing, singing, music, from using garlands, perfume, cosmetics and ornaments. It stresses on abstinence from all forms of sensual lust and development of control over them. A man who gets addicted to these lusts devises means to be always in contact with them. He is unware of the underlying suffering in these sensual lusts. Abstinence from these help the mind to develop right mindfulness paving the way for *Nibbāna*.

8. I undertake the vow to abstain from the use of high seats (*Uccāsayana mahāsayanā veramaṇī sikkhāpadaṁ samādiyāmī)*

Abstinence from the use of the high seats refers restraint upon a luxurious style of living. Addiction to luxurious style of life adds to the ego of man, which is not conducive to achieving the highest goal. The mind gets entangled in the pursuit of mundane pleasures, which are full of suffering. The Buddha exhorts his followers to practise simple living—wherein one makes use of things only to the extent essential. Such a 'detached mind' can lead one to higher regions of right mindfulness, leading to *nibbāna*.

(iii) Dasa Sīla

By adding two more precepts to the eight mentioned above, the Buddha makes it *dasa sīla* or ten precepts. It is prescribed by the Buddha for the Bhikkhus to be practised life-long. Here, the seventh precept of *aṭṭaṅgasīla* is divided into two, making it seventh and eighth precepts, the eighth precept of *Aṭṭaṅgasīla* becomes the ninth precept. The tenth precept is:

10. I undertake the vow to abstain from accepting gold and silver (*Jāta-rūpa-rajata-paṭiggahanā veramaṇī sikkhāpadaṁ samādiyāmī*)

This precept lays emphasis on abstinence and developing control over the desire to accept gold and silver, the most valuable of material possessions. Only when the mind has overpowered the desires of material possessions, it possesses the capacity of leading one to the realisation of the Truth-the truth of *dukkha*.

Thus, the ten precepts advocated by the Buddha help the aspirant to gain over the forces disturbing the mind's progress towards *Nibbāna*. He develops a 'healthy mind' in a sound body, which is an essential pre-requisite for one entering the stage of *samādhi*.

(iv) The Fruits of Sīla

The constant observance of ten-fold precepts leads to five-fold benefits, covering both the mundane and the supramundane realms. Firstly, he acquires a large fortune due to his habitual diligence; Secondly, he earns great fame and reputation; thirdly he is respected and honoured in public assemblies, fourthly, he dies unperturbed for he is free from anxiety-he is calm; and fifthly, he is reborn in the 'heavenly world'[46]. He also gains a mental state of non-remorse, which helps destroy the cankers (*āsavas*).

The aspirant, though by cultivating the practice of *Sīla*, gains ethical perfection and resultant happiness, yet is not free from the cycle of birth and death. Ethical perfection, an essentially preparatory state, should be used to ascend to the stage of *samādhi* in the path towards *Nibbāna*.

Samādhi

'*Samādhi*' is made up of three terms 'Sam+ ā + dhā. '*Sam*' stands for 'properly', '*ā*' for 'completely' and '*dhā*' for 'holding'. The total expression '*samādhi*' means 'holding properly and completely'. It means the unification of the moral consciousness with its mental states, properly and perfectly, on the desired object. Thus, '*samādhi*' is the one-pointedness of moral consciousness[47]. The English word 'concentration' is treated as synonymous to *Samādhi*[48]. *Samādhi* has 'non-distraction' as its characteristic. It destroys all forms of distraction and enables the mind to develop one-pointed concentration.

(i) The Ten Impediments (Palibodhas)

The Buddha speaks of ten impediments (*palibodhas*), which the Bhikkhu has to overcome in order to enter *samādhi*. They are

1. *Dwelling (Āvāsa):* Dwelling refers to a place of residence- a room, a hut, or a monastery. Attachment to the dwelling and its possessions is a great impediment to concentration. Mere residency devoid of attachment to its possession however does not constitute and impediment.[49].

2. *Family (Kulaṁ):* Family stands for an aggregate of relatives. It is an impediment for a Bhikkhu who attaches and identifies himself with their well-being. 'He is pleased when they are pleased'.[49] But for a person who has cultivated detachment, nobody, including his parents, can serve as an impediment to his concentration. He must not have *ātmatā* and *mamatā* (I-ness and mineness).

3. *Gain (Lābho):* The Bhikkhu receives a large supply of requisites from lay-followers, in return for teaching the *Dhamma* and blessing them. It is likely that his temptation of gain does not give him enough time to concentrate on

the duties as an ascetic. Thereby, it hinders his progress in the path towards perfection. Hence, the Bhikkhu should cross the obstacle of the temptation 'of gain'. He should leave them and wander like a stranger devoting all his time and energy in meditation.[50]

4. *Class* (*Gaṇo*)*:* Class stands for a group of students of *Sutta* or *Abhidhamma*. It is likely, that a class acts as an impediment, since Bhikkhu is kept busy in imparting instructions to his students. In order to concentrate on his duties as an ascetic he should make alternative arrangements for instruction or advise them to seek guidance from another instructor.

5. *Building* (*Kammāṁ*)*:* Building refers to construction work. The Bhikkhu who involves himself in building work finds his mind completely absorbed in it. He does not find time or energy to attend to his daily ascestic duties. He should, therefore, overcome this impediment by handing over the work to others and free his mind from such an absorption. He should leave the place and meditate on the 'Truth'.

6. *Travel (Addhānaṁ):* The Bhikkhu, if he has to make a journey for some useful purpose, should perform it first. Even if he practises his ascetic duties, the thought of the intended journey is likely to impede his concentration and his duties as an ascetic.

7. *Kin (Ñāti):* Kin refers to preceptor, co-resident, pupils and others in a monastery; and at home it includes father, mother, sisters, brothers and the like. The illness of anyone of the members either in the monastery or home is likely to serve as an impediment to concentrate and discharge his duties as an ascetic. To ensure effective concentration, he is advised to take precautions to cure them with loving care.

8. *Affliction (Ābādho):* Affliction refers to illness. Since illness acts as an impediment to concentration, the Bhikkhu should get over it by treatment. If he cannot overcome the illness, he has still to discharge his ascetic duties.

9. *Books (Gantho):* Books herein refer to the Buddhist Scriptures-Tipitakas. If the Bhikkhu merely concentrates on reciting the texts and not gaining an insight into the truths stated, they act as an impediment. Hence, he has to overcome this impediment by understanding the essence of the scriptures, instead of indulging in mere recitation.

10. *Super-sensory Power (Iddhis):* Super-sensory powers stand for the powers obtained by an ordinary man through concentration. They become an impediment for one who is in search of inward vision (*vipassanā*) and should be relinquished.

(ii) Kalyāṇa-Mitta

The Bhikkhu after having overcome the ten impediments approaches a kalyāṇamitta a spiritual guide. A *kalyāṇamitta* is a person, who acts as a good friend, guide and philosopher to the Bhikkhu in selecting the object of meditation, depending upon his temperament. He should be a man of wisdom (*paññā*), one possessing an insight into the teachings of the Buddha.[51] The *kalyāṇamitta* prescribes the two-fold meditational objects: (i) Generally useful meditational objects and (ii) Special object for meditation. The first category of general meditational object involves cultivation of loving kindness towards other fellow Bhikkhus and all beings of the world. Later, he has to develop mindfulness of death and foulness.[52] It helps him to realise the transitory nature of all things and he cultivates the practice of detachment.

The *kalyāṇamitta* also prescribes the special object of meditation from amongst the forty objects of meditation,[53] depending upon the temperament of the Bhikkhu. Everyman exhibits a certain trait of character more prominently than the others. These dominant traits constitute the temperament of that person.[54] The mental dispositions of 1. greed, 2. hatred, 3. delusion, 4. faithfulness, 5. intelligence and 6. reasoning are displayed depending upon their temperament. The object of special meditation should be chosen bearing in mind that it should not only counteract these traits, but should also render them conducive to meditation. This is decided by the *kalyāṇamitta* after careful observation and study of the temperament displayed by the Bhikkhu.[55] For instance, a Bhikkhu who has a greedly temperament, the ten kinds of foulness (*asubhas*)[56] are recommended as useful.[58] Selecting the object of meditation therefore, is a technique, which is not possible for all. For instance, Elder Sariputta, as a *kalyāṇamitta* of a young Bhikkhu, chose a special meditation object to help him to meditate and thereby attain freedom from lust. But the Bhikkhu failed to attain freedom from lust as the object of meditation did not correspond to the temperament displayed by the Bhikkhu. They approached the Buddha to suggest a special meditation object. Buddha with his deep insight into the past history of the Bhikkhu who happened to be a gold smith in his past life, decided to prescribe a lotus made of gold, as the special object of meditation. The object being suitable to the Bhikkhu's temperament helped him to concentrate and realise the three marks of conditioned existence, of imperamance (*anicca*), essencelessness (*anattā*) and suffering (*dukkha*) leading him to the attainment of arhatship.[59].

(iii) Place of Meditation (Vihāra)

After the prescription of the special object of meditation, the Bhikkhu sets out in search of a suitable place for meditation. The Buddhist texts[60] speak of the criteria to be taken into consideration while selecting the place of meditation. It should be free from the eighteen faults of: 1. being a large monastery, 2. a monastery under construction, 3. a dilapidated monastery, 4. situated on a highway, 5. near a pond, 6. surrounded by creepers having edible leaves, 7. small trees with fruits, 8. shrubs having flowers, 9. near an entry port, 10. being famous, 11. being near a city, 12. situated among timber trees, 13. near an arable field, 14. located among incompatible people, 15. on borders, 16. frontiers of a kingdom, 17. having unsuitable objects and 18. one without a *kalyāṇamitta*. Such a place is unsuitable, for it does not provide solitude, which is a necessary pre-condition for development of concentration.

The Buddhist texts[61] further recommended outer dwelling places, forests, the foot of a tree, a mountain and an open field as suitable places for meditation. The *Visuddhimagga*[62] mentions the following five factors which should be borne in mind by the Bhikkhu while selecting the place for meditation:

1. It should neither be too far nor too near from the alms resort and should be approachable.
2. There should be very little disturbance.
3. It should be free from gadflies, extreme sunlight and creeping creatures, like snakes.
4. It should be a place where robes, food and medicine can be procured easily and
5. Where there are Bhikkhus, who are well-versed in the Scriptures to provide guidance.

The Bhikkhu after having selected the place for meditation gets his head tonsured, nails and body hair removed. He has to keep his bowl, bed, chair and other essentials clean. He has to maintain his old robes by mending, patching or dyeing them whenever required.[63] He follows the step of 'Right effort' (*Sammā-Vāyāmo*), which involves a four-fold duty; 1. preventing the origination of immoral states which have not arisen,

2. discarding the immoral states already possessed, 3 giving rise and developing moral states which have not yet arisen, and 4. promoting the growth of moral states, already existing.[64] Right effort can be successfully practised when Right mindfulness is also put into practice. Both of them mutually help each other in checking the advent of immoral states. Right minduflness involves the cultivation of vigilance with regard to the functioning of 1. the body, (*kāyānupassanā*) 2. feeling (*Vedānupassanā*) 3. mind, (*Cittānupassanā*) and 4. mental objects (*dhammānupassanā*)[65]. With the help of both 'Right effort' and 'Right mindfulness', the Bhikkhu is capable of maintaining his mind on the right path of concentration.

(iv) Rūpa Samādhi

The Bhikkhu having selected a suitable place for meditation begins his endeavour of purfying the mind by cleansing consciousness of its defilements and increasing the capacity to concentrate. In this state he is known as a 'yogavacara', one who has taken to concentration. He selects, with the guidance of *kalyāṇamitta*, the material objects of meditation out of the thirty-six material objects of meditation.[66] Meditation on these material objects constitutes *Rūpa-samadhi*.[67]

The material objects is reviewed as a '*nimitta*' or sign. It serves as a three-fold sign namely *parikamma-nimitta*, *Uggaha-nimitta*, and *paṭibhāga-nimitta*. *Parikamma nimitta* stands for the actual object itself. To begin with, the Yogavacara concentrates solely on the objects, withdrawing his mind from the rest of the world. He develops a state of concentration, wherein he can recall the image of the object even in the absence of its physical existence. This mental disposition gives rise to *Uggaha-nimitta*. (after image). The transformative after-image rise to *Uggaha-nimitta* (reflex-image). For instance, a Yogavacara selects and adopts *paṭhavi-kasiṇa-maṇḍala* as on object of meditation. By deep meditation his mind obtains the uggaha-nimitta or after-image of the object. The characters of the object vanish from sight and the uggaha-nimitta appears, having a shining lustre, resembling the disc of the moon, just emerged out of a cloud.

The *paṭibhāga-nimitta* helps the yogayacara to attain access concentration (*Upacara samadhi*), which enables him to overcome the five defilements (*nīvaraṇas*). These defilements (*nīvaraṇas*) are subdued only with the help of Jhāna[68] factors known as *Jhānāṅgas*.[68a]

These *Jhānāṅgas* are five in number

1. *Vitakka:* Vitakka stands for the initial application of the mind on the object of meditation.[69] It helps the mind withdraw itself from other 'objects' and directs

it towards the specific object. This helps the mind to overcome the defilement of inactivity and drowsiness (*thīnamidda*).[70]

2. *Vicāra: Vicāra* refers to the sustained application of the mind on the object of meditation.[71] It helps the mind overcome the defilement of doubt and wavering (*vicikicchā*).[72]

3. *Pīti: Pīti* refers to the pleasant sensation which one gains in meditation.[73] He develops a joyful psychic ambience and inspires confidence in realisation. It helps the mind overcome the defilement of malevolence (*Vyāpāda*).[74]

4. *Sukha:*[75] Sukha stands for the composure of the mind which one experiences after the realisation of the object.[76] *Sukha* makes both the mind and body composed and saturates them with serenity. It helps the mind overcome the defilement of worry and flurry (*Uddhaccakukkuca*).[77]

5. *Ekagatā*[78]*:* Ekaggatā refers to the character of one pointed- ness of the mind on the object of meditation.[79] It helps the mind overcome the defilement of sensual desires (*kāmacchanda*).[80]

Rūpa-Jhāna

With the suppression of the five-fold defilements by the *Jhānāṅgas*, the mind becomes disciplined and is able to concentrate on an object with form and colour. This is called *Rūpa-jhāna*. In the rupa jhana there are five stages.[81] Each stage is a step towards purification and absorption of consciousness.

In the first stage of *Rūpa Jhāna, paṭhama-rūpa-jhāna,* all the five jhānāṅgas namely *Vitakkā, Vicāra, pīti, Sukha* and *Ekaggatā* are cultivated. Functioning individually and also in association, they generate the one-pointendness of the consciousness. Before proceeding to any higher stage of *rūpa-jhāna,* the Yogāvacara has to consolidate and gain proficiency through the constant practice of the five-fold vasi, the five-fold masteries of: 1. mastery of adverting (*āvajjāna vasī*), 2. mastery of attaining (*samāpajjana vasī*), 3. mastery of resolving (*Adhiṭṭhāna vasī*), 4. mastery of emerging (Uṭṭhana vasī) and 5. mastery of reviewing (*paccavekkhana vasī*) of the *jhāna* attained.[82]

After perfecting the first *rūpa jhāna* stage, he reviews the nature of the five *Jhānāṅgas.* He realises that *vitakkā* is gross in nature, apart from being akin to the sensual plane. With constant practice, the mind is relieved of its fickle nature. By itself, it tends towards the object. He meditates on the object and repeats the process undergone while attaining the first state. He succeeds in dropping '*vitakkā*' and strengthens faith

(Saddhā), which helps the mind to gain tranquility and concentration. He enters the second stage of *rūpa-jhāna* namely *Dutiya-rūpa jhāna*.

As the yogāvacara proceeds from the first stage of rūpa *Jhāha* to the second stage of *rūpa-jhāna*, the level of concentration increases and the grossness of the objects of concentration decreases. In other words, as he enters the second stage, he does not require a captivating object for his concentration. He does not require much effort to concentrate as he was prone to in the first stage, in other words concentration becomes relatively easy whereby, his ability to concentrate increases.

In the second stage on reviewing, he finds *Vicāra* to be gross in nature. He finds that his mind is so trained, that there is neither the need of applying it on the object nor that of sustaining it. He is able to drop *vicāra* and is contented with the remaining three *Jhānaṅgas* of *pīti*, *sukha* and *ekaggatā*. He enters the third stage of *rūpa-jhāna* namely. *Tittiya-rūpa-jhāna*. Here again, on reviewing, piti finds it very alluring and disturbing for deeper meditation. There is no need for generating joy in the hope of realising the desired object, but it is by that time naturally realised. He concentrates and is able to drop *pīti* and is left with *sukha* and *Ekkagatā Jhānāṅgas*. At this stage, he enters the fourth stage of *rūpa-jhāna*, known *as catuttha rūpa jhāna*. Due to his gradual *Jhānic* maturity he starts experiencing serenity 'within' and 'without'. The external wandering of the consciousness is gradually curtailed, so that it may not develop attachment to the object of meditation itself. On reviewing '*sukha*', he finds it gross and absorbing for the Yogavacara to maintain equanimity towards it. There is the possibility of developing a craving for this joyful and pleasant state. It is against the principle of meditation. He becomes alert and replaces *sukha* and *upekkha*. Thus, in the fifth stage of rupa-jhana *Pañcma rūpa jhāna*. He has equanimity and one-pointed consciousness is pure form devoid of any disturbance. The yogavacara's consciousness at this stage becomes pure, free from defilements. His mind is mild, pliable, steadly and concentrated. He can now take up a formless object and exert for *arūpa jhāna* for making his consciousness more subtle.[80]

The progress in the direction towards purity of consciousness stands for the ascent from the *rūpa* to *arūpa samādhi*, from concentration on an entity with form and colour to an entity devoid of form and colour, from the gross to the subtle. The progress of concentration can be measured by one's ability to concentrate even in the absence of an object with form and colour that is non-material objects.

Moreover, the materiality or images of the materiality are sources of distraction. The material world is full of objects and their respective events, their images are agitating us, threatening us and makes our lives insecure and unhappy. To quote *Visuddhimagga* 'it is in virtue of matter that wielding of sticks, wielding of knives, quarrels, brawls and disputes take place'.[84] Naturally, concentration in the midst of such agitation would be difficult. Hence the need to transcend from the world of materiality to the world of the immaterial, which is relatively free from the disturbance of the materiality.

(v) *Arūpa Samādhi*

Arūpa Samādhi is concentration on non-material objects[85], which include objects devoid of form and colour. The yogavacara having attained mastery over rupa jhana by constant practice, is able to reduce or extend the power of concentration, as he desires. He with his increased powers of concentration, as the desires. He with his increased powers of concentration, removes it and finds before his mind 'Infinite space', *ananta ākāsa*. By strict practice of meditation, his mind gains concentration of this formless object, of 'infinite space' (*ananta-ākāsa*). At this stage, he enters the first stage of *arūpa jhāna* namely *Ākāsānañcāyatanaṁ*.[86] By his gradual maturity of concentration, he comes to understand that infinite space is nothing but the manifestation of his consciousness. It is his consciousness which is pervading all over as infinite space and therefore, it is real. Gradually he gives up the infinite space and takes the 'infinite consciousness' (*Ananta-viññāṇa*) as an object of concentration. He finds this stage to be more peaceful and calm than the previous one. He exerts and cultivates concentration on it. After due practice and continuous efforts, he gets one-pointendness over it. At this stage, he enters the second stage of *Aūpa jhāna*, known as *dutiya arūpajhāna-Viññāṇañcāyatanaṁ*.[87].

In this *Jhānic* pursuit, after thorough analysis of the nature of consciousness, he understands that it is void, empty and without reality; there is nothing in it. He gives up the 'infinite consciousness' and takes up the 'nothingness of consciousness' as an object of concentration. He concentrates on the idea of nothingness of consciousness. It is a replacement of his previous thought concerning the infinity of consciousness by a new thought that there is nothing (*natthi kiñci*) in it. With his ability to concentrate on the nothingness of consciousness, he enters the third stage of *arūpa-jhāna* namely *Akiñacaññāyatanaṁ*.

The Yogāvacara, having gained mastery over the third stage of *arūpa jhāna*, reflects on it. His reflection reveals that even preception is a source of disturbance. He realises that it is only the state of 'neither perception' nor 'non-perception' (*n'eva saññā nāsaññaṁ*) is peaceful and sublime. He concentrates on this state and develop one-pointendness on it, he enters the fourth and final stage of his jhānic pursuit known as Nevasaññānāsaññāyatñaṁ.

The Yogāvacara's mind herein is immensely subtle. His mind is now capable of realising the supreme knowledge (paññā) leading to Nibbāna. His mind is as clear as a crystal which denotes the colour of the object presented. He has a direct perception of things as 'they really are'.

(vi) Fruits of Samādhi

The yogāvacara by constant practice and cultivation of concentration gains five-fold benefits and also has access to five kinds of direct knowledge.

The five—fold benefits are

1. Attainment of a peaceful abiding, pure mindfulness devoid of any disturbance.[90]
2. Insight with concentrated consciousness on the tilakkhanas[91].
3. Ability to be a witness of any state realisable by direct knowledge to which the mind inclines, whenever he desires[92].
4. Improved forms of existence, such as a place in *arūpaloka*, in the company of Brahma's retinue[93].
5. Helps the yogāvacara attain the knowledge necessary for cessation, leading to *nibbāna*[94].

The five kinds of direct (*Iddhividha*) knowledge that the Yogavacara has access to are:

1. The ten kinds of super sensory powers[95] -psychic powers, which enable him to perform miracles.[96]
2. Knowledge of the divine ear: He has access to divine knowledge and can listen to both the divine and the human sounds with this power[97]
3. Knowledge of the penetration of minds: The Yogāvacara, having developed the medium of light, penetrates into the heart base, which is the seat of the mind[98].
4. Knowledge of recollection of past life: He can recall the past events of his present life and can trace the relation of these events to the present existence[99].
5. Knowledge of the passing away and reappearance of beings: He visualizes the phenomenon of beings passing away and being born in accordance with the law of *kamma*.[100]

The yogāvacara should not involve himself in these supersensory powers. He should exercise all his faculties and energies making them conducive to attain the state of higher form of meditation (*vipassanā*). This will help him realise the supreme knowledge (*paññā*) leading to *Nibbāna*.

Pañña

Meaning, Character and Function

'Paññā' is a compound of two words 'pa' and 'ññā'. 'pa' means 'properly,' 'rightly', clearly' and 'ññā' means 'to know' or 'understanding'. Thus, *paññā* means 'proper understanding', to gain insight, into the nature of reality and to know 'what reality is'. It is the right understanding of existence, life and things as being characterised by impermanence (*anicca*), essencelessness (*anattā*) and suffering (*dukkha*). This knowledge will enable the aspirant to develop complete detachment from them.

In the *Visuddhimagga*,[101] pañña is defined as 'knowing in a particular mode, separate from the modes of perceiving (*sañjānana*) and congnising (*vijānana*). Though *paññā* involves 'knowing', it is distinguished from the knowing through the insight and it stands for our understanding of the true nature and character of the object, which is not involved in knowledge attained through perceptual cognition. A clear distinction between them can be brought about by an illustration. A heap of coins is seen by three persons, a child, a villager and a money lender. For the child, the coins are objects of attraction by way of figures, shapes and so on, but he is not aware of the value. The villager, apart from knowing the shape, also knows the value and utility of the coin. But the money lender, apart from knowing both about the shape and utility of the coins is also able to discriminate between the genuine and non-genuineness, and the value of the coins. Perception (*Saññā*) is comparable to the child without discrimination, wherein the mode of appearance of the object is only seen. Cognition (*Viññāṇa*) is like the villager, who apprehends the mode of appearance and penetrates the character. Understanding (*paññā*) is like the moneylender, who apart from apprehending the mode of appearance and knowing the character goes further, reaching the manifestation of the path. Thus, *paññā* refers to 'total and complete perception of' or penetration into the object's true nature, the nature of reality.[102] Its function is to remove the darkness of delusion, which conceals the individual's perception and provides insight into the nature or reality.[103]

(i) The Subject Matter of Paññā

Paññā stands for the rising above sense knowledge; it involves the gaining of a right understanding of several material and mental states of reality, which are categorised in Buddhist texts as;

1. Aggregates (*khandhas*), 2. Bases (*Āyatanas*), 3. Elements, (*Dhātus*), 4. Faculties (*Indriyas*), 5. Four Noble Truths, (*Cattāri Ariya Saccāni*) and 6. Doctrine of dependent origination (*paṭiccasamuppāda*).

Aggragetes (khandhas)

The Buddha, in the *Vacchagotta Saṁyutta*[104] opines that man's failure to understand the true nature of existence and the cause for varied views about its nature, arises due to his ignorance of the aggregates. The aggregates are five-fold namely, *Rūpa*, *Vedanā*, *Saññā*, *Viññāna*, and *Saṅkhāra*. They are characterised by the three marks of existence, namely impermance (*anicca*), essencelessness (*anattā*) and suffering (*dukkha*). The entire phenomenal existence, *saṁsāra*, is nothing but an interaction of these aggregates. There is nothing underlying the five *khandha* aggregation, which constitute man's personality. (A detailed analysis of each of the five aggregates has been made in Chapter 4).

Bases (Āyatanas)

Āyatana stands for the base of our experience.[105] Such bases are the six sense organs and their corresponding sense objects.[106] They constitute the 'base' of their respective type of consciousness and psychic factors. They are:

Six Sense Organs	Six Sense Objects
1. Eye (*Cakkhu*)	7. Visual object (*rūpāyatana*)
2. Ear (*Sotam*)	8. Sound object (*Saddāyatana*)
3. Nose (*Ghāna*)	9. Smell object (*ghānāyatana*)
4. Tongue (*Jivhā*)	10. Taste object (*Rasāyatana*)
5. Body (*kāya*)	11. Touch object (*phoṭṭabbāyatana*)
6. Mind (*Mano*)	12. Mental object (*dhammāyatana*)[107]

The Buddha, in the *Salāyatana Saṁyutta*[108] speaks of these 'bases' as being transitory in nature. Seeking attachment with them would only produce suffering. Renunciation of the desire that governs the 'bases' and feeds the thirsty will, alone can help one avoid suffering.

Elements (Dhātus)

Etymologically, 'dhatu' means those elements which 'uphold a being'. It refers to the six sense organs, their objects and six related types of consciousness.

1. Eye (*Cakkhu*)
2. Ear (*Sotam*)
3. Nose (*Ghāna*)
4. Tongue (*Jivhā*)
5. Body (*kāya*)
6. Mind (*Mano*)
7. Visual object (*rūpāyatana*)
8. Sound object (*Saddāyatana*)
9. Smell object (*ghānāyatana*)
10. Taste object (*Rasāyatana*)
11. Touch object (*phoṭṭabbāyatana*)
12. Mental object (*dhammāyatana*)[107]
13. Visual consciousness (rūpa viññānāyatana)
14. Auditory consciousness (saddaviññānāyatana)
15. Nasal consciousness (ghānaviññānāyatana)
16. Gustatory consciousness (rasviññānāyatana)
17. Tactual consciousness (phoṭṭabbaviññānāyatana)
18. Mind consciousness (dhammaviññānāyatana)

The Buddha, in the *Dhātu Saṁyutta*[109], observes that the nature of phenomenal existence can also be probed and understood through a study of eighteen dhatus. These dhatus are transitory in nature, and seeking attachment with them would only produce suffering.

Faculties (Indriyas)

In the *Indriyabhāvanā sutta*[110] the Buddha speaks of twenty-two faculties besides the twelve ayatanas and eighteen dhatus a 'being' requires for his existence. The analysis and understanding of these faculties help one to gain an insight into the real nature of phenomenal existence. These twenty-two faculties can be brought under two categories depending upon their nature and role in the production of suffering and liberation. The first category consisting of faculties which are sources of suffering begins with the set of six sense organs, followed by masculinity (purisa), feminity (*itthi*), vitality (*jīvta*), pleasure (*sukha*), physical suffering (*dukkha*), mental pleasure (*somanassa*), mental displeasure (*domanassa*), and equanimity (*upekkhā*). The second category consists of faculties connected with liberation namely self-confidence (*saddhā*), energy *(viriya)*, watchfulness (*sati*), concentration (*samādhi*), exertion for knowledge (*paññā*), the determination to gain knowledge about the 'unrealised' (*anaññātaññasāmit-)*the determination to gain knowledge and work for the practical realisation of the highest truth (*añña-*) and the determination for the final realisation (*aññātañ-*).[111]

Four Noble Truths (Cattāri Ariya Saccāni)[112]

The four Noble Truths form the foundation of Buddhist philosophy. They are:

(i) The Truth of Suffering (Dukkhaṃ Ariyasaccāṁ)

That suffering exists, is a fact that none can deny. It springs from the attachment to the five-fold *khandha* aggregate taking the form of birth, death, lamentation, and so on.

(ii) The Truth of the Cause of Suffering (Dukkhaṃ Samudayao Ariyasaccaṁ)

Suffering, being an effect, should have a cause. The cause is 'craving' (*taṇhā*), which is three-fold: (a) craving for sensual pleasures, (b) craving for becoming, and (c) craving for non-becoming. Craving motivates action in a man leading to the accumulation of *kamma* and the process of *saṁsāra*.

(iii) The Truth of the Cessation of Suffering (Dukkhanirodhao Ariyasaccaṁ)

When the cause, 'craving' is removed or annihilated, the effect, 'suffering' ceases to exist. Such a state of freedom from suffering is referred to as *Nibbāna*.

(iv) The Truth of the Path Leading to Nibbāna (Dukkhanirodhanagāminī Paṭipadā Ariyasaccaṃ)

The noble eight-fold path is prescribed by Buddha as a 'means' to gain freedom from suffering. The eight stages are : Right view (*Sammā diṭṭhi*), Right thought (*Sammā saṅkappo*), Right speech (*Sammā-vācō*), Right action (*Sammā kammanto*), Right livilhood (*Sammā sati*) and Right concentration (*Sammā samādhi*). (All these stages are explained in detail in the preceding section).

(v) Paṭiccassamuppāda

The Buddha, on the third night of attaining *saṁbodhi*, realising the phenomenal existence, which consists of *khandhas*, *āyatanas, dhātus* and so on was not an happazard affair, but a connected whole, administered by a law. This law which explains the process of phenomenal and individual existence is known as *paṭiccasamuppāda*. It explains the way causal relations operate and set in the process of *saṁsāra*. The Buddha, stressing on the importance of *paṭiccasamuppāda*. States that, one who has understood *paṭiccasamuppāda* has understood the *dhamma*' rightly.

The twelve links of the causal chain (*bhava-chakra*) are 1. Ignorance (*Avijjā*), 2. Impressions (*Saṅkhāra*), 3. Consciousness (*Viññāṇa*), 4. Psycho-physical complex (*Nāma-rūpa*), 5. Six sense organs (*Salāyantana*), 6. Contact (*Phasso*), 7. Feeling (*Vedanā*),

Craving (*taṇhā*), 9. Clinging (*Upādāna*), 10. Becoming (*Bhava*), 11. Birth (*Jātai*), and 12. Ageing and death (*Jāramaraṇa*).[113] A detailed study of *paṭiccasamuppāda* has been presented in chapter 4 under the section paṭiccasamuppāda.

STAGES OF PURIFICATION

In the path towards freedom from *dukkha*, the *Yogāvacara* despite his knowledge of the various categories that entagle man in bondage, does not find himself liberated. He has to proceed further through the following stages in order to reach the state of ultimate perfection.[114]

(i) Purity of View (Diṭṭhi Visuddhi)

In this stage, the *yogāvacara* making use of his concentration directs his mind towards the analysis of the body. He trealises that the body is made up of the five *khandha* aggregate, which is perpetually in a state of flux, that which is impermanent (*anicca*) is devoid of any essence (*anattā*) and can only be a source of suffering. This realisation helps him overcome the notion of 'I-ness' and he is able to gain more purity and enter into the next stage of purification.

(ii) Purity by Overcoming of Doubts **(Kaṅkha Vitaraṇa Visuddhi)**

In this stage, the aspirant realizes that phenomenal existence is neither a divine creation nor a chance happening. It has a cause and the cause has to be removed or extinguished. He also acquires insight into suffering and its origin. He gains this through the right understanding of the law of dependent origination, which stresses upon the conditioned co-production of all events in phenomenal existence. He is now equipped to enter into the next state of purification.

(iii) Purity of Knowledge and Insight Into the Path and what is not the path (Maggāmaggañāṇa Dassana Visuddhi)

In this stage the aspirant meditates on the three-fold characteristics of objects, tilakhaṅas: impermanence, essencelessness and suffering and perceives a void around himself. He is able to draw a clear distinction between the mundane and supramundane forms of the path, by his insight.

(iv) Purity of Knowledge and Insight into the Path of Progress (Paṭipadāñāṇadassana Visuddhi)

The aspirant, having perceived the right path, resumes his meditation on the tilakkhaṇha. He attains deeper insight and clarity about the nine-fold knowledges.

1. The knowledge of the arising and disappearing of things.
2. The knowledge of the dissolution of all things.
3. The knowledge that perceives with fear the five aggregates of existence. He gains knowledge that the five groups of aggregates being impermanent are full of suffering and hence, is a source of fear.
4. The knowledge that perceives with misery the five aggregates of existence. The whole world appears to the aspirant as a pit of burning embers and this knowledge is a source of misery.
5. The knowledge associated with disgust and aversion from existence. On reflection of the wretchedness and vanity of the fearful and wicked world that one gains this knowledge.
6. The knowledge associated with the will for deliverance. Feeling disgusted with the world and its nature, the will for deliverence arises.
7. The knowledge associated with deliverance from all forms of existence.
8. The knowledge associated with equanimity of all formations. One meditates on the *tilakkhaṇa* and realises the sameness of all formation *i.e.*, conditionedness.
9. The knowledge of adaptation: One becomes completely indifferent to all conditioned things by developing neither attachment nor aversion to any worldly object.

(v) The *Yogāvacara*, having gained mastery over the nine-fold knowledges, enters the final stage of purification, that is (*ñāṇadassana visuddhi*) purity arising from knowledge and insight. He develops complete repulsion for all things of the world. He leads a detached life in the world just like a drop of water on a lotus leaf.

The *Yogāvacara*, has thereby gained not merely perceptual knowledge, but conceptual knowledge about the real nature of things in existence. In the pursuit of further perfection to attain *Nibbāna*, he has to transalate this insight gained into 'action'. Therefore, in the Early Buddhist path of purification, we have two clearly defined stages. 1. Theoretical stage, wherein insight or understanding about the different laws and operational mechanism at the physical, mental and moral realms of human existence is gained. 2. *Practical stage*: In this stage, equipped with the understanding of the true and real nature of the universal categories and their working, one has to avoid what is illusory and practise the truth gained till this understanding becomes a permanent part of his psyche. Thereby, the path of purity no longer remains at the theoretical level but advances into the realm of the practical (*sadhāna*). It is the translation of what are intellectually conceived into 'actions' or practise. This further stages are aimed at purging the mind of its tendency towards attachment to wrong or false conceptions of the Universe, and to follow the path towards perfection. The stages of further perfection are termed as *Sotāpanna*, *Sakadāgāmin*, *Anāgāmin* and *Arhat*.

Sotapanna

Sotapanna is a compound of two words, '*Sota*' meaning 'stream' and '*apanna*' meaning 'one who has entered'. Thus, *sotapanna* refers to 'one who has entered the stream, which merges into the Ocean, namely *nibbāna*.

In this stages, the aspirant in his pursuit for purification strives to gain freedom from the three-fold fetters (*Saṁyojanas*) of (1) Delusion of the 'self' (*Sakkayadiṭṭhi*) (2) Doubt (*Vicikicchā*), and (3) Rituals (*Sīlabbataparāmāsa*).

(i) Freedom for the Delusion of 'Self' (Sakkayadiṭṭhi)

The aspirant becomes equipped with the understanding that there is no permanent 'self' in the five aggregate complex and that 'self' (attā) is a name merely referring to the five-fold aggregate, which is impermanent and produces unsatisfactory experiences. He develops aversion (*doso*) for any form of attachment deterimental to the *khandhas*. He practises detachment from all froms of passions. He maintains a constant vigil over the functioning of the *pañcakkhanadhas* and by non-identification with them gains freedom from the delusion of the 'self'.

(ii) Freedom for Doubt (Vicikicchā)

All though one has gained insight and cultivates the practice of developing the thought of 'essencelessness' or 'non-substantiality' of the worldly objects in creation, one is likely to be gripped by the old habit of thought that there still exists a substantial thing or a 'Core' that is a self. To overcome this obstacle, one has to continuously contemplate the truth of 'essencelessness' and never allow the mind to waver. All thoughts in the mind about 'substantiality' or 'essence should be rooted out; he should cultivate the truth of 'anatta'.

(iii) Freedom from Rituals (Sīlabbataparāmāsa)

The practice of rituals with the belief that there exists a 'Superpower' who will liberate him is an obstacle to one on the path of purification and perfection. One should realise and cultivate the truth, that *Nibbāna* can be attained only through one's own effort. To quote the Buddha 'strive for your salvation with deligence'.[115] The Buddha was never tired of exhorting his disciples to work out their salvation with diligence. The practice of a detailed ethical code (*Sīla*) coupled with a course in meditation (*Samādhi*) and wisdom (*Paññā*) alone holds the key to liberation.

The *Sotāpanna's* mind, having gained freedom from the these fetters, is comparable to the sun, which has driven the clouds of darkness from the sky and shines brightly. He can be born in the human realm, at the most for seven times, with all excellences, but never in the lower realms.[116] He has access to the divine palaces of devas and *Brahmas*.[117]

Sakadāgāmin

In this stage, the aspirant works for the weakening of the fetters of sensual lust *(kāma)* and anger *(krodha)*. These two are obstacles in the path of perfection. Having realised the unsatisfactoriness of the experiences generated by the ephemeral desires and hatred one cultivates the practice of closely guarding the mind from the influences of these evil forces. By constant meditation on the 'transitoriness' and 'unsatisfactoriness' of these wordily desires and aversion to the objects of the world, he is able to weaken and control the two fetters of sensual lust and anger.

This state of *Sakadāgāmin* is referred to, as a state of 'once-returner', in the sense that he can be born only once in the human plane, but in the next birth, he is assured of attaining arhantship. He has conquered completely all the gross desires like power, money, and so on, but he still has to conquer certain subtle desires like the desire to become *Arhat*. Due to these subtle desires, may be born only once, again. In this next birth, working out his salvation with diligence and with the power of *paññā*, he visualises his previous birth and the folly of attachment to subtle desires, he practises and develops control over even these subtle desires. He attains the next state of *Anagāmin*.[118]

Anagāmin

In this state, the aspirant completely redeems himself from the remaining impressions of the fetters of sense-desires (*kāmaccahanda*) and ill-will (*Vayāpāda*) in the mind. Even the meagre clinging to the body within him is completely overcome. Such a person no longer returns to the human world. He enters the pure world of *Arūpa loka*.[119]

Arhat

Arhat' means 'one who is worthy', in the sense that he is qualified and equipped for ultimate realisation. In this state, the aspirant has to overcome and gain complete freedom from the remaining five fetters, of attachment for form (*Rūparāga*), attachment for formless (*Arūparāga*), spiritual pride (*Māno*), self-righteousness (*Uddhacca*) and ignorance (*Avijjā*).

(i) Attachment for Form (Rūparāga)

The aspirant has to overcome the attachment for world of form, an obstacle for one who is on the path to perfection. He should not desire for birth in the world of form, for it is an imperfect state.

(ii) Attachment for the Formless (Arūparāga)

Even the desire for rebirth in the formless world is an obstacle for one who seeks *nibbāna*. He should overcome this desire of birth in the formless world, which is not free from suffering, for further perfection leading to *Nibbāna*.

(iii) Spiritual Pride (Māno)

Just as a wealthy person possesses the pride of his possessions, the aspirant should not possess the feeling of superiority on his achievement or on the perfections attained. For, this is also an obstacle to be overcome by one who wants to realise *Nibbāna*.

(iv) Self-righteousness (Uddhacca)

The buddhist texts point that, one who is wedded to the summum bonum which is *Nibbāna*, has to liberate himself completely from this feeling of self-righteousness. It is an obstacle, an ethical fetter wherein one thinks that being almost perfect, what he does alone, is the 'right' way.

(v) Freedom from Ignorance (Avijjā)

It is against ignorance (*avijjā*) the root cause for bondage that man has been waging a battle. It is true that by the time one passes through the stages of perfection, one would have scored victory over ignorance, but ignorance is such a tenacious enemy that haunts the aspirant constantly even at the final stages of enlightenment. In other words, even the aspirant, who has reached the stage of *enemy* is likely to be affected by this devil of ignorance, unless one is extremely cautious. Therefore, Buddhism lays caution that even the *Arhat* has to take care, not to lapse into the peril of ignorance. With the annihilation of all forms of ignorance, the aspirant has attained *Arhatship*.

The *Arhat* having purified his mind and having gained an insight into the truth of *dukkha* has attained the state of *Nibbāna*.

REFERENCES

1. *Dhammapada.* 1.1: Manopubbaṅgamā dhammā manoseṭṭhā manomayā, manasā ce paduṭṭhena bhāsati vā karoti vā tatonaṁ dukkham anveti cakkaṁ vavahato padam.

2. *Dīgha Nikāya* 2 Sāmmaññaphala sutta: *Dīgha Nikāya*.I. 71-73.

3. *kāmacchanda* fr. *kāma* (Vedic) meaning to desire : *Dīgha Nīkaya* I. 156, 246, *chanda* meaning excitment of sensual pleasures. It is synonyms with (1) *Chanda*-impulse; (2) *rāga*-excitement, (3) *nandi*-enjoyment, (4) *taṇhā*-thirst, (5) *senha-love*, and (6) *Pipāsā*-thirst. Ref. *pali. Eng. Dic.* p. 205. *Digha Nikaya* III. 258 (kāme avigāta-rāga, chanda, pema, pipāsā' paritāha, taṇhā).

4. The Sumaṅgala Vilasīni Vol. I. p.213. (ed) Rhys Davids T.W.

5. *Majj. Nikāya* 54 (Potaliya Sutta): *Majj Nikāya* i.364.

6. Ibid., Winternitz, Maurice, *History of Indian Literature*, Vol. II. P.72.

7. Vyāpāda: (fr. vyāpajjati) meaning doing harm, desire to injure, malevolence, ill-will, *Dīgha Nikāya* 1.72, 246, *Majj. Nikāya*. III.3. *pāli-Eng. Dic.* p. 654.

8. *Sumaṅagala Vilasīni*, Vol. 1. p.213.

9. *Thīna-midda*: '*Thina*' meaning 'stiffness' + '*middha*' meaning torpor, lack of urgency and vigour: Thīnanca middhaca, *Vis. Magga.* XIV, 167, p. 530., Pāḷi-Eng. Dic., p.309;

10. *Uddhaccakukkucca*: fr. *ud+dharati*; ud + dhṛ, + kukkucca meaning flurry and worry, *Dīgha. Nikāya.* 1.71, 246, Ref. *Pāli Eng. Dic.* p. 136.

11. *Vicikicchā.* fr. *vicịkicchati* meaning doubt, perplexity, uncertainity. *Digha Nikaya.1.* 246. *Vis. Magga.* 471. *Pāli. Eng. Dic.* p.615.

12. *Majj. Nikaya*.1.36: Vatthūpama sutta: *Majj. Nikāya*.7.

13. *Aṅg. Nikāya* 1.10 pabhassaramidaṁ bhikkhave, cittaṁ. Taṁ ca kho agantukehi upākkilesehi upākkilittham' ti. pabhassaramidam, bhikkhave, cittam, Tam ca kho agantukehi Upakileshi Vippamuttam".

14. Dhammacakkappavattana sutta (*Saṁ. Nikāya* V. 420-21)

'Dve' me, bhikkhave, antā pabbajitena na sevitabbā katame dve? Yocāyaṁ kamesu kāmāsukhallikānuyogo hīno gammo, pathujjaniko, anariyo, anathasaṁhito. Yocāyaṁ attakilamathanu yogo dukkho anariyo anatthasaṁhito. Ibid.

15. *Ibid.* "Ete te, bhikkhave, ubho ante anupgamm, majjhīmāpaṭipāda Tathāgatena...Ayam 'eva ariyo aṭṭhaṅgiko maggo...."*Setting in motion the wheel of Truth p.2.* Trans. Acharya Buddharakkhita.

16. *Digha Nikāya* Mahāparinibbāna sutta (Trans: H.C. Warren Buddhist discourses, p. 109.)

17. Dhammacakkappavattana sutta. (*Saṁ. Nikāya*. V.420-21)

"Ayam eva ariyo aṭṭhaṅgiko maggo, seyyathīdam: Sammā diṭṭhi, sammā saṅkappo, sammā vācō sammā kammanto, samma ājīvo, sammā vāyāmo, sammā sati, samma samādhi'' Trans. Acharya Buddharakkhita, *Setting in motion the wheel of truth*, p.4.

18. *Digha Nikāya*-10. Subha sutta. (Trans) T. W. Rhys Davids,. *Dialogues of the Buddha*, part I. Introduction to Subha sutta, p. 265.

19. *Vis. Magga*, I, 10-15, pp. 5-6 (*Nñānamoli*).

20. *Vinaya Texts* part I, Vol. XIII (SBE). p.107.

21. *Aṅg. Nikāya* i.9.

22. *Digha Nikāya* 16, *Dīgha Nikaya* iii. 123, Mahāparinibbāna Sutta. Rhys Davids, T. W. Buddhist Suttas, Vol. IX, pp. 64-65.

23. Macdonell, Arthen Anthony, *A Practical Saṅskrit Dictionary*, p. 315.

24. Humphreys, Christmas, *A Popular Dictonary of Buddhism*, p.182.

25. The ten immoral acts: three physical, four vocal and three mental acts; for details refer (1) Tin. pe Maung (Trs) The *Expositor* (Buddhaghosa's Atthasālinī) pp. 128-135 (2) Hardy R. Spence, *A Manual of Buddhism*, p. 460

26. The Ten moral acts are enuamerated in Kashyap. J. Bhikku, *Abhidhamma Philosophy*, Vol. I, Chap. 5, p. 157.

1. Dāna 2. Sīla, 3. Bhāvanā, 4. Apacāyāna, 5. Veyyāvacca, 6. Pattidāna, 7. Pattanumodana, 8. Dhamma-desana, 9. Dhamma saraṇa and 10. Diṭṭhiujukarama.

27. *Dhammapada*, Chap. x. 2, 130 (Trans) S. Radhakrishanan, Oxford University press, Delhi, (1950), 1982, p. 103.

"Sabbe tasanti daṇḍassa sabbesaṁ jīvitam piyam attānam upamaṁkatvā na haneyya na ghātaye''. All men tremble at punishment all men love life likening others to oneself, one should neither slay nor cause to slay.

28. *Majj. Nikāya*. I. 129. kakac-/pamasutta, (Chalmers Vol.I.p. 90)

29. Taking of life, of course, is permitted, it is a food and medicine but indiscriminate killing for the sake of sport or seeking vengenance is forbidden. Killing does not constitute a valid means for earning one's living. It goes against the principle of right livelihood. Mv. Nalanda Series pp. 229-256. and Jat. A. (Kulāvaka Jātaka)

30. *Karanīya Mettā* Sutta: Nineth Book of *Khuddaka patha*, the first book of *khuddaka Nikāya*.

"Mettan ca sabba lokasmiṁ

Uddhaṁ adho ca tiriyañcā

Asaṁbādnaṁ averaṁ asapattaṁ'' Buddharakkhita (Trans), Ninth Book of *khuddhaka patha*, pp. 62-65.

31. *Telakatahagāthā* V. 79. Yo yacako bhavti bhiṇṇakpalhatho, mundo dhighakarsatahi ca tañjyan to bhikhaṁ sadanibhavane sakucelvaso, dehe parvitthro naro so. cf. Malasekhera G. P., *The Pāli literature of Ceylon*, p. 162-163.

32. *Digha. Nikāya*, 31. (Sigalovada sutta), *Dīgha. Nikāya* iii. 188.

33. *Itivuttaka Aṭṭhakatha* (It.A) third part of the fifth sutta of third Nipāta.

34. *Dhammapada* Chap. I. 13: Yathā agāram succhannaṁ vuṭṭhi na samativijjhati evaṁ subhāvitam cittaṁ rāgo samativijjhati.

35. *Ibid*. Chap.III. 10 .2. diso disaṁ yaṁ taṁ kariyā verī vā pana verinam micchāpaṇihitaṁ cittaṁ pāpiyo naṁ tato kare.

36. *Aṭṭhaka Nipāta*, Trans. Hare, E.M., Vol. IV., p. 169.

37. *Uposatha*: The word '*Uposatha*' refers to the day preceding the four stages of the moons' waxing and waning 1st, 8th, 15th and 23rd nights of the lunar month, a weekly sacred day. These days were utilised by pre-Buddhistic reforming communities for the expounding their views. *Uposatha* for Buddhist stands for the 15th day of the half-month. On this day, they would use it for recitation of paṭimokkha, or expound the "*Dhamma*". Refer: T. W. Rhys Davids & Stede, *Pāli. Eng. Dic.* pp. 150-51.

38. *Sn*. 396. Hare, E. M., Woven Candences of Early Buddhists, p. 59, cfs. Dh. p. 309, 310.

39. *Itivuttaka Aṭṭhakatha* - Third part of the fifth sutta of third Nipāta.

40. *Dhs. A.* 131.

41. *It. A.* third part of the fifth sutta of third Nipāta.

42. *Sutta Nipāta* (Dhammika Sutta) 398-399

43. Vin. 1. 205.

44. *A.A.ṭṭhaka Nipāta* (Duccarita-vipāka sutta) see Here E.IV, p.169.

45. *It. A.* Third part of the fifth sutta of third Nipāta.

46. *Dīgha. Nikāya* 16. Mahāparinibbāna Sutta: Dīgha Nikāya. ii. 86, Rhys Davids, T.W., (Trans.) Buddhist Suttas, p. 17.

47. *Vis. Magga.* III. 2.2. (ft) p. 84.

48. The English word 'concentration' has several expressions. It is an essential 'quality' for people practising different professions, if, they want to succeed, for instance, the scientist or surgeon has to concentrate on their object of work, in order to achieve successful results. But there is a difference between the concentration practicsed by them and a Bhikkhu. Apart from different motivating factors, concentration herein, has a spiritual content. To bring this difference, 'samādhi' is described as the one-pointedness of moral consciousness aimed at the purification of the mind.

49. He who dwells in a closed area must practise *jhāna* in abhokāsā (Open air).

50. *Dh. P.* Chap. Vi. 8.

51. Qualities of a *kalyāṇamitta* are described in *Aṅg. Nikāyai.* iv, 32, *Saṁ. Nikāya*, i. 88, V. 3, 32.

52. *Vis. Magga.* p. 66. piyo garu bhavaniyo vatta ca vacanakkhamo, gambhiram ca kathakattā no catthane niyojaye (B.V.B)

Foulness refers to the process of decay and death at every moment.

53. *Vis. Magga.* III, 104, p. 112.

The forty objects of meditation are:

1 *The ten totalities (kasiṇas)*:-

(i) Four elements earth, water, fire and air,

(ii) Four colours, Blue, Yellow, Red and White.

(iii) Light (dloka) and limited space (paricchinae-ākāsa)

II. *Ten repulsives or foulness*:-

The ten corpses, swollen; livid; Festening; Fissured; gramed;

Scattered; hactked and scattered; Bleeding; worm infested and skeleton.

III. *Ten reflections (anussatis)*:-

Buddha, Dhamma, Samīgha, Virture, Generaosity; devas, death, thirty two parts of the body; peathiry, and pcace.

IV. *Four sublime States* (Brahma vihāras):-

Friendliness compassion, sympathic joy and equanimity.

V. *Four immateñal State (arupas)*:-

Infinity of space, infinity of consciousness, Nothingness and neither consciousness nor unconsciousness.

VI. *One perception (Saññā)*.-

perception of the loathsomeness of food (ahara)

VII. *One definings (Vayaṭṭāne)*:-

defining of the four elements. Ref. *Vis. Magga*. III. 104, p. 112-113. (*ñānmoli*)

54. The Buddhist texts speak of six kinds of temperaments: (1) hating (2) greedy, (3) deluded, (4) faithfull, (5) intelligent, and (6) speculative temperament. Vis. Magga. III. 74. p. 102.

55. Vis. Magga. III. 87, p. 105-106. By observing the posture, action, eating habits, seeing and the mental states functioning, one can decide a person's temperament.

56. Perception of the ten asubhas and the ten corpses; swollen, purple and so on are prescribed objects of meditation. *Vis. Magga*. p. 77. (B.V.B).

57. The thirty-two parts of a body are: hairs of head, hairs of the body, nails, teeth, skin, flesh, sinews, bones, marrow, kidneys, heart, liver, pleura, spleen, lungs, intestines mesentery, gorge, faeces, brain, bile, phlegm, pus, blood, sweat, fat, tears, oily fat, saliva, mucus, synovial fluid and Urine.

58 *Vis. Magga*. p. 77. (B. V. B)

59. Burlingame, Eugene Watson (Trans) '*Buddhist legends*' part I, p. 23 also see; Tittha Jātaka.A. No. 25.

60. *Vis. Magga*. p.82, (B.V.B.) L. *Vis. Magga* IV., 2, p. 122.

61. *Majj. Nikāya*. 10 (Satipaṭṭhānasutta), Majj. Nikāya. 1:56.

62. *Vis. Magga*. IV., 19, 125.

63. *Vis. Magga*. p. 122, (B.V.B), Dhs. A., 168.,

64. *Saṁ. Nikāya*. V. (Sammappadhāna Saṁyutta).

65. *Majj. Nikāya*.10. (Satipaṭṭhāna Sutta): *Majj. Nikāya*. i. 56.

66. The forty objects of meditation consists of thirty-six material objects and four immaterial objects of meditation.

67. Here Rūpa means an object associated with form and colour. It is generally gross in nature.

68. jhāna ref. *Vis. Magga*. IV., 119, p.156.

68a. Jñāna:-'na' root-means to learn. Therefore, Jhāna helps in the learning of the five (*Nīvaraṇas*) defilemnts.

The pali term' Jhānaṅga' is a compound of 'ñāna+aṅga', where' ñāna' means absorption, meditation and so on, and 'anga' means factor, constituents, limits and so on. Thus, jhānaṅga stands for the constituents of meditation.

69. Vitaka (fr. vi+takka), reflection, thought, thinking, initial application; Defined as vitakkanan vitakko *jhānānti* vuttan hoti.

70. *Atthasālini*p. 94. Vitakko thīnamiddassa.

71. Arammane tena cittom Vicārati ti vicāro; Vicāranaṁ va vicāro. Anusanucāranam ti vuttaṁ hoti. Svayaṁ, arammana numajjana lakhaṇo. Tattha Sāhajataruyopana raso. Cittāso anuppabandha pacupatthano. *Atthāsalini. p. 94.*

72. *Ibid*. p. 135. Vicikiccihāya Vicāro.

73. piti is five-fold: Minor happiness (khuddikāīti) such as raising is five-gold: Minor happiness (khuddikāpīti) such as raising the hair on the body, (2) momentary happiness (khaṇikāpīti), (3) Overwhelming happiness (Okantikāpīti), (4) Uplifting happiness (Ubbegāpīti) and (5) pervading happiness (pharanāpīti). *Atthasālini p.95, Vis. Magga.* Chapter IV. (para) 94, Vol. I (Bom. Univ).

74. *Ibid*. piti cal Vyāpadassa.

75. There is need to draw a distinction between pīti and sukha. Pīti arises when a person gets the hope of obtaining the object and sukha when it is attained and enjoyed. Pīti creates an interest in the object, while sukha enables one to enjoy the object. For instance pīti is like the sight of an oasis to a weary desert traveller while drinking water, and bathing in it is sukha.

76. *Atthasālini*. p. 95.

77. *Ibid*. p. 135, Sukham Uddhaccakukkuccam.

78. *Ekkāggatā*- Eka+a-/ggatta: Eka-one, āgga - object, tā-tendency of the mind to concentrate on a single object is called Ekkāggatā. *A Manual of Abhiddamma*, Nārada Mahāthere. Buddhist Pub. Society, Colombo, 1980 p.55.

79 *Ibid.*

80 *Atthasālini* p.135. kāmacchandassa pakkhu ti petake.

81. In the traditional sources (Sutta) there is mention of four stages only. The difference is due to the fact that the two jhānaṅgas vitākka and vicāra are absent in the second stage of rūpa jhāna. The above five stages are in the Adhidhamma description.

82. To gain mastery of attendance, the Yogāvacara has to discipline the mind so as to enable him to switch over to the jhāna state irrespective of time and place. He must be able to sustain such a state of mind as long as he desires. Mastery of attaining refers to the

capacity of the Yogavacara to readily recall the state of jhāna whenever and for whatever length of time he is desireous. Mastery of resolving involves tuning oneself with jhāna for any length of time. Mastery of rising to a place as he desires. Mastery of reviewing the jhāna at any place for any length of time is to be cultivated.

Vis. Magga. IV., 131, p. 160 (ṭāmamoli).

83. For a detailed analysis of the five jhanas refer: The path of purification Visuddhimagga. (Trans) Bhikkhuñṭānamoli, Chapter IV, 79-202, pp. 144-176.

84. *Vis. Magga*. X.1 p. 354. cf *Majj. Nikāya*. 1. 410.

85. Generally an object stands for an 'object' or its image in space and time. Here, space as 'objectless' entity is to be understood as different, and not the ordinary object which exists in space and time.

86. *Dhs*. 73: *Dīgha Nikāya*. i. 153.

87. *Ibid*.

88. *Dhs*. 73: D.i. 154. *Vis. Magga*.228.

89. *Ibid*. For a detailed analysis of the four arupa-jhanas, refer to *The Path of Purification* (*Vis. Magga*) Trans. Bhikkhu ñānamoli, Chap. X. 1-66, pp. 354-371.

90. *Majj. Nikāya*, I. 40

91. *Saṃ. Nikāya* III, 13.

92. *Majj. Nikāya*, III, 96, *Aṅgṅ. Nikāya*. I. 254

93. *Vibhaṅga*. 424.

94. *Ps*. I. 97.

95. The ten supersensory powers are: 1. Miracle of will, (*adhiṭṭhana iddhi*) 2)-of transformation, (*vikubbāna iddhi*), 3.-of mind, (*manomaya iddhi*) 4.-of knowledge, (*ñānavipphāraiddhi*), 5.-of concentration (samādhi vipphāra iddhi). 6. - of noble ones, (*ariya iddhi*), 7.-born of kamma, (*kamma vipākajaiddhi*), 8.-of meritorious ones, (*suññavata iddhi*) 9. - of (*śamapayaoga iddhi*) *Vis. Magga*, Chap. XII (1) p. 410.

96. Ibid. *Sam. Nikāya*. Iddhipāda saṁyutta No.7.

97. *Vis. Magga*. Chap. XIII, p.446.

98. *Ibid. Chap*. XIII, 8, p.448-9.

99. *Ibid, Chap*. XIII, 13, pp. 450.

100. *Ibid*, Chap, XIII, 72, p. 464.

101. *Vis. Magga* (437), XIV, 3, p. 480.

102. *Vis. Magga*. XIV., 4 & 5, p. 480-81.

103. *Ibid*. XIV, 7, 481.

104. *Sam. Nikāya*, III. 260.

105. *Vis. Magga*. Chap. XV 4, p. 548.

106. *Vis. Magga*. Chap. XV, 1, p. 547.

107. *Ibid*.

108. *Saṁ. Nikāya*. IV, 1-6.

109. *Saṁ. Nikāya*. II, 140.

110. *Majj. Nikāya*. 152, iii. 298-302.

111. *Abhidhammakośavyākhaya*, II, p.1.

112. Dhammacakkapavattana sutta, *Saṁ. Nikāya*, V. 420-21.

113. *Digha Nikāya* II. 55-71, 15.

114. *Majj. Nikāya* 24. Rathavinita Sutta. The yogāvacara having attained sīlavisuddhi and cittāvisuddhi proceeds to attain the remaining five types of purification.

115. Mahāparinibbāna Sutta. *Digha Nikāya*. 16., *Dīgha Nikāya*. II.93.

116. *Saṁ. Nikāya* ii: 134.

117. *Digha. Nikāya*. I. 156

118. *Aṅg. Nikāya*, 232, Woodward Vol I. p. 212.

119. *Ibid*.

6

Nibbāna

INTRODUCTION

The philosophical ideal of Buddhism is *Nibbāna* and the *Ariyo Aṭṭyo Aṭṭangiko Maggo* is the means. Lot of controversy surrounds this concept, whether it refers to a positive state of bliss or merely to a state of freedom from pain. In this chapter, it is proposed to discuss the nature of the state of *Nibbāna* and the controversy surrounding it with special reference to early Buddhism in comparison with the later Buddhist conception.

Meaning of Nibbāna (Skt. Nirvāṇa)

Etymologically, the term '*Nirvāṇa*' admits two interpretations. Firstly, '*Nirvāṇa*' is a compound of Ni-Vā-Na[1] and secondly, that it is a compound of '*Nir+vāṇa*'[2]. The former explains that '*Ni*' means 'absence', 'out; the root '*vā*' means 'to go' or 'blow out', and '*Nā*' is the suffix used in the auxiliary sense[3]. This expression of 'to blow out' suggests 'blowing out of fire'. This phenomena takes the form of a simile of the wind and fire. The Buddha made use of similes and metaphors for effective communication with his disciples. The sermon of fire[4] is one such, wherein he points to the fact that 'everything is on fire', on fire with the flames of desire, hate and delusion. 'Blow out', conveys the idea of the extinction of these flames and the five-fold aggregate, the idea of annihilation of all activities, a form of nihilism. It goes against the fact that the Buddha led an active life even after attaining sa-upādisesa - nibbāna. It also goes against the conception of *arhat*, the 'prefect being', which is accepted by the Theravādins.

Worship of the Bodhi Tree

Triratna

Birth of the Buddha

Dharma chakra-Worship

Maras' Assault

Mahabhinishkramana

Purna Kumbha

Stupa - Slab

Moreover, any form of 'nihilism' was not acceptable to the Buddha. The putting out of the flames of desire, hatred and illusion by 'blowing out', is not suggestible, for at times this act of 'blowing out' can result in inciting the flames. This extinction of fire and flames can be brought about by covering up or depriving it of further fuel or by withdrawing the cause for its production. This is suggested in the popular usage of '*va*' fused with '*vr*' meaning covering up[5]. According to the latter view, '*Nirvāṇa*' is a compound of '*Nir+vāṇa*', '*Nir*' stands for 'absence, 'leaving of; '*Vāṇa* for forest', 'the dense forest' full of desires, hatred and illusion. The expression '*Nirvāṇa*' therefore, refers to a state which is free permanently of the dense forest of khandhas, of the 'fires' of desire, hatred and ignorance and of the three attributes of things namely, impermanence (*anicca*), essencelessness (*anattā*) and suffering (*dukkha*). Buddhaghosa, in his *Visudhimagga* opines that '*Vāṇa*' the second component of '*Nirvāṇa*' means 'weaving' or 'fastening'. *Taṇhā* is interpreted as '*Vāṇa*', in the sense of 'fastening', because it ensures successive 'becoming', the succession of birth, that is rebirth. Thus, the compound '*Nirvāṇa*' refers to the absence of craving (*taṇhā*) the cause for suffering. The different (etymological) interpretations of the term '*Nibbāna*' points that it is a state of freedom from the fires of desire, hatred and delusion; freedom craving (*taṇhā*) and from all forms of successive birth, becoming leading to the cessation of *saṁsāra*.

Kinds of Nibbāna

The Buddhist texts[7] speak of two kinds of *Nibbāna* namely *Sa-upādi-sesa-nibbāna* and *An-upādi-sesa-nibbana*. The key term in both is '*Upādi*', which refers to an 'entity', in the form of the psycho-physical complex, the five-fold aggregate. *Sa-upādi-sesa-nibbāna* refers to the extinction of the defilements with *upādi*, that is the psycho-physical complex remaining intact, or in other terms liberation while yet one is alive. *An-upādi-sesa-nibbāna*, refers to the extinction of both the defilements and the five-fold aggregate.

Sa-upādi-sesa-nibbāna

Sa-upādi-sesa nibbāna refers to the attainment of liberation with the psycho-physical frame (five-fold aggregate) remaining intact. It is a state of deliverance, both from the subjective bondages known as fetters (*Saṁyojanas*) and also from the objective bondages of being tied onto the wheel of becoming-*Bhavacakka*.

It is a state, wherein, there is no more continuity of the life affirming process, manifested as various mental defilements such as greed, hatred, delusion and so on. Here, clinging to existence and the endless cycle of birth and death in the three lokas of *kāma*, *Rūpa* and *Arūpa*, which these mental defilements produce has ceased. The conditions leading to the future birth are destroyed. This is his last birth. He is like a fish in the water, which has broken the net.[8] But he has not yet attained khandha-nibbāna or freedom from the five-fold aggregate complex, as he has to undergo the effects of his *prarabḍa kamma*, fruits of his past actions or deeds. The law of *kamma* continues to govern him just as the potter's wheel continues to revolve, even after the potter has removed his operative hand, due to the stored energy in the wheel.[9] This state of *sa-upādi-sesa-nibbāna* is an earlier state of liberation through which a 'liberated man' passes, before attaining the state of *an-upādi-sesa-nibbāna*:

The 'liberated man' is an embodiment of uprightness (*sīla*), self-concentration (*Samādhi*) and wisdom (*pañña*). To quote the Buddha, "Uprightness is purified by wisdom, wisdom is purfied by uprightness; where there is wisdom, there is uprightness, and the wisdom of uprightness and the uprightness of wise have all the uprightness and wisdom of the world, the highest value.''[10] There is absolute integration and harmony among all the three modes of his action, physical, mental and verbal. His mind and body work in harmony as an integral unit, with the sole aim of eliminating all suffering. There is no gulf between precept and practice, which we find in the unliberated man.

The 'liberated man's actions are not 'volitional', for they are devoid of the elements of 'willing'. They may be called 'barren acts', which will not produce any resultants. His thoughts, words and deeds are termed as inoperative functions, devoid of resultants, just like a burnt seed, which is incapable of sprouting even when all other auxiliary conditions prevail. He lives like any other normal human being, but with a difference; He is not overwhelmed with passion for the worldly objects, as he can perceive their true nature, being characterised by tilakkhana,in other words, impermanence, essencelessness and suffering with his perfectly well-developed mind. His mind is like the trunk of a large, majestic tree firmly anchored, which does not quiver or shake, even to the force of a strong wind. He has cultivated detachment for the evanescent worldy objects and their experiences. He is in the world and yet out of it. To quote the Buddha, 'with past fully extinct, with no fresh becoming, their minds forever severed from rebirth, are like burnt seeds, their desires sprout no more'[11].

Though the five senses are operative, they are under control. He does not let them commit any misdeeds. He experiences all sensations, pleasant, unpleasant and neutral.[12] Though he experiences the conditions of suffering, he is not affected by them.[13] When we say that the 'liberated man' is not affected by the pain caused by the senses, one should not understand that he is not affected by fever, cold and other diseases. That he does suffer fever, cold and other diseases, the sting of a scorpion, the bite of a cobra, injuries inflicted by other fellow beings, animals, is obvious. Aṅgulimāla, an *arhat*, while on his way begging for alms, got beaten with stones and sticks, and returned to the Buddha with blood flowing from his injuries.[14] The fact that the 'liberated man', an *arhat* does under go the conditions of pain is also obvoius from the Buddha's ailment in the last days of his life. As long as the five *khandha* complex continues, one cannot but experience the pains and pleasures that are characteristic of them. The liberated man realises this with his insight into the true nature of worldly existence. But, one might ask that if this is so, in what way the 'liberated man' can be considered free and perfect? He is free and perfect in the sense, that the life he is habituated to or decided to live, is such that it does not allow him to take to such acts which will allow the influx of fresh *kamma*. When he is confronted with a situation that would normally breed contempt and hatred, anger and lust, the 'liberated man' would not succumb to them ; he would rise above them. A person who has made this type of conduct as his way of life, when he dies, never returns to suffer the chain of birth and death. It is in this sense, that we have to interpret the view, that the 'liberated man' is not affected by the ordinary modes of pains and gains.

The 'liberated man's mind does not have any of the twelve types of immoral consciousness[15] rooted in greed, hatred and delusion. It is free from the four *āsavas* namely sensual pleasure (*kāma-*), desire for continued existence (*bhava-*), false views (*diṭṭhi-*), and ignorance (*avijjā-*). It has also destroyed the four kind of ties (*ganthas*), of convetousness (*Abhipa*), ill-will (*vyāpāda*), indulgence in wrongful rites and ceremonies (*śilabhataparāmāsa*) and adherence to one's dogma as truth (*idaṁsaccabhinesa*). His life is anchored in the five virtures, of faith (*saddhā*), mindfulness (*sati*), energy (*viriya*), concentration(*samādhi*) and wisdom (*paññā*).[16]

The 'liberated man's takes into consideration the 'goodness' of mankind whenever he contemplates to act. He will never do an act, which will result in the slightest injury to any living being. For, he has given up all pride and prejudice, he is not jealous of, or bears hatred towards any living being.[17] His sole motive is to help, remove the suffering of others. His speech, which is guided by his calm and tranguil mind, is soft, soothing and conveys only the 'truth'.[17] He uses his speech to communicate to all beings the truth of suffering and its annihilation.

The 'liberated man' has no fixed abode, he has no attachment to any place or people.[18] He travels, spreading the truth of *dukkha*', the *dhamma* and maintains his living by collection of alms. No house or land belongs to him. Perceiving the impermanence in worldly objects, he has sought and gained the permanent, that is, *Nibbāna*.

His entire outlook is tranformed and the normal course of functioning of the five-fold aggregate is totally changed. The inflow of impurities has ceased, causality operates, but with a difference. The change is as follows: The elimination of ego-consciousness produces revulsion (*nibbāda*) with regard to 'objects', which were earlier grasped as being substantial and permanent. Revulsion produces detachment (*virāga*). Detachment produces freedom (*vimutti*) and leads to the attainment of stability (*ṭhitatā*) of the mind. His mind is unruffled and unagitated when confronted either with gain (lābha) or loss (*ālabha*), good repute (*yasa*) or disrepute (*ayasa*), praise (*pasaṁsā*) or blame (*nindā*), hapiness (*sukha*) or suffering (*dukkha*).[19]

The 'perfect being' has found a solution to the trackless hard maze of *saṁsāra* by attaining the wisdom and realising the truth of *dukkha*. He has crossed over and reached the shore of safety, namely *nibbāna*. He has reached the place of safety, an abode free from fear and anxiety, a state of calmness, tranquility and peace (*samatā*). He goes around conducting himself in a righteous manner, discharging his duties, of helping others to overcome suffering. He meditates in peace on the truth of *dukkha*, whenever he is free. The 'perfect being' of the Buddha is *sa-upādi-sesa-nibbāna* it is comparable to the *jīvanmukta*.

The perfect being, who has attained this state of freedom from evil forces and resultant *dukkha* has attained a state of purity, he is known by different names in different schools of Buddhism. In early Buddhism (*theravāda*), he is known as *Arhat*, whereas, the same is termed by *Mahāyāna* as '*Bodhisattva*'.

W. Rahula opines that there is no such fixed rule that the Hinayana ideal is '*Arhat*' and *Mahāyāna* is '*Bodhisattva*. He cites passages from the *pāli* scriptural texts, which mention *Bodhisattva* ideal. He further states that, it is left to the individual's discretion, that he can select either the ideal of *Arhat* or *Bodhisattva*, depending upon his temperament and attitude.[20]

(i) Arhat

Etymologically '*Arhat*' means 'worthy', in the sense that, he is equipped to attain final liberation. He is one, who has overcome all afflictions (*kilesas*) and fetters (*saṁyojanas*). He is the ideal, perfect man and saint. He is free from all desires, hatred and illusion, the germs of *dukkha*. Subjectively, with this knowledge (*viññāna*), understanding (*paññā*) and meditation (*samādhi*) he has realised the goal of *Nibbāna*. Subjectively, he is convinced that he has attained '*Arhatship*'. Objectively, he possesses the capacity to examine the mind of others and ascertain whether it is freed or not. The ideal of '*Arhatship*' can be attained by anyone who practices, develops and cultivates the path of *sīla*, *samādhi* and *paññā*.[21]

There is a view, that the ideal of *Arhat* refers to 'individual enlightenment'. He does not render a helping hand to fellow-beings for showing them a way out of bondage. He believes that others, troubled by the miseries of the world and life, should take to the path of *Nibbāna* on their own. He simply isolates himself from society and takes to monastic life, awaiting the final release. But, this view seems to be misfounded. We have ample evidence from the Buddhist texts to show that the *Arhat* does help his fellow-beings in bondage to attain *nibbāna*. This fact is very well brought out by W. Rahula in his scholarly essay "*Bodhisattva Ideal in Therāvāda and Mahāyāna*.'[22] Here, he observes that it is wrong to say that *Arhat* spends his left over period of life in solitude and does not help others. On the other hand, Rahula observes that the *Arhat*, being fully qualified with *Dhamma*', teaches others and strives for their freedom from *dukkha*.

Narada Mahāthera,[23] refuting the charge that *Arhat* is a selfish ideal', states that there is nothing selfish in the noble ideal of *Arhat*, for *Arhat* is gained only by eradicating all forms of selflessness. Self-illusion and egoism are some of the fetters that have to be eliminated in order to attain-*Arhat*. The wisemen come to attain *Arhat* after undergoing the entire process of ethical and psychological perfection.'*Arhatship*' is an irreversible condition. Once achieved, it is impossible for one to fall back on lust, hatred and delusion. An *arhat* is completely incapable of greed, anger and egoism and generates no unwholesome physical, mental or verbal activities. He continues to act, think and feel as any other normal person, until death. With his 'death' (*parinibbāna*) there will be a complete cessation of the cycle of birth and death in any of the three planes of existence, *kāma*, *rūpa*, or *arūpa lokas*.

Bodhisattva: 'Bodhisattva' is a compound of two terms 'Bodhi'and '*sattva*', wherein '*Bodhi*' means 'perfect wisdom' or 'enlightenment' and *Sattva* means 'essence' or 'potential devoted to'. Therefore, '*Bodhisattva*' refers to 'one who has the essence or potential of transcendental wisdom'. He is one, who is on the way to the attainment of transcendental widom. Unlike the '*Arhat*', he does not seek, the goal of 'individual enlightenment', he during his incalculable period of births is always working for the salvation and removal of others suffering before the last birth in which he fulfils his great destiny of becoming a *Saṁbuddha*.

The *Bodhisattva* posseses two characters, *Bodhi-citta*' and '*praṇidhānabala*'. '*Bodhi-citta*' is made up of two aspects namely '*Prajñā*' (wisdom) and *karuṇā* (compassion);

whereas '*Praṇidhānabala*' is the resolve, to remove the *dukkhas* of all living beings. The *Bodhisattva* is utterly grieved by the magnitude of the suffering to which all living beings are exposed.[24] He resolves to suffer the torments and agonies of the different realms of existence, if need be, so that he may lead all beings to enlightenment.[25] It is his universal compassion (*Mahākaruṇā*) for all sentient beings undergoing the repeated cycle of birth and death, who are plagued with suffering, that gives him immense spiritual energy to carry out this mighty work of removing others suffering. He loves all beings as a mother loves her only child.[26] In order to liberate other beings from suffering, he takes birth in bad states (*durgati*) at 'will' as he likes. This is possible through an exchange (*parivattanaṁ*) of the effects of *karma*. The *Bodhisattva* relieves the miseries of others and with his own good deeds thereby suffering the resultants of their *karma*. He makes himself subject to the law of *karma* not caused by his *karman*, but by the transferred *karman* of the suffering beings.[27] Though he undergoes repeated existences, he is free from all defilements. He is comparable to an immaculate, undefiled flower which grows out of mire, yet is not contaminated by it.[28] The *Bodhisattva* adopts a difficult life pattern, one which is full of struggle and self-sacrifice. Nothing gives him greater delight than working towards the removal of others' suffering. For him, work is happiness and happiness is work. There is mention in *Jākatamala* of King Siri, a *Bodhisattva*, who distributed all his wealth among the people, and yet remained dissataisfied to see some small insects for whom he had not done anything. He inflicted several wounds on his person and shed his blood to feed these insects.[29] This spirit of selfless service is one of the chief characteristics of a *Bodhisattva*. He forgets himself in this disinterested service to others. He does whatever work he feels is appropriate to his station in life, to the best of his abilities. He does not grade or differentiate any kind of job as high or low, superior or inferior, all are equally important for him. The 'motive' of the act is more important than its context. His sole motive is to mitigate the suffering of the masses, an universal ideal. This altruistic ideal of *Bodhisattva* is comparable to the 'Gnostic Being' of Aurobindo, who also strives for the ideal of 'Divine life' on earth. He is ready to sacrifice his life if it could be of help to others. There is also mention in the *Jātaka* of a *Bodhisattva*, who threw himself before a hungry tigeress or else owing to excessive hunger, she was on the verge of devouring her own little cubs.[30] He teaches and enlightens the masses about the truth of *dukkha* -the *Buddhadhamma*.

Though the ideal of *Bodhisattva* is altruistic, one may doubt thus: Is he a liberated one or not? for, he entangles himself in the cycle of birth and death (*saṁsāra*). The *Bodhisattva* is liberated, in the sense, that he possesses the knowledge about the true nature of existence (*saṁsāra*), as being characterised by impermanence (*anicca*), the essenceless (*anattā*) and suffering (*dukkha*). He is ready to undergo others' suffering for 'perfection' that is, 'true perfection' which is not merely 'self-perfection', but a state of perfection in which all beings are 'perfect'. All of them are liberated from suffering. His suffering is not out of ignorance (*avijjā*), but it is out of his compassion (*mahākaruṇā*) for others, suffering. He undergoes repeated existence due to this 'desire' to liberate others' It is this 'desire' 'to live for others' that forms the 'motiving will' for his repeated existences. But, his existence is now with difference, for he has only the aim of removing others suffering and does not have to work out for his salvation. But, this will lead to the criticism and question-whether this Ideal of *Bodhisattva* being a long drawn process running into repeated existences will finally cease; when will the *Bodhisattva* attain final salvation? Is it possible at all? But, yet, by this doctrine of *Bodhisattva*, the *Mahāyāna* school gains more popularity and scores over *Hīnayāna*. It counteracts the criticism that a tendency of a placid and inert monastic life, only to remove ignorance of *Buddhadhamma*, is practised in Buddhism.

An-upādi Sesa-Nibāna

The 'perfect being', having attained the supreme wisdom (*pannñā*) about existence and life, does not bother about death. His attitude towards death has undergone a radical change. By his perfection, he has attained freedom from craving (*tanhā*) and thereby freedom from all becoming (*bhava*). He is no more attached to the 'present life', nor concerned with 'life after death', which does not exist for him. He has, in a way, conquered death and is not afraid of it. To quote the *Theraghāthā*, 'Not fain am I to die nor yet to live.'[31] The 'perfect being' is like a servant, who awaits his reward after having completed the assigned job. He has to wait till all the effects of his past *kamman* (prarabadha kamma) have completely worked or worn out and there is no trace of any *kamman* left. He waits for this with a fully alert and watchful mind. In the words of the Buddha, 'the body of the perfect one subsists cut-off from the streams of becoming'. 'As long as this body subsists, so long will men see him'. 'If his body is dissolved, his life runs out.'[32] With entry into *Anupādi sesa-Nibbāna*, all perception, all sensations and the consciousness have attained a state of rest. There is complete cooling of all feelings, sensation and perception. Not only the fires of passions (*Rāgo*), hatred (*doso*) and ignorance (*avijjā*) have been destroyed, but also the psycho-physical complex (*pañca-khandha*)-five *khandha* aggregate, the seat of suffering disintegrates with the absence of the motivating forces of 'the desire to live' - 'the moral will'.[33]

The state of the 'perfect being', who has attained this state of *parinibbāna*, has been expounded by the Buddha in the *Aggivacchagotta sutta*. To quote, 'All things material, all feelings, all perceptions, all *kammic* forms,-all consicousness everthing by which the truth finder might be denoted, has passed away for him, grubbed and stubbed, leaving only the bare, cleared site, where once a palm tree towered - a thing that once has been and can be no more. Profound, measureless, unfathomable is the truth-finder, even as the mighty ocean reborn does not apply to him or not reborn, nor any combination of such terms. Everything by which the truth finder might be denoted has passed away for time utterly and forever'.[34]

The Buddha contends that, after the five *khandha* aggregate complex becomes 'extinct' at the time of *parinibbāna*, the perfect being is to be described as existing in some other identifiable form or he is totally annihilated; which would lead to the extremes of eternalism and annihilationism. He prefers to either remain silent or replies in paradoxical languages.[35] Just as the bourn of a blazing spark of fire struck from the anvil gradually fading cannot be known, the perfect being who has won realisation cannot be denoted or pointed to.[36]

CONTROVERSY CONCERNING THE STATE OF NIBBĀNA

Unlike other systems of Indian Philosophy, which have clearly defined the state of final freedom, that is liberation, here, there is no clear-cut definition. The Buddha did not want to discuss and discourse over it, since, he thought these questions would lead to endless metaphysical speculation, discussion and controversy. In the *Majjhima Nikāya*, *Māluṅkyaputta Sutta*, there is mention of the Buddha's dislike for metaphysical discussion.[37] Further, he also contends in the *Mūlapariyāya Sutta* that, 'no conception should be made of *Nibbāna*, nor of its attainment by any person, as that would be admitting individuality and its relation to an entity.'[38] Moreover, to denote it as either existing (Is) or non-existing ('Is not'), would lead to the extremities of eternalism (*Sassata*) or annihilationism (*Uccheda*). The Buddha's prime concern was to show the way out of suffering (*dukkha*). But this does not mean that the Buddha altogether avoided saying anything about (*Nibbāna).* His teachings about *Nibbāna* appear in the form of small dialogues with his disciples. The concept of *Nibbāna* in its nebulous form is present in the original Buddhist literature of *Tipiṭakas* (mainly the *Suttapiṭaka*, that is *Nikāyas*). The Buddha, himself, has not elucidated this concept. When confronted with the challenges from his opponents and requests of his disciples as to the meaning of this conception, the Buddha took to certain analogies, metaphors and similes to elucidate the meaning of this concept.

Nibbāna in Pāli Texts: The Buddha has made use of the analogy of 'extinction of fire' to explain the state of *Nibbāna*. Just as fire is extinguished by removal of the fuel, the source of its existence and continuance, herein, with the removal or absence of the evil forces of (*rāgo*), hatred (*dveṣo)* and ignorance (*avijjā*), *Nibbāna* is attained. *Nibbāna* refers to a state, wherein, there is complete destruction of these evil forces, which produce craving (*taṇhā*) and resultant 'becoming' (*bhava*), is a state of 'freedom for rebirth'. To quote the *Saṁyutta Nikāya*[39], 'as the fire would go out, bereft of food (fuel); because the former supply being finished, no supply is forthcoming'. With the absence of all 'becoming' and 'craving', there is complete absence of 'rebirth'[40]. This expression of *Nibbāna* as a state of freedom from passion, hatred and ignorance also derives support in the *Dhammapada*, wherein, the Buddha says, 'cut down the whole (forest), not the tree (only); danger comes out of the forest. Having cut down both the forest and desire, O mendicants, do you attain freedom'.[41]

The Buddha while explaining the nature of *Nibbāna* to Venerable Radha in the *Saṁyutta nikāya* cites the analogy of children building sand-castles on the sea-shore for playing and destroying them after their desire to play with them has been satisfied, without leaving any trace behind. *Nibbāna* is a state of destruction of desire, passion, hatred and ignorance without leaving any trace behind. The empirical man caught in building and safe-guarding of his own 'sand castles', that is property, children, social status and so on, develops desire for them, identifying them as sources of pleasure. The realisation that these empirical things are impermanent, essenceless and generate only fleeting 'pleasures' and unsatisfactoriness creates aversion for them. This leads to the cultivation of detachment, just as children trample over sand-castles and carry no impressions, once their play is over; the perfect being is also free from the sense-impressions in the state of *Nibbāna*.[43]

The Buddha's description of *Nibbāna* as a state of complete destruction and absence of passion, hatred and ignorance has been construed by Venerable Yamaka as referring to *Nibbāna* as a state of annihilation and complete extinction.[44] To quote, "I understand the doctrine taught by the Blessed one that on the dissolution of the body, the '*Arhant*' who has lost all depravity is annihilated, perishes and does not exist after death'.[45] It was left to Venerable Sariputta to bring out the correct interpretation of Buddha's description and avoid *Nibbāna* being branded as 'annihilation' (*Ucceheda*).[46]

In the *Udāna*,[47] the Buddha has expounded and expressed *Nibbāna* as one. In *Nibbāna* the 'perfect being' is 'independent', there is no wavering; in the absence of wavering, there is tranquility. Further, with the absence of passionate delight, there is no coming and going (rebirth). In the absence of rebirth, there is no falling from one state to another; there is no 'here', no 'beyond'; no 'there and no yonder'. There is complete absence or ceasing of all 'becoming'. With the cessation of all 'becoming', impermanency ceases. The absence of inpermanency refers to a state of permanency and eternality. Eternality implies that it is 'One'. The Buddha compares the 'perfect being' to various streams which flow and finally culminate into the ocean namely, *Nibbāna*. To quote from the *Udāna* 'Just as monks, whatsoever stream flows into the mighty ocean and whatsoever rain falls from the sky, there is no shrinkage nor overflow seen thereby in the mighty ocean. Even so, though many 'perfect beings' pass finally away in that condition of *Nibbāna*, which has no remainder, yet there is no shrinkage, nor overflow in that condition of *Nibbāna* seen thereby. The experience of a 'perfect being' about *Nibbāna* is the same as experienced by other 'perfect beings'. There is no change in the state of *Nibbāna*.[48]

Further, in the *Udāna*[49] there are passages which point to the fact that the Buddha expressed *Nibbāna* as a state of infinite, pure consciousness. In this text the Buddha expounds unto Venerable Dabba that *Nibbāna* is attained when the body is consumed completely, all perception is dissolved, all feeling is cooled, the component parts have ceased and the consciousness of the mind has reached its end'. The consciousness in *Nibbāna* is free from all impurities and agitations. The Buddha, in the *Aṅguttara Nikāya*[50] has described this 'consciousness' as being brilliant white (*pabhassaram*). This white consciousness is polluted by impurities (*Upakkilesa*) due to various activities of the 'Being', the 'perfect being' through the practice of *sīla*, *samādhi* and *paññā* is able to purify this consciousness to the state of brilliant whiteness. This pure consciousness cannot be localised. This fact derives support in the *Saṁyutta Nikāya*[51], wherein the Buddha referring to Mara's search for the consciousness of Vakkali, who has attained '*parinibbāna*' the consciousness herein, has no need for any support (*apatiṭṭhita*). It is unconstituted, devoid of growth and independent of any cause and condition, and hence is free.

There is also mention in *Udāna* of the Buddha having characterised *Nibbāna* as a state which is unborn (*ajatam*), unbecome (abhavam), unmade (*akatam*) and not compounded (*asamkhatam*). The reason for such a conception, the Buddha contends, is necessary if one has to believe in the notion that there is escape from the born, becoming and compound existence. Moreover, this negative import is necessary to motivate his disciples and fellow-beings to work for salvation. This negative method is in accordance with the Buddha's method of inquiry, who begins acknowledging *dukkha* as an existential reality and finally succeeds in finding a way out for the suffering humanity.

It is not that the Buddha has merely characterised *Nibbāna* as a negative state, he has also expressed it as a positive state of 'the highest bliss', the highest happiness to be attained by man following the 'path', which is the *ariyo aṭṭaṅiko maggo*. In the *Dhammapada*,[53] he speaks of *Nibbāna* as the highest happiness. The word happiness - '*sukha*' is used at times as a synonym for *Nibbāna*. There is bound to be confusion, for '*sukha*' is generally used to denote the pleasures of the empirical realm. There is mention in the *Aṅguttara Nikāya*[54] of this confusion being confronted by Udayin, a disciple of the Buddha, who approached Sariputta for clarification. Sariputta draws a distinction by pointing that the happines ('*sukha*') herein is cut-off from sense pleasure. In this way, *Nibbāna* is not categorised as *Vedanā* that operates as a great obstacle on the path to *Nibbāna*.

The positive aspect of *Nibbāna* is further strengthened by the passages in the *Mahāvagga*, wherein, the state of the Buddha on attaining *Sambodhi* is described. To quote, 'happy the solitude in him who is full of joy who has learnt the 'Truth', who has seen the 'Truth'. Happy he, who in this world, has no ill-will, self-restrained to all beings that have life. Happy is freedom from lusts, the getting way from these. The highest bliss is freedom from the pride of the thought 'I am'.[55]

Nibbāna has also been positively and negatively defined by the Buddha in terms of 'health' in the *Majjhima Nikāya*. Negatively, it is a state of freedom from disease (*abyadhi*)[56] and positively a state of perfect health (*anitika*).[57] To be 'healthy' means to have a 'healthy mind', not merely physical but also psychological. It should be a mind psychologically healthy- which does not identify 'Oneself' with any of the five khandhas, and is able to perceive the true nature of things and existence (*saṁsāra*), which is plagued with the germs of impermanence, essencelessness and is full of suffering.[58]

But as we know, analogies, metaphors and similes used by the Buddha to elucidate *Nibbāna* led themselves to different interpretations. Accordingly, Buddha's notion of *Nibbāna* was interpreted differently by different thinkers.

The reasons for this diversity are as follows

1. The pali scriptural texts, *Nikāyas* as a whole, do not present a coherent system of philosophy and doctrine. They constitute a mosaic of the Buddha's teachings at different places on various occasions wide apart from each other. Scholars have cited portions which lent support to their views and interpretations, whenever disputes arose.

2. The *Nikāyas* are only a collection of Buddha's saying put into an uniform setting and given the garb of *suttas*.

3. Each of these *Nikāyas* developed itself under the special attention of a group of reciters called *Bhānakas*. These *Bhānakas* confined themselves exclusively to the presentation of that collection. Buddhaghosa observes that these *Bhānakas* differed among themselves regarding the interpretation of certain technical expressions in the texts.[60]

4. Vasubandhu in his *Adhidhammakośa* has pointed to the fact that many of the *Suttas* that is Buddhas' sayings, were lost. Some underwent slight modifications and that new interpretations were given to them, in such a way that the acreditions conveyed a sense different from that of the kernel around which they were set.[61]

5. The followers and scholars taking advantage of the contradictory teaching of the texts and obscure meaning of the words and dialogues, imposed their own views on them. Therefore, it is natural that divergent interpretations of the conception of *Nibbāna* have crept into Buddhist literature.

Interpretations of Nibbāna: These diverse interpretations can be broadly considered under four categories:

1. *Nibbāna* as a state of annihilation.
2. *Nibbāna* as a state of eternal, pure and infinite consciousness.
3. *Nibbāna* as an inconceivable and inexpressible state and
4. *Nibbāna* as a notion left undefined by the Buddha.

1 Nibbāna as a State of Annihilation:

The Buddhist scholars such as Oldernberg,[62] Paul Dalkhe,[63] Poussin[64] and Bigandet Burnouf, subscribe to this conception of *Nibbāna*. It is described as 'the bottomless gulf of total annihilation'.[56]

This conception of *Nibbāna* as a state annihilation derives its sustenance from the *Majjhima Nikāya* passages, where the Buddha, in response to Vacchaghotta's enquiry, on the nature of the liberated person after death, compares the state attained by a 'perfect being' after death to be similar to that of the fire which has been extinguished. To quote *Majjhima Nikāya*: "What do you think, Vaccha? If a fire were burning before your eyes, would you then know there, before me, a fire is burning". "Yes, Reverend Gotama". "But, Vaccha, if someone should ask you", "through what is the fire before your eyes burning, what would you answer him"? Reverend Gotama, I should answer, "The fire before my eyes is burning, because it keeps grasping wood and hay. "If now the fire before your eyes should be extinguished, would you then know that the fire is extinguished?" "Certainly, Reverend Gotama". "But Vaccha, if you were asked towards which region of the world has the fire departed, that is extinguished before your eyes, towards the East, the West, the North or the Soth?" "What would you then answer". "The fire before was burning because it kept grasping wood and hay, having totally consumed and being without any further fuel, owing to the lack of food is to be called as extinguished one". "Exactly the same with the perfected one, Vaccha". "His body, his sensations, his perception, his cognition, his consciousness that might be the thought of, when speaking of him. are done with, are entirely got rid of beyond all possibility of their ever gaining arising in the future...."[62]

Thus, the Buddha has expounded *Nibbāna* as a state comparable to the extinction or blowing out of the fire. Taking clue from this conception of *Nibbāna* as 'blowing out' and Buddha's denial of the 'permanent self', some scholars understood that the finality reached by a perfect being is a state of complete annihilation, the absence of existence altogether - a state of 'eternal death'.

But, we must first grasp the meaning underlying the simile of the Buddha, 'of blowing out of the flame, to gain a correct understanding of the concept of *Nibbāna*. If we equate *Nibbāna* to blowing out, we have to first answer the question, Whether this 'blowing out' stands for the annihilation of the agitations, passions, desires and delusions of the person in bondage, or the annihilation or elimination of the person in bondage as such. If we subscribe to the latter, we have to dispense with the conception of *Arhat* in Buddhist philosophy. If on the other hand, we accept the former alternative, we will be offering an intelligible explanation of the Buddha's conception of *Nibbāna* without dispersing with the concept of *Arhat*.

The former alternative of the meaning of 'annihilation' does not mean the complete destruction of the personality. It refers to the annihilation and complete destruction of all the evil forces, of craving for wordly objects, the desire to live, rebirth, becoming and ignorance. There is the absence of all *rāgo*, *doso*, *moho* and *ahaṅkaro* in the state of *Nibbāna*. The Buddha, in the *Dhammapada*[69] compares man to a boat loaded with all types of goods on a voyage. If the boat is heavily loaded, there are chances of it caspsizing and sinking, or the voyage being rough, whereas a lightly loaded boat has better chances of reaching its destination. He wants man to acquire mastery over the triple principles of *sīla*, *samādhi* and *paññā*, to cross the ocean of *saṁsāra* and reach the banks of safety, that is *Nibbāna*. The cultivation and development of these principles do away with all the evil forces which influence and generate bondage and the resultant suffering (*dukkha*).[70]

The latter alternative that 'annihilation' refers to the total elimination of the person in bondage leads to the extreme view of 'annihilationism (*Ucchhedavādo*), which is repudiated by the Buddha in the *Brahmajāla sutta* as faulty and incorrect. This interpretation of the simile, of the blowing out of the flame, is disputed by Professor Keith. In his book *Buddhist Philosophy* Professor Keith points to the fact that the extinction of the flame does not mean complete destruction. On the other hand, it is to be understood as the lapsing of the flame into its pure, original state of fire. It is the state, in which it existed prior to its manifestation as flame.[72]

The *Vaibhāśika* school of early Buddhism[73] understands *Nibbāna* as a state, wherein, the conciousness is dissociated from all its impurities, of fetters and defilements such as passion, hatred and ignorance.

2. Nibbāna as a State of Eternal, Pure and Infinite Consciousness:

In the *Pāli* text *Udāna*, *Nibbāna* is described as a state in which the consciousness (*viññāṇa*) is free from all fetters and defilements, which proudce *dukkha*. The consciousness herein, is free from all the dualities of pleasure and pain, good and bad, and also from the impurities of passion (*rāgo*), hatred (*doso*) and ignorance (*avijjā*), which produce *dukkha*. Consciousness is signless, infinite and radiant in all directions, in *Nibbāna*. It is pure and untainted. The Buddha compares the 'tainted consciousness' in the 'imperfect being' to the waves in a rough sea, wherein the consciousness is in a state of agitation. It is in a state of change, a state of impermanence that leads to suffering. In the 'perfect being' the consciousness is devoid of all stress and strain. Such a state is comparable to the calm waters of the sea after the turmoil has died down.

This conception derives support from the *Milandapañha* also wherein, Nagasena contends that 'final deliverance as declared by the Buddha, to be nothing other than a faultless state of consciousness'. It is free from all agitations *rāgo, doso* and *moho*.

The Buddha, in the *Kevaddha Sutta*[76] equates *Nibbāna* to 'infinite consciousness'. In this Sutta, the Buddha explains to the *Bhikkhus* that the place where all distinctions like water, earth, fire and air have no footing, where long and short, fine and coarse, good and bad, or name and form cease absolutely is *Viññāṇa* namely consciousness. *Nibbāna* is a state where all distinctions disappears and where the constituted *viññāṇa* after cessation disappears. The Buddha, in the Samyutta Nikaya II points out that *Māra* will not be able to get at Vakkali's consciousness, who has attained *parinibbāna*. For consciousness herein, is pure and perfect. It does not require any support (*apatiṭṭhita*). The infinite consciousness is unconstituted, devoid of growth and independent of any cause and condition and hence is free.[77]

The *Yogācāra* school of Mahāyāna[78] Buddhism subscribes to the view that *Nibbāna* is a state wherein absolute consciousness is completely pure, being freed from the delusion of '*ahaṅkāro*' its resultant activity and the experiences of *sukha* and *dukkha*. In this state, there exists pure harmonious consciousness: Harmonious, in the sense, there is the complete absence of all agitations.

The *Yogācārins* contend that with the attainment of *Nibbāna*, the 'perfect being' realises that *saṁsāra* is illusory. Reality is nowhere, but it is 'itself'. It is just like a musk deer which searches for the source of the fragrant smell of *kṣturi* throughout the jungle, not realising that it is present within its own body. Asaṅga observes that with the destruction of illusoriness '*Nibbāna*' can be attained[79]. This can be attained on the realisation of both *pudgala-nairātmya* and *dharma-nairātmya*. *Pudagala-nairātmya* is the realisation of *anicca* and *anattā* of the external objects, whereas '*dharma-nairātmya*' is the realisation that the external world is a mere illusion. The external world is a result of cosmic illusion. It is a super-imposition. Man, under the notion of a permanent 'self', attaches himself to the world, performs actions resulting in experiences of *sukha* and *dukkha*. Asanga contends that with the realisation of *pudagala-nairātmya* all the *kilesas*, the veil of *kilesāvaraṇa*, the Veil of *Jñānāvarana* covering pure consciousness is destroyed. *Nibbāna* is a state, wherein the two veils are completely destroyed. In this state, there is purified absolute consciousness, freed from the evil forces of greed, hatred and ignorance.

3. Nibbāna as an Inconceivable and Inexpressible State:

This conception of *Nibbāna* gains substance from the dialogue, which took place between the Buddha and Upasiva regarding the state of existence of the liberated[80]. The Buddha describes *Nibbāna* as a state above and beyond the four categories of thought. 'Is' 'Is not'; Both 'Is' and 'Is not' and 'Neither Is' nor 'Is not'. The inconceivability of *Nibbāna* is also stressed by the Buddha in the *Sutta Nipāta*. Just as the flame of a lamp struck by a gust of wind disappears and cannot be traced, similarly a perfect being freed from name and form that is, an *Arhat*, disappears without leaving behind any trace[81].

Radhakrishnan, commenting on this, states that "Buddha's real attitude is probably a state of perfection inconceivable by us, and if we are obliged to offer a description of it, it is best to bring out its inconceivability by negative description; the richness of content by positive predicates, realising all the time that such descriptions are at best approximations only"[82]

Nibbāna, which is a felt experience and a discursive thought can hardly be comprehended and communicated to others. There are many experiences in the mundane world which can hardly be described or expressed to others such as the aesthetic experiences gained on observing carvings and statues at Ajanta and Ellora caves. Whatever may be the description offered, it is not the same as experiencing it oneself. All means of communication available through the use of language have limitations, since these belong to the empirical level of reality. They cannot explain the trans-empirical namely, the transcendental. The alternative way left for communication of these experiences is that they can be described through analogies and similes, which were adopted by the Buddha to communicate to the common man, the nature of *nibbāna.*

Nāgārjuna, the propounder of the *Madhyamika* school of *Mahāyāna* Buddhism[83], with the use of dialectical arguments has shown that *Nibbāna* is an inexpressible state. He takes the four postulates arising regarding the state of *Nibbāna* for dialectical analysis. They are:

1. *Nibbāna* as a state of *bhava;*
2. *Nibbāna* as a state of *abhava;*
3. *Nibbāna* as a state of both *bhava* and *abhava* and
4. *Nibbāna* as a state of neither *bhava* nor *abhava.*

1. *Nibbāna as a state of bhava*: Nāgārjuna, analysing this conception, points if it is a kind of existence ('*bhava*'), then it must be subject to the laws of death, decay and impermanence. Moreover, every existence ('*bhava*') is a product of a cause. Similarly, if *Nibbāna* is an existence ('*bhava*'), it is also a product of a cause. This is untenable, for *nibbāna* is not a product of any kind of production, it is uncaused. It does not have a substratum from which it can be produced[84].

2. *Nibbāna as a state of abhava* : It is a state of absence of all defiling elements and individual existences produced by them. Nāgārjuna raises the objection that this would lead to the belief that the impermanence of these defiling elements and personal existence would attach to *nibbāna*, thereby, making

nibbāna a state of impermanence, which is not acceptable. Secondly, *nibbāna* being an *abhava* is not independent. For, every non-existent entity is dependent on its positive counterpart, which is not acceptable in the case of *nibbāna*[85]

3. *Nibbāna, as a state of both existence* ('*bhava*') *and non-existence* ('*abhava*'): '*Abhava*', in so far as the defiling elements of existence (*kilesas*) and elements of existence are extinct in it and in itself, this, lifeless condition is '*abhava*'. Nāgārjuna points to the fact that if '*nibbāna*' is both '*bhava*' and *abhava*', then final liberation would be both a 'reality' and '*abhava*', then final liberation would be both a 'reality' and 'unreality' together, a state, wherein both the energies of life are active and extinct. But how can deliverance and phenomenal life be the same? It is not conceivable. Secondly, if *nibbāna* would be relative and dependent on the totality of its causes and conditions, it would not be absolute for, both '*abhava*' and '*bhava*' are relative. But *nibbāna* does not come within the realm of relativity. It is uncaused. It is impossible to conceive such a notion, contends Nagarjuna.[86]

4. *Nibbāna is neither 'bhava' nor 'abhava'* : Nāgārjuna feels that we cannot conceive of a state, which is neither '*bhava*' nor '*abhava*'. We cannot understand this negation. This negation is absurd. It is underfinable and cannot be labelled as a definite judgementy[87].

   Nāgārjuna, further rejects all the four postulates of *nibbāna*, for they tend to lead man to the extremes of eternal death and eternal life.

5. *Nibbāna as a notion left undefined by the Buddha*: The Buddha intelligent as he was, sensed the inadequacies of giving an expression to *Nibbāna*, left it undefined. Scholars like Radhakrishnan opine that 'Buddha did not trouble himself about the definition of these transcendental concepts such as *nibbāna*, which he felt to be real, for they do not help life and progress'[88]. An appropriate illustration of this is found in the dialogue which took place between the Buddha and Malunkyaputta[89]. The Buddha's aim is intensely practical to motivate the common man, not to speculate, but to develop the 'awareness' of the magnitude of *dukkha* and to remove it. The Buddha's conception of life and the universe are derived from his practical outlook to help man realise his predicament and strive to overcome it.

The existence of everything depends upon a cause. With the removal of the cause, the effect will cease to exist. If the sources of all suffering are destroyed, suffering itself would disappear. The only path through which we can remove the cause of suffering is by purifying the mind and following the moral law-dhamma. Metaphysical doctrines which take away the urgency of the moral task and prevent cultivation of individual character are repudiated by the Buddha. The Buddha further opines, that interest in metaphysical doctrines such as *nibbāna* and its speculation, diverts the attention and energy from ethical values and the understanding of actual conditions by means of which their realisation may be furthered. The Buddha observed that man should use the power they possess to advance 'good' in life, to attain liberation, which has to be accomplished by their own efforts. It is human effort or individual effort alone that will help man liberate himself from the clutches of *dukkha*, To quote the last words of the Buddha[90], '*Vayadhamma Saṁkhāra*, *Appamedana Sampadetha*' (All composities are perishable by nature, strive deligently). 'Truth' can be realised by personal effort, and ethical striving for this is essential. 'In the world of spirit, none can see who does not kindle a light of his own'[91]. The Buddha has repeatedly pointed to the fact that man alone is responsible for the situation in which he finds himself. Man, by his 'will' and action can determine his future. Human effort alone counts, if man wants to liberate himself from suffering.

The Buddha's silence on metaphysical issues, such as *Nibbāna*, has been construed as his ignorance about 'anything' beyond the empirical realm. Does his silence imply that he did not know 'anything' beyond the empirical realm or about the reality. This can be confirmed by many of his utterances, in which the Buddha makes out that he knows more than what he has given to his disciples. To quote the Buddha, "what think ye, my disciples, which are the more, these few 'Siṁsāpa' leaves which I have gathered in my hand, or the other leaves yonder in the 'Siṁsāpa' grove. The few leaves which the exalted one holds in his hand are not many; but may more are those leaves yonder in the 'Siṁsāpa' grove". "So also my disciples, that much more which I have learned and have not told you, than that which I have told you" "and, therefore, my disciples, I have not told you that, because it does not lead to the turning from the earthy, to the subjection of all desires, to the cessation of the transitory, to appease the knowledge, to illumination, to *nibbāna*"[92] The Buddha realises the futility of such a metaphysical inquiry. Man has to be freed from suffering. He offers to man the immediate necessary knowledge about awareness of *dukkha* and its annihilation.

The Buddha knew that the nature of absolute reality was 'supra-logical', and it would be a waste of energy and time to insist on giving logical accounts of it. The unconditioned absolute cannot be conceived by means of logical categories[93]. It is something to be experienced and realised. Any amount of descriptions of conceptualisation of a trans-empirical reality, in terms of empirical language, would be an exercise in vain. Realising the above stated difficulties, he felt that it would be better to leave the concept of *nibbāna* undefined. To quote Radhakrishnan. 'whatever metaphysics we have in Buddhism, is not the original *Dhamma*, but added to it[94]

Nibbāna, the state of freedom from *dukkha*, the Truth or Reality discovered by the Buddha, is beyond discussion (atarkavācana). It can be realised only by the wise, within one's own mind. Based on the above discussion of the various interpretations of *nibbāna* we can draw some conclusions. The early Buddhists present two aspects of *nibbāna* namely ethical and 'metaphysical'.

Nibbāna, as an ethical state, has received the largest amount of attention in the *pāli* texts. *Nibbāna* is described negatively as the destruction of attachment (*rāgo*), hatred (*doso*) and delusion (*moho*), of desire (*taṇhā*), impressions (*saṅkhāra*) and firm grasp of wrong views (*micca diṭṭhi*), of impurities (*āsava*) and afflictions (*kilesa*), and of desire for existence (*bhava*), birth (jab), old age and death (jaramarana) and thus of suffering (*dukkha*). Positively, it is a state of peace (*Sama*) and tranquility (*santa*). It is a state of eternal bliss.

The 'metaphysical' aspect of *nibbāna* has also been presented in the pāli texts. It is an eternal state beyond the scope of discursive and discriminatory thoughts. It has neither origin or decay. It is without past, present or future. It is unconditioned and unconstituted. It is unlimited and unsurpassable, unfathomable and immeasurable. It is supramundane and beyond the three spheres of existence. It is beyond the four propositions of thought.

REFERENCES

1. Chatterjee, H. "*The Buddhistic Conception of Nirvāna*", *Mahābodhi*, Vol. 63. p. 195.
2. *Vis. Magga*. Chap. VIII., 247. p. 319 (ff)
3. Op. Cit.
4. *Saṁ. Nikāya*. 19.
5. *Pāli-Eng. Dic.* p. 362.
6. *Vis. Magga*. 293. (ff) Chatterjee, Heramba, 'The Buddhist conception of Nirvāna', *Mahābodhi*, Vol. 63, p.195.
7. *Itivuttaka*, 38. Saupādisesā ca nibbāna dhātu anupādi sesa ca nibbānadhātu.
8. *Sutta Nipāta*, p. 61.
9. Silve Lynn A de. *The Problem of Self in Buddhism and Christianity*, p. 67.

10. Oldenberg, H. *The Buddha, His life, His doctrine, His order*: p.288.

11. *Ratana Sutta*, Majj. Nikaya.2.

12. *Itivuttaka*, 38, tassa tiṭṭhanteva pañca indriyāni yesam avihātattā manāpāmanāpaṁ paccanubhati sukhadukkham patisamvedi yati. ...Saupādisesa nibbānadhātu.

13. *Vis. Magga*. XVI, 90 (Nñānamoli). For, there is suffering, but none who suffers. Doing exists, although there is no doer; extinction is but not extinguished person; Although there is a path, there is no goer. p. 587

14. *Majj. Nikāya*. 86. Aṅgulimāla Sutta.

15. Twelve kinds of immoral consciousness are mentioned under section viñāña, Chapter II p. Foot-notes pp. 149-150.

16. Saṅgharaksihita, Mahāsthavira, *Human Enlightenment*, p. 43.

17. *Dh. p.* VII. 94.

17a. *Dh. p.* VII, 96, 'Sanata Vāca'.

18. *Dh. p.* VIII, 91 & 92.

19. Kalupahana, David J., *Buddhist Philosophy*, p. 73, *Digha Nikaya*, 260, Aṭṭhaloka - dhammā lābho, ca alābho ca yaso ca ayaso ca nindā ca passṁsā ca sukhañ c dukkhaṁ ca.

20. *Mahābodhi*, Vol. 79, May-June 1971 Nos. 5 & 6, pp. 139-143 Bodhisattva Ideal in Theravāda and Mahāyāna.

21. This ideal of 'Arhat' can be realised by either adopting the means of 1. *Śrāvaka Yāna* or 2. *Pracceka buddhayāna*.

    (1) *Śrāvaka Yāna*: Srāvaka means, 'hearer'. The follower of this path adopts the means of hearing and learning the truth from the Buddha or any realised *Arhat*, to gain *Arhatship*. (2) *Praccekabuddha yāna*: pracceka means 'private', individual, single or solitary. The followers of this path do not derive any support from any external sources to gain 'Arhatship'. It is attained by 'solitary singleness', in independent study and meditation of the truth of *Dukkha*.

22. *Mahābodhi* Vol. 79, May-June 1971, Nos. 5 & 6 pp. 139-43.

23. *Mahābodhi*, Vol. 80, Oct-Now. 1972, Nos. 10-11, pp. 481-85.

24. *Jātakamāla*, 41.1.

25. Hardayal, *Bodhisattva Ideal in Saṅskrit Literature*, p, 178.

26. *Latitavistara* 244.8; *Avadana ṣataka*, I. 412.

27. The conception, of the transfer of karma is accepted and advocated by the Andhaka school of Buddhism. Malasekara in his article titled "Transference of merit in Ceylonese

Buddhism" (*Philosophy of East and West*, Vol. XVIII, No.1-4, Jan-Oct, 1967) has discussed about this conception.

Acharya Shantideva's Bodhisattvacharyavatara -*A guide to the Boddhisattva's way of life*, (trans) Stephen Batchelor, library ofTibetan works Archives, Dharmasala, 1979; Chap. VIII, Meditation 136, Chapter X, dedication, 2.

28. Suzuki, D. T. *Qutlines of Mahāyāna Buddhism*, p. 298-99.

29. *Jātakamāla*, 6ff, *Avadanaṣataka* I, 182.ff.

30. *Jātakamāla*, I.ff, *Avadanakālpalata* II, 95ff, II.907.

31. *Therāghāta*: 1002-1003; Rhyś Davids, C.A.F. Psalms of the Early Buddhist, Part.II. p. 346.

32. *Saṁ. Nikāya*. IV. 294.

33. The other two *khandas* namely *rūpa* and *saṅkhāra* are rendered ineffective and infruitious; Rupa, which refers to the material aggregate is at rest, for there is no more saṅkhāra to bring it into action due to wearing off of the kammas completely.

34. *Majj. Nikāya*. 72 (Aggi-Vacchagatta Sutta), *Majj. Nikāya*. 1.486 f. Chalmers. Vol. 1. p.344.

35. *Udāna* 80-81 (Woodward, *The Minor Anthologies*, part. II. p. 114.)

36. *Ibid*. 93.

37. *Majj. Nikāya*: 1: 63: For the above discussion between Buddha and Māluṅkyāputta on the futility of metaphysical questions and their discussion, please refer to pages 45-6 of chapter I (Second section).

38. *Majj. Nikāya*. I.1.

39. *Saṁ. Nikāya* 88. 'Aggikkhando purimassa upādānassa pariyadana annassa ca anupāhāra anāhāro nibbāneyya.

40. *Ibid*.

41. *Dh.p.* Chap. XX: 283. (Trans) Radhakrishnan pp. 148-49. 'Vanaṁ chindatha, mā rukkham, Vanato jāyati bhayam Chetava vanaṁca vanathaṁca nibbānā hotha bhikkhavo. cf. M:1,487, *Sn. 1094*; *S*:1:236, *J*:1:212, *Miln*: 346.

42. *Sam. Nikāya*, III. 190: Woodward part III, p.156.

43. *Ibid*.

44. *Ibid*, XXII 851. (Warren. pp.138-39).

45. *Ibid*.

46. *Ibid*

47. *Udāna* 81

48. *Udāna* 55.

49. *Udāna*, VIII. 9.

50. *Aṅguttara Nikāya*, I, pp. 10, 257.

51. *Saṁ. Nikāya*, III, p.124.

52. *Udāna*. 81.

53. *Dhammapada*, 204. nibbāṇaṁ paramaṁ sukham.

54. *Aṅguttara Nikāya* iv 414.f. "Sukham Idam, āvuso nibbānaṁ", ti— kiṁ panettha āvuso Sāriputta, Sukhaṁ, yad ettha natthi Vedayitaṁiti? Pañcime".. kāmaguṇā — idaṁ vuccatāvuso. kāmasukhaṁ — vivicc eva kāmehi, Hare, E.M. Vol. IV, p. 279-80.

55. *Majj. Nikāya*. 2., Rhys Davids. T.W., *Early Buddhism*, p. 39.

56. *Majj. Nikāya*, 75, (Magandiya Sutta).

57. *Majj. Nikāya*, 511 : (arogya: health)

58. *Sam. Nikāya*, iii. 46.

59. *Sum. Vil*. p. 15.

60. *Vis. Magga*. p. 95.

61. *Adhidhammakośa*, ii, 55, p. 278ff.

62. Oldenberg, H. *The Buddha, His life, His doctrine, His order*, p.273.

63. Dalkhe, Paul, *Buddhist Essays*, pp. 47-48.

64. Poussion, M, *Way to Nirvāna*, p. 150.

65. Max Muller, *Studies in Buddhism*, p. 57.

66. *Ibid*., p. 51.

67. *Majj. Nikāya*, 72. Aggi-Vacchagotta Sutta (M:1:486) (PTS).

68. In the *Vis. Magga* Buddhaghosa (cf. *Sam. Nikāya*. Jaṁbukhadaka sutta) warns that mere cessation cannot be the nature of Nibbāṇa, in that case, the state of *Arhatship* will have to be regarded as a state of cessation. But the Buddha has not given the specific character of this state as it can only be gained by intutive experiences. It is an inexpressible state.

69. *Dh.p.* Chap. 25, 10-p. 173.

70. *Ibid*. Siñca bhikkhu imaṁ nāvam sittā te lahum essati chetvā rāgaṁ ca dosām ca tato nibbāṇam ehisi (369)

71. *Dīgha Nikāya* I.1.

72. Keith, *Buddhist Philosophy*, p. 66.

73. Vaibhāśikas: The Vaibhāsikas school of radical pluralism are continuators of the Sārvastavādas. They derive their name because they accepted the commentary (*vibhāṣsa*) of the *Abhidhamma* as more authoritative than the original suttas. The exponents of this school are Dharmottara, Dhamatrata, Vasubandhu, Vasumitra, Buddhadeva and Guṇaprabha. They contend that Nibbāna is existent (dravya), real and eternal. It is the dharmasvabhāva, which remains on cessation of dharamalakṣhṇāh. Ref. Stcherbatsky, The Conception of Buddhist Nirvāna, pp. 27-87. The individual here is conceived as a series of momentary states of consciousness, which constitute a stream. In the agitated man, this stream of consciousness is impure with passion, hatred and delusion. With the practise of *Sīla*, *Samādhi* and *Paññā* this stream is cleansed and the agitation is reduced to an inoperative state. The last moment of consiousness is devoid of the potency of self-reproduction and thereby rebirth ceases.

74. *Udāna*. VIII. 9.

75. *Miln*. (PTS) III, 5.10.

76. *Dīgha Nikāya*. I. p.223. *Sum. Vii.* (IHQ ii.1) *Majj. Nikaya*., p. 239. *Papañcasudani*, I. p.413.

Viññāṇam anidassaam anantaṃ sabbato pabhaṃ

Ettha āpo ca paṭhavi tejo na gādhati,

Ettha dīghan ca rassañ ca anuṃ thūlaṃ subhāsubhaṃ

Ettha nāmañ ca rūpan ca asesam uparujjhati,

Viññāṇsassa nirodhena etth', etam uparujjhati, (Dīgha Nikāya I. p. 223).

Buddhaghosa, Commenting on the above passage, opines that there is ambiguity in the meaning of the term '*Viññāna*. He clarified the meaning and implication of the term '*Viññāṇa*' by stating that its meaning should be made on the basis of the root '*ñā*' *i.e.* to know; that which is to be known *i.e.*, *Nibbāna*. He says that as the first '*Viññāṇa*' is another name for *nibbāna* whereas, the second Viññāna is one of the five aggregates (*Vis. Magga*. p. 689).

77. *Sam. Nikāya*. II. 66. &, III. 53.

78. Yogācāra school of Mahāyāna Buddhism was founded by Maiterya (3rd century A.D.). Asaṅga (4the century A.D.), Vasubandhu (4th century A.D.), Sthiramati (5the centry A.D.), Diṅnāga (5the century A.D.), Dharmapāla (7the century A.D.), Dharmakiriti (7the century A.D.), Santaraksita (8th century A.D.) and Kamalasīla (8the century A.D.) are the exponents of this school.

79. *Laṅkāvatara Sūtra* speaks of absolute consciousness (ālaya vijñāna) alone as being real and all other dharmas are unreal. The eternal world and its objects are mere creation of absolute consciousness. Individual consciousness (*pravṛṭṭi-vijñāna*) consists of the seven *pravṛṭṭi vijñanas*. The Seventh *kliṣta mānovijñāna* represents the continuous consciousness, it acts as intermeditary link between the absolute consciousness and individual consciousness. It is here, that the potentialities of absolute consciousness are actualised. Vasubandhu, in *Trimshika*, also holds that the reality is pure consciousness. But this reality has three types of modifications. First of all, it manifests itself as *Ālaya-Vijñāna* (universal consciousness). This universal consciousness manifests as the individual subject (*kliṣta mānovijñāna*) and secondly as various mental states -*Viṣaya-vijñāna*. Behind these three modifications is the eternal and exchanging pure consciousness (*vijñāptimatra*). The *Ālaya-vijñāna* of Lankāvatara is identical with the Vijnapatimra os Vasubandhu.

80. Thomas. E.J, *Road to Nirvāna*, p. 69.

81. *Sutta Nipāta* (p.206-7) (as quoted by Dutt N. in *Early Monastic Buddhism*, p. 280).

82. Radhakrishnan, S., *Indian Philosophy*, Vol. I, p. 453.

83. Madhyamika School of Mahāyāna Buddhism is said to have originated with Nāgārjuna (2nd century A. D.). He was followed by Aryadeva (3rd century A. D.), Buddhapalita (5the century A. D.), Bhavaviveka (5the century A,. D), Candrakiriti and (6the century A. D.) and Saṇtideva (7the century A. D.)

84. Stchehbatsky, Th., *The Conception of Buddhist Nirvāna*, 1977, pp. 200-203.

85. *Ibid.*, pp. 203-205.

86. *Ibid.*, p. 209-210.

87. *Ibid.*, p. 99.

88. Radhakrishnan, S., *Indian Philosophy*, Vol. I. p. 455.

89. For details of the above dialogue refer to Chap. I, Section IIp.

90. *Mahāparinibbā=na Sutta*. M. *Dīgha Nikāya*. 16, *Dīgha Nikāya*. ii. 91f.

91. *Dīgha Nikāya*. ii. p. 217. Vis. Magga 211. Chapassa imem dhammamti, Evaṁ pavaṭṭaṁ ehi passa vidham arahititi.

92. *Sam. Nikāya*. V. 437.

93. *Saṇtideva - Bodhicaryāvatara* (ix.2).

94. Radhakrishnan, S., *Indian philosophy*, Vol. 1., p. 358.

7

Conclusions

Philosophical inquiry in Indian tradition started with man's endeavour to overcome *duḥkha*. Philosophy, in India, is never divorced from life. It is primarily meant to meet the demands of man in ensuring freedom from *duḥkha* and leading him to ānanda. The Buddha, wise as he was, realised the futility of an inquiry, which was not relevant to the elimination of human misery and recognised rightly that metaphysical inquiry, instead of solving man's suffering, lands him in a futile intellectual exercise and unending disputes. Therefore, he avoided all such futile intellectual exercises and concentrated on the factors underlying human misery and their elimination.

Buddha's primary task was to awaken the 'slumbering man', to the magnitude of suffering, engulfing his existence. His threadbare analysis of the various manifestations of suffering, from conception to death, from craddle to grave is aimed at making man realise the limitations and uncertainties of existence. In a philosophical sense, *dukkha*, according to the Buddha, is aimed at the illumination of the true significance of life embroiled with suffering of repeated births. It points to an unenlightened mode of existence and an intensive search to overcome it. It shows that life is not to be spent drawing meaning and nourishment from one's attachment to material objects and false concepts, such as an abiding 'ego' or 'self'.

The Buddha points out explicitly to this misdirected mode of human existence, in his inquiry into the truth of *dukkha*. The ignorance (*avijjā*) about the true meaning of life is more paralysing and harmful than any other form of physical or mental suffering. But this suffering is neither visualised nor experienced by one, who does not transcend the physical existence. Awareness of this kind of suffering needs a sensitive mind that can penetrate beyond the physical and mental suffering of man. It motivates one to seek what is beyond the mind and body.

Suffering arises when one's desires, which get translated as volition are unfulfilled. Suffering may result: (a) when a desire is curbed by the mind through the knowledge that the desire sought cannot be fulfilled. This results in frustrated will and helplessness, which are forms of suffering, (b) Once a desire is satisfied, it leads to repeated desires, but my not be satisfied, suffering is to be understood firstly, as a 'frustruated will'-a feeling of helplessness and secondly, as a restless state of the mind gripped by unsatisfied desires.

The early Buddhist analysis of the concept of man, points to the fact, that man is nothing but a mere aggregation of the *pañcakkhandhas*, which are in a state of perpetual flux. There is no 'self' or 'ego' either permanent or impermanent, over and above this five-fold aggregation (nāma-rūpa). 'Self' or 'ego' is nothing more than a mere name, an appellation, or an abstraction, which refers to this relatively existent psycho-physical aggregation. By pointing to the fact of impermanence (*anicca*) and the resultant essenceless (*anattā*) nature of existence the Buddha observe that any identification with any one or the whole of the five-fold aggregation as permanent or impermanent, single and independent principle, leads one to misdirected acts, whose resultants are one of suffering.

This teaching of the Buddha about 'emptiness' and 'selflessness' has a significant role to play in the present day materialistic society. We find that man, under the veil of ignorance, identifies himself and his existence with this false idea of a 'self' as a permanent and independent entity, to overcome fear and gain security. He strives to satisfy its unending desires, for he identifies living with the satisfaction of the 'self', little realising the folly and futility of such an exercise.

When the Buddha exhorted his disciples not to hanker after things (*taṇha*), he was always alive to the distinction between 1. Basic desires and 2. Excessive desires of man. Basic desires refer to those which are essential for man's bare existence, such as a reasonable quota of food, clothing and so on. These basic desires, the bare essential necessities for man's existence, can be termed as 'need'. 2. Excessive desires refer to craving in man to hoard, amass material objects more than what is needed. This excessive craving can be termed as 'greed'. The Buddha was never averse to the 'needs', but he was against the life based on 'agreed'. Man, making use of this knowledge should avoid craving by cutting down his 'greed'. This can be achieved by the practice and cultivation of detachment for the fleeting objects of the world.

The Buddha, in his analysis of *kamma*, explictly points to the fact that man is the maker of his destiny. *kamma*, herein, refers to the 'willed' actions, that is, deeds of the beings with the full consent of the conscious mind. These deeds shape the character of the being, which plays an important role in determining the birth and experiences of man. Therefore, if one has to liberate oneself, one can achieve it through self-effort by the development and cultivation of *kusula kamma* avoiding the *akusula kamma*.

The law of dependent origination, discovered and expounded by the Buddha, explains that there is nothing like a self-independent entity. Everything comcs into being depending upon the other. When one exists, there is the possibility of existence of the other, when one does not exist, the possibility of existence of the other is also not seen. The twelve 'links' or nidānas, which make the wheel of becoming, are dependent upon each other. With these nidānas, the three circle of existence have been shown. The first two *nidānas* namely *avijjā* and *saṇkhāra* belong to the past. The last two *nidānas*, *jāti* and *jarā maraṇa* belong to the future. The remaining eight *nidānas* namely, *viññāṇa*, *nām-rūpa*, *salāyatana*, *phassa*, *vedanā*, *taṇha*, *upādāna* and *bhava* in the middle, belong to the present state of life. The bhava-chakra shows that, belonging to the past life, there is the existence of the present one, and depending upon one's present, there is the possibility of the arising of the future life. It is in this way, the circle of existence and the suffering present in *saṁsāra* is exhibited as a fact of life.

The Buddha, rightly identifies craving (*taṇha*) as the cause of suffering. It is the craving for attachment towards the objects of the phenomenal world, which leads to fueling the revolution of the *bhava-chakra*. It generates in man, a three-fold urge: 1. for relishing the sensual pleasures, 2. for maintaining the individuality of one's own and 3. the strong sense of hatred and antipathy towards others in general and their prosperity in particular. Craving, which essentially refers to man's excessive desires 'greed', has to be controlled and curbed by one, who wants to gain liberation. It points to the urgent need in man to cut down his wants to the bare minimum, that is, a shift from 'greed oriented' living to 'need oriented' living. Man's life should be based on the dictum 'simple living and high thinking'. The development and cultivation of this attitude by man is very essential for the harmonious and peaceful co-existence of man on this planet.

Ignorance (*avijjā*) is identified as the root cause of human suffering and his repeated existence. Ignorance generates psychic darkness, bewilders the consciousness and does not allow one to visualise the truth. Under its influence the facts of suffering, its origin, causes, cessation, path leading to *nibbāna*, the existence in the past, future, the state of existence in the present and dependent origination are not understood. It makes man take the fleeting objects as permanent sources of joy and cling to them. The apparent is taken for the real, the untruth for truth, the impermanent for permanent and so on. It is because of the lack of knowledge and understanding of the nature of reality and life that one wastes his vital energies, seeking satisfaction from the fleeting objects of the world. This form of ignorance keeps man entangled in the web of *saṁsāra*.

The Buddha contends that, *avijjā* and *taṇhā* are the two fountain heads, that is, accelerating forces behind the cycle of existence (*bhava-chakra*). The chain of suffering is headed by *avijjā,* which lies dominant at the root and is conditioned by *taṇhā*. *Avijjā*, the dominant, determines the weak and is a condition of *taṇhā Avijja* determines *taṇhā,* which is born out of a condition of the latter's profilement. *Avijjā* functions in the root and generates a bewildered state of psychic darkness in viewing objects. The objects, which are subject to change, lack an essence, and suffering appears to be permanent, full of essence and the pleasant. The sensual pleasure, which is like a blaze of fire appears to be a source of joy. It inspires thirst for the phenomenal and gives rise to a leaning to have them that is, *taṇhā*.

The Buddha, having identified *avijjā* as the root-cause of *dukkha*, directs his energies towards dispelling it. Unless the mind is purified of its defilements, there is no real chance of one ever gaining perfect wisdom about the reality, to liberate himself from the clutches of *saṁsāra*.

The Buddha repeatedly pointed out in his discourses, such as the *Dhammacakkappavattana sutta*, to the follies of adopting the extremes of self-mortification and self-indulgence as means to attain freedom from *dukkha*. These means are improper, for they are ingrained with the germs of *dukkha*. He prescribes the *madhyomo-maggo*, practised by himself, to attain *nibbāna*.

This technique consists of three components namely sīla, *samādhi* and *paññā*, which are aimed at developing a three-fold control: 1. control over our relationship with fellow-beings, 2. control over the forces of nature, and finally, 3. a control over ones' own self (physical and mental control). Unlike other systems of Indian philosophy, which have laid emphasis on one aspect of the 'means', such as Advaita Vedānta on 'knowledge', (*jñāna*), herein, equal stress is laid on all the three components for an all-round control, development and cultivation of all the three aspects. Each of them has a specific and important role to perform in the process of purification, leading to *nibbāna*. *Sīla*, which stands for ethical perfection, removes the defilements arising from wrong speech, wrong action and wrong conduct. *Samādhi* stands for mental perfection, through the development and cultivation of concentration whereby one overcomes the defilement of craving (*taṇhā*) the cause for suffering. *Panna* stands for perfect wisdom which is directed to overcome the defilements of false views, of ignorance (*avijjā*), the root cause for suffering and it leads to the cutting off all becoming, leading to *nibbāna*.

The perfected man(arhat) of early Buddhist conception does not isolate himself from society. He renders selfless service to fellow-beings apart from spreading the message of *Buddha dhamma*. His prime aim is to help alleviate the sufferings of his fellow-beings. He is a selfless worker striving towards establishing harmony in this world of strife, conflict and suffering.

Regarding the question whether the liberated man is free from suffering, the Buddha makes it clear that even the liberated man, as long as he has a body, that is, the psycho-physical complex (*nāma-r-ūpa*) suffers, but there is a difference between his suffering, and that of the man in bondage. The liberated man knows that his suffering which the body is undergoing is the effect of the past deeds, which will cease with his final death. But the man in bondage is not aware of the way out.

Early Buddhists conceive of liberation as the absence of, cutting-off all forms of rebirth. For rebirth even in the *arūpaloka*, is not desirable for it is not free from the fetters of suffering, though the intensity of suffering is less. *Nibbāna* is essentially state of absence of rebirth, cessation of becoming, and thereby a state of freedom from suffering.

The Buddha's analysis of the orgin and annihilation of suffering has given a new meaning, direction and purpose to philosophical inquiry. His influence is visible in all directions. The present day society has absorbed all the 'goods' and put the best of his ethics into practice. A new respect for life, kindness towards fellow-creatures, a sense of responsibility and an endeavour for higher life are brought out with a renewed force. He started a revolt against the craving for material objects by showing that they are of the nature of transitoriness, essenceless and suffering.

The discussion that centres around the issues regarding the origin of *dukkha* and its annihilation is relevant at all times. Though scientific progress has urshered some comfort into man's life at large, it is threatening man's existence every moment, for the stockpile of nuclear armaments is sufficient to wipe out the entire humanity, several times. The very existence of the entire humanity is in peril. Man lives in a world wherein he is not sure of himself, his wants, his values, and the meaning and purpose of his very existence. An ethical crisis has broken out, man is set to destroy his fellow-beings and himself by plunging into ego-centric desires and material pursuits. He has failed to realise the gravity and intensity of the suffering in store for him from such a misdirected endeavour. It appears that yet another Buddha will have to be born on this planet to infuse the true meaning of life in man and lead the entire humanity from disorder to order, from suffering arising out of repeated births and death to the cessation of rebirth namely, *nibbāna*.

Bibliography

SYSTEMS OF INDIAN PHILOSOPHY

1. Cārvāka

1. Dakshinaranjan Shastri — *A Short History of Indian materialism*, Book Company, Calcutta, 1930.

2. Debiprassād Chattopadhyaya — *Lokāyata: A study in Ancient Indian Materialism*, Peoples Publication House, New Delhi,1973.

3. Madhavācārya — *Sarva-darśana-saṁgraha*, Bhandarkar Institute, Poona, 1924. English Translations by Cowell and Gough, Chowkhamba, Varanasi, 1961.

4. Haribhadra — *ṣaḍ-darśana-samuccaya*, Asiatic Society, Calcutta, 1905. English Translation by Prof. K. S. Murthy, Eastern Book Linkers, Delhi, 1986.

5. Vātsyāyana — *Kāma-Sūtra*, Chowkhamba, Varanasi, 1920, Ch. I-II.

2. Sāṅkhya

1. Īśvara kṛṣṇa — *Sāṅkhya kārikā*. Trans. H. H. Wilson, Theosophical Society Publication, Bombay, (1887), 1975.

——— Trans. S. S. Sastri, University of Madras Publications, Madras.

2. Vācaspati Miśra — *Tattva kaumudī*, Comm. on Sāṅkhya Kārikā. Trans. Mahamahopadhyaya Ganganath Jha, Oriental Book Agency, Poona, 1965.

3. K. P. Bahadur — *The Wisdom of Sāṅkhya*, Sterling Publishers, Pvt. Ltd, New Delhi., 1978.

4. Kapila — *Sāṅkhya Aphorisms*. Trans. J. R. Ballantyne, Chowkhamba Sanskrit Series, Varanasi, 1963.

3. Yoga

1. Pātañjali — *Yoga Sūtras with comentary of Vyāsa and Gloss of Vācaspati Miśra* . Trans. Rama Prasada, Oriental Book reprint Co., New Delhi-1978.

2. K. P. Bahadur — *The Wisdom of Yoga*, Sterling Publishers Pvt. Ltd., New Delhi-1977.

3. S. N. Dasgupta, — *The study of Pātañjali* Calcutta University, Calcutta, 1920.

4. P. N. Mukeerji — *Yoga Philosophy of Pātañjali*, Calcutta University, Calcutta, 1963.

5. Swami Prabhavananda (Trans) — *The Yoga Aphorisms of Pātañjali* Sri Ramakrishna Mutti Madras (1953)1982.

4. Nyāya

1. Gautama — *Nyāya Sūtra and commentary of Vātsyāyana Bhāṣya*, Trans. Mrinalkanti Gangopadhaya, Indian Studies Past & Present, Calcutta, 1976.

Trans. Mahamahopadhyaya Satish Chandra Vidyabhusana, Oriental Book Reprint Co, New Delhi-1975.

—Trans. Ganganatha Jha. Vol. I to IV. Motilal Banarsidass, Delhi 1984.

2. Gautama — *Nyāya Sūtra with Vātsyāyana's Bhāṣya, Uddyotakara's Nyāya-vārttika, Vācaspati's Nyāya-vārttika-tātparyaṭīkā and Viśvanāth's Vṛtti*, Critically edited with notes by Tarnatha Nyaya tarkatirtha, and Amarendramohan Tarkatirtha, Munshiram Manoharlal Publications, New Delhi, 1985.

3. Bhāsarvajña — *Nyāyasārah* ed. by S. S. Sastri & V. S. Sastri, Govt. Oriental Manuscripts Library, Madras, 1961.

4. S. K. Mitra — *The Ethics of Hindus*, Asian Publication Services, New Delhi, (1925) 1978.

5. Vaiśeṣika

1. Kaṇāda — *Vaiśeṣika Sūtras*- Trans. Nandalal Sinha, The Panini Office, Bhuvaneswari Ashram, Allahabad, (1911), 1974.

2. Prāsatpāda — *Padārtha-dharma-Saṅgraha* Chowkhamba, Benares, 1923.

6. Mīmāṁsā

1. Jaiminī — *Mīmāṁsā Sūtras*, Part I & II, Trans. Mohanlal Sandal, Motilal Banarsidass, New Delhi, 1980.

2. Kumarila Bhatta — *Ślokavārtika*, Comm. Kasika of Sucarita Miśra and Nyayaratnakara of Pārthasārathi Miśra. Trans. Ganganath Jha, Sri Satguru Pub, Delhi (1900), 1983.

3. Pārthasārathi Miśra — *Śāstradīpikā*, tarkapada, Nirnayasagar, Bombay, 1915.

4. Śālikanātha — *Prakaraṇa pañacikā* with *Nyāya Siddhi*, Trans. A. Suryanarayana Sastri, BHU, 1961.

7. Advaita Vedānta

1. Badarayana — *Vedānta Sūtras* with comm. by Baladeva. Trans. Rai Bahadur Srisa Chandra Vasu, Panini Offic, Allahabad, (1912), Sacred book of the Hindus, Series No. 5. AMS Press, New York, 1974.

2. Śaṅkara — *Brahma-Sūtra-bhāṣya*, Trans. Swami Gambhirananda, Advaita Ashram, Calcutta, 1983.

3.———— — *The Bhāṣyas on the ten Upaniṣads* with Ānanda Giri's Gloss, Ānandaṣrama Editions.

4. Nikhilānanda — *The Upanishad*, Trans. Harper, New York, 1962.

5. Paul Deussen — *The Philosophy of the Upaniṣads*, T. & T. Clark, Edinburgh, 1908.

6. T. M. P. Mahadevan — *The Philosophy of Advaita*, Luzac & Co., London, 1938.

7. Bhāratītīrtha Vidyāraṇya — *Pañcadaśī*, trans. Swami Swahananda, Sri. Ramakrishna Math, Madras. Ed. 1980.

8. Adi Śaṅkarācārya — *Vivekacūḍāmaṇi*, Trans. Swami Madhvānanda, Advaita Ashrama, Calcutta, 1978.

9.——— *Tattva Bodha*, Chinmaya Mission Trust, Bombay, 1982.

8. Jainism

1. Hermann Jacobi (Trans) — *Jaina Sūtras* I & II. Trans. from Prākrit by Hermann Jacobi, Dover pub. Inc., New York, 1968.

2. B. C. Law — *Some Jaina Canonical Sutras*, Monograph No. 2, Royal Asiatic Society Bombay, 1949.

3. K. C. Sogani — *Ethical Doctrines in Jainism*, Jaina Saṁskirti Saṁrakshaka Sangha, Sholapur, 1967.

4. Rev. J. Stevenson (Trans) — *The Kālpa Sūtra and Navatatva*. Bharati-Bharati, Varanasi, 1972.

5. Nathmal Tatia — *Studies in Jaina Philosophy*, Jain Cultural Research Society, Banaras 1951.

6. Jain Muni Uttam Kamal — *Jain Sects and Schools*, Concept Publishing Co., Delhi, 1975.

7. S. Gopalan — *Outlines of Jainism*, Wiley Eastern Pvt. Ltd., New Delhi, 1973.

8. S. Stevenson — *The Heart of Jainism*, Oxford University Press, London, 1916.

9. Mohanlal Mehta — *Outlines of Jaina Philosophy*, Jaina Mission Society, Bangalore, 1954.

BUDDHISM

Text

1. Vinaya Piṭaka

Vinaya Piṭaka, Ed. H. Oldenberg, Pāli text Society (P. T. S.), London, 1964-77, 5 Vols.

Vinaya texts, Trans. T. W. Rhys Davids & H. Oldenberg, Delhi, 1974-75, 3 Vols.

The Book of Discipline-Vinaya Piṭaka, Trans. I. B. Horner, Sacred books of the Buddhists, London, 1966-75, 4 Vols.

-*Samanta-pāsādikā*, Buddhaghosa's Commentary on *Vinaya Piṭaka*, Ed. J. Takakusu and Makoto Nagai, P. T. S, London, 1947-75, 8 Vols.

2. Sutta Piṭaka

1. Dīgha Nikāya

-Ed. Bhikkhu J. Kashyap, Nālandā Devanāgarī Pāli Series (NDPS), Pāli Publishing Board (P. P. B.), Bihar 1958, 3 Volumes.

-Ed. T. W. Rhys Davids and J. E. Carpenter, P. T. S., London, 1966-76, 3 Volumes.

-*Dialogues of the Buddha*, Trans. T. W. and C. A. F. Rhys Davids, P. T. S., London, 1977, 3 Volumes.

-*Sumaṅgala-Vilāsinī; Buddhaghosa's Commentary on Dīgha-Nikāya*, Ed. T. W. Rhys Davids, J. E. Carpenter and W. Stede, P. T. S., London, 1971, 3 Volumes.

-*Dīgha Nikāyya tika Linatthapakasini*, Ed. Lily de Silva, P. T. S., London, 1970, 3 Volumes.

2. *Majjhima Nikāya*

-Ed. Bhikkhu J. Kashyap, NDPS, P. P. B., Bihar, 1958, 3 Volumes.

-Ed. V. Trenckner & Robert Chalmers, P. T. B., London, 1977-79, 4 Vols.

-*The Middle Length Sayings, Majjhima Nikāya*, Ed. I. B. Horner, P. T. S., London, 1975-77, 3 Volumes.

-*Pāpañcasūdanī - Buddhaghosa's Commentary on Majjhima Nikāya*, Ed. J. H. Woods, D. Kosambi & I. B. Horner, P. T. S., London, 1976-79, 5 Vols.

-*The further dialogues of the Buddha*, Trans. Lord Chalmers, 4 Vols, S. B. B., Ed. Rhys Davids.

3. *Saṃyutta Nikāya* -Ed. Bhikkhu J. Kashyap, NDPS, P. P. B., Bihar, 1959, 3 Volumes

-Ed. L. Feer and Rhys Davids, Pali Text Society, London, 1970-80, 6 Volumes.

-*The Book of Kindered Sayings, Samyutta Nikāya.*

Ed. Rhys Davids and F. L. Woodward, P. T. S., London, 1972-80, 5 Volumes.

-*Sārattha-ppakāsini - Buddhaghosa's Commentary on Saṃyutta nikāya*. Ed. F. L. Woodward, 3 Volumes, P. T. S., London, 1977.

4. *Aṇguttara Nikāya* -Ed. Bhikkhu J. Kashyap, NDPS, P. P. B, Bihar, 1960, 4 Volumes.

-Ed. Richard Morris, E. Hardy and C. A. F. Rhys Davids, P. T. S., London, 1960-79, 6 Volumes.

The Book of the Gradual Sayings, Aṇguttara Nikāya, Ed. F. L. Woodward and E. M. Hare, P. T. S. London, 1972-79, 5 Vols.

-*Manorathapūraṇī-Buddhaghosa's Commentary on Anguttara Nikaya*, Ed. Max Walleser & H. Kopp, P. T. S., London, 1966-79, 5 Vols.

5. *Khuddaka Nikāya* (K.N) -Ed. Bhikkhu J. Kashyap, NDPS, P.P.B., Bihar, 1959, A Volumes,

-*Khuddakapātha with Commentary: Paramatthajotikā-I*, Ed. Helmer Smith, P. T. S., London, 1978.

-*Minor Reading and Illustrator; Khuddakapātha and Commentary*, Ed. Bhikkhu Nñānñ'amoli, P. T. S., London, 1978.

Dhammapada-Ed. Bhikkhu J. Kashyap, NDPS, P. P. B., Bihar, 1959, K. N. Vol. I.

-*The Commentary on the Dhammapada*, Ed. H. C. Norman, P. T. S., London, 1970, 5 Volumes.

Udāna -Ed. Bhikkhu J. Kashyap, NDPS, P. P. B., Bihar, 1959, K. N. Volume. I.

-Ed. Paul Steinthal, P. T. S., London, 1948.

-*Paramatta - Dīpanī Udānattha-katha of Dhammapalacariya*,

Ed. F. L. Woodward, P. T. S., London, 1977.

Itivuttaka -Ed. Bhikkhu J. Kashyap, NDPS, P. P. B., Bihar, 1959, K. N. Vol. I.

-Ed. E. Windisch, P. T. S., London, 1975.

-*Itivuttaka Commentrary Parmatthadī-panī*, Ed. M. M. Bose, Complied by H. Kopp., P. T. S., London, 1977-79, 3 Volumes.

Sutta Nipāta -Ed. Bhikkhu J. Kashyap, NDPS, P. P. B., Bihar, 1959, K. N. Vol.1.

-Ed. Dines Anderson and Helmer Smith, P. T. S., London, 1965.

-*Paramatthajotikā II*, Commentary on *Suttanipāta*, Ed. Helmer Smith, P. T. S., London, 1966-72, 3 Volumes.

Vimāna Vatthu and Peta Vatthu -Ed. Bhikkhu J. Kashyap, NDPS, P. P. B., Bihar, 1959, K. N. II.

-Ed. N. A. Jayawickrama, P. T. S., London, 1977, 2 parts.

-*Minor Anthologies Vol. IV: Stories of Mansions and Stories of departed*, Ed. I. B. Horner and H. S. Gehsman, P. T. S., London, 1974.

Theragāthā -Trans. K. R. Horman, P. T. S. London 1969.

-*The Elder's Verses I, II Theragāthā*, Trans. K. R. Horman, P. T. S., London, 1969.

-*Psalms of Early Buddhists, Sisters & Brethren*, Ed. Rhys Davids, P. T. S., London, 1980.

-*Paramatthadīpanī* V., Commentary on *Theragāthā*, Ed. F. L. Woodward, P. T. S., London, 1971-77, 3 Volumes.

Therīgāthā -Ed. Bhikkhu J. Kashyap, NDPS, P. P. B., Bihar, K. N. II.

Thera-Therīgāthā -Ed. H. Oldenberg and R. Pischel, P. T. S., London, 1966.

Jātakas -Ed. Bhikkhu J. Kashyap, Nālandā Devanāgarī Pāli Series, P. P. B., Bihar, 1959, K. N. II.

-*Stories of the Buddha's Former Births* Trans. under Editorship of E. B. Cowell, London, 1973, 3 Volumes.

Jātakaṭṭhavaṇṇanā - Buddhagohosa's Comm. on Jātaka verses.

Mahāniddesa -Ed. Bhikkhu, J. Kashyap, Nālandā Devanāgarī Pāli Series, P. P. B., Bihar K. N. II.

-*Saddhamma - Pajjotikā* - Comm. on Mahāniddesa, Ed. A. P. Buddhasatta, P. T. S., London, 1980, 2 Volumes.

Cullaniddesa -Ed. Bhikkhu J. Kashyap, NDPS, P. P. B., Bihar, 1960.

Patisaṃbhidāmagga -Ed. Bhikkhu J. Kashyap, Nālandā Devanāgarī Pāli Series, P. P. B., Bihar, 1960.

-Ed. Arnold C. Taylor, P. T. S., London 1979, 2 Volumes.

-*Saddhammappakasinī*, Comm. on patisaṃbhidāmagga, P. T. S., London 1979, 3 Volumes.

Apadāna -Ed. Bhikkhu. J. Kashyap, Nālandā Devanagarī Pāli Series, P. P. B., Bihar, 2 parts, 1959, K. N. II.

Buddhavaṃsa and Cariyāpiṭaka -Ed. Bhikkhu J. Kashyap, Nālandā Devanāgarī Pāli Series, P. P. B., Bihar, 1959.

-Ed. N. A. Jayawickrama, P. T. S., London 1974.

-*Minor Anthologies*, Vol.III, Ed. I. B. Horner, P. T. S., London, 1975.

-*Buddhavaṃsa, Comm. Madhuratthavilasinī*. Ed. I. B. Horner, P. T. S., London, 1979.

-*Clarifier of Sweet Meaning, Buddhavamsa* Commentary, Ed. I. B. Horner, P. T. S., London, 1978.

Cariyāpiṭaka -Ed. Bhikkhu J. Kashyap, Nālandā Devanāgari Pāli Series, P. P. B., Bihar, 1959, K. N. Vol. VII.

-*Achariya Dhammapala's Paramatthadīpanī* Comm. on Cariyāpiṭaka. Ed. D. L. Barua, P. T. S., London, 1979.

3. Abhidhamma Piṭaka (A.P.)

1. *Dhammasaṅgaṇi* -Ed. Bhikkhu J. Kashyap, Nālandā Devanāgarī Pāli Series, P. P. B., Bihar, 1960, A. P. Vol. I.

-Ed. Edward Muller, P. T. S. London, 1978.

-*Buddhist Psychological Ethics - Dhammasaṅgaṇi*.

Ed. Rhys Davids, P. T. S. London, 1974.

-*Atthasālinī* Buddhaghosa's Comm. on Dhammasaṅgaṇi Ed. Edward Muller, P. T. S., London, 1979.

-*The Expositor - Atthasālinī*. Ed. pe Maung Tin, P. T. S, London, 1976, 2 Volumes.

2.*Vibhaṅga* -Ed. Bhikkhu J. Kashyap, Nālandā Devanāgarī Pāli Series, P. P. B., Bihar, 1960, 2 volumes.

-Ed. Mrs. Rhys Davids, P. T. S., London, 1978.

-*Vibhaṅga Comm. Samoha-Vinodanī*. Ed. A. P. Buddhadata, P. T. S., London, 1980.

-*The Book of Analysis-Vibhaṅga*. Ed. U. Thittila, P. T. S., London., 1969.

3.*Kathāvatthu* -Ed. Bhikkhu J. Kashyap, Nālandā Devanāgarī Pāli Series, P. P. B., Bihar, 1960.

-Ed. Arnold C. Taylor, P. T. S., London, 1979, 2 Volumes.

-*The Points of Controversy-Kathāvatthu* Ed. S. Z. Aung and Rhys Davids, P. T. S., London, 1979.

-*Comm. Kathāyātthuppakaraṇa-Aṭṭhakathā* Ed. N. A. Jayawickrama, P. T. S. London, 1979.

4.*Puggala Paññatti* -Ed. Bhikkhu J. Kashyap, Nālandā Devanāgarī Pāli Series, P. P. B., Bihar, 1960.

-Ed. R. Morris, G. Landsberg and Rhys Davids, P. T. S., London, 1972.

5. *Dhātukathā* -Ed. Bhikkhu J. Kashyap, Nālandā Devanāgarī Pāli Series, P. P. B., Bihar, 1960.

Ed. E. R. Gooneratne, P. T. S., London, 1963.

Dhātu-katha pakaraṇa and its Commentary, Ed. U. Narada, P. T. S., London, 1977.

6. *Yamaka* -Ed. Bhikkhu J. Kashyap, Nālandā Devanāgarī Pāli Series, P. P. B., Bihar, 1961, 3 Volumes.

7. *Paṭṭhāna* -Ed. Bhikkhu J. Kashyap, Nālandā Devanā=garī Pāli Series, P. P. B., Bihar, 1961, 5 Volumes.

-*Conditional Relations, Paṭṭhana*, Vol.I Ed. U. Narada, P. T. S., London, 1969.

Milandapañha: *The Questions of Kind Milanda*- Trans. T. W. Rhys. Davids, Motilal Banarasidass. Delhi, 1975, 2 Vols.

Visuddhi Magga: Ed. Swami Dwarikadas Sastri, Buddha Bharati Series, Varanasi, 1977.

The path of Purification. (Trans) Bhikkhu ñānamoli, Buddhist publication Society, Kandy, 1979.

Mahāyāna Texts: Buddhist Sanskrit Series, Ed. P. L. Vaidya. The Mithila Institute of P. G. Studies and Research in Sanskrit learning, Darbhanga, Bihar.

Saddharma Pundarika: *The Lotus of the True Law*, (Trans) H. Kern, Motilal Boanarasidass, Delhi, 1981.

Mula-Madhyamika Kārikā: Ed. H. Chatterjee, Firma KLM Pvt. Ltd, Calcutta, 1962.

Sika-Samuccaya: Complied by Santideva, (Trans) C. Bendall & W. H. D. Rose, Motilal Banarasidass, Delhi, 1981.

Bodhisattvacharyavatara: By Acharya Santideva *A Guide to the Boddhisattva's way of life*, Trans. Stephen Batchelor, Library of Tibetan Works & Archieves, Dharmasala, 1979.

Alabaster, H. *The Wheel of the Law*, Indological Book House, Delhi, 1972.

Alexander, David Neel. *Buddhism — Its Doctrine and Its Methods*, B. J. Publications, London, 1972.

Allen, G. F. *The Buddhist Philosophy*, George Allen and Unwin Ltd., London, 1959.

Ambedkar, B. R. *The Buddha and His Dharma*, Siddarth College Publication, Bombay, 1957.

Anacker, Stefan.*Seven Works of Vasubandhu*, Motilal Banarasidass, Delhi, 1984.

Ashby, Elizabeth.*Our Reactions to Dukkha*, Buddhist Publication Society, kandy, 1965.

Bahm, A. J. *Philosophy of Buddha*, Rider and Company, London, 1958.

Banerjee, N. V. *The Concept of Philosophy*, University of Calcutta, 1968.

Bapat, P. V. (ed.). *2500 Years of Buddhism*, Government of India Publication, New Delhi, 1959.

Barth Elemy, Saint Hilaire J. *Life and Legend of Buddha*, Sushil Gupta, Calcutta, 1957.

Barua, B. *Prolegomena to a History of Buddhist Philosophy*, Munshiram Manoharlal Publication, Delhi, 1974.

Barua, B. *A History of pre-Buddhistic Indian Philosophy*, Motilal Banarasidass, Delhi, 1981.

Baser, R. N. *A Critical Study of the Milindapanha*, Firm KLM Private Ltd., Calcutta, 1978.

Basu Rabindranath. *A Critical Study of the Milindapanha*, Firma KLM Private Ltd., Calcutta, 1978.

Beyer. *The Buddhist Experiences, Sources and Interpretation*, Dickenson Publishing Co., California, 1974.

Bhagwat, N. K. *The Buddhist Philosophy of Theravada*, Patna University Readership Lectures, Bihar.

Brewester, E. H. *The Life of Gotama, The Buddha*, Bharatiya Publishing House, Varanasi, 1975.

Buddharakkita, Acharya. *Living Legacy of the Buddha*, Buddha Vachana Trust, Bangalore, 1979.

Banerjee, Nikunjavihari. *Glimpses of Indian Wisdom*, Munshiram Manoharlal Publication, New Delhi, 1972.

Chandra, pratap. *Metaphysics of Perpetual Change*, The Concept of Self in Early Buddhism, Somaiya Publications Private Ltd., Bombay, 1978.

Chang Gama, C. C. *The Buddhist Teaching of Totality*, George Allen and Unwin Ltd., London, 1971.

Chatterjee, A. K. *The Yogacara Idealism*, Motilal Banarasidass, New Delhi, 1975.

Chaudhuri, Sukomal. *Analytical Study of Abhidharma Kosa*, Government Sanskrit College, Calcutta, 1976.

Chaudhury, B. N. *Abhidhamma Terminology in the Ruparupavibhanga*, Calcutta Sanskrit College Research Series No. CXIII, Government Sanskrit College, Calcutta, 1983.

Clarence, O. Mc Muller (Ed). *The problem of Death and Suffering in Indian Religions*, Lit House publications Ltd., Delhi, 1983.

Conze, E. and Horn. *Buddhist Texts Through the Ages*, Philosophical Library, New York, 1954.

Conze, Edward.*Buddhist Meditation*, George Allen and Unwin Ltd., London, 1968.

Coomaraswamy, Ananda. *Buddha and The Gospel of Buddhism*, Associate Publishing House, Madras, 1956.

Cowell, E. B. (Trans). *Buddhist Mahayana Texts*, Motilal Banarasidass, Delhi, 1978.

Cowell, E. B. and Et. al. *Buddhist Mahayana Text*, Sacred Books of the East, Dover publications, New York, 1969.

Davids, T. W. Rhys. *Gotama, The man*, Luzac & Co., London, 1928.

——— *Dialogues of the Buddha*, Bharatiya publishing House, Delhi, 1976.

———*Early Buddhism*, Bharatiya publishing House, Delhi, 1976.

———*Indian Buddhism*, Rachna Prakasan, Allahabad, 1972.

———*Manual of Buddhism*, Oriental Book Reprint Co., New Delhi, 1975.

———*Buddhist India*, Motilal Banarasidass, Delhi, 1981.

———(Trans). *Buddhist Sutras*, Motilal Banarasidass, Delhi, 1973.

———(Trans). *The Questions of King Milinda*, 2 Volumes, Motilal Banarasidass, Delhi, 1975.

Dayal, Har. *The Bodhisattva Doctrine in Buddhist Sanskrit Literature*, Motilal Banarasidass, Delhi, 1978.

De, Silva Chales, lambert, Albert. *A Treatise on Buddhist Philosophy*, Carlton Publishing Work, Colombo, 1937.

Dharma Sena, C. *Aids to Abhidhamma Philosophy*, Buddhist Publication Society, Kandy, 1963.

Dube, S. N. *Cross Currents in Early Buddha*, Manohar Publications, Delhi, 1980.

Dumovlin, H. *Buddhism in the Modern World*, Collier Macmillan publications, London, 1976.

Dutt, Nalinaksha. *Buddhist Sects in India*, Motilal Banarasidass, Delhi, 1981.

Dutt, Nalinaksha. *Early Monastic Buddhism*, Firma KLM Pvt., Ltd., Calcutta, 1981.

———*Mahayana Buddhism*, Firma KLM Pvt. Ltd., Calcutta, 1976.

———*Mahayana Buddhism*, Indological Book House, Delhi, 1973.

———*Buddhist Sects*, Firma KLM Pvt. Ltd. Calcutta, 1977.

Dutt, Sukumar. *Early Buddhist Monachism*, Asia publisher, London, 1960.

Edward Elbridge Sausbury. *Buddhist Papers*, Sanskrit Pustak Bhandar, Calcutta, 1972.

Edward, J. Thomas. *The Life of Buddha*, Routledge and Kegan Paul, London, 1975.

Evola, J. *The Doctrine of Awakening*, Luzac and Co., Ltd., London, 1951.

Fatone, Vicente. *The Philosophy of Nagarjuna*, Motilal Banarasidass, Delhi, 1981.

Fuminaro, Watanabe (Ed.). *Philosophy and Its Development in the Nikāyas and Abhidharma*, Motilal Banarasidass, Delhi, 1983.

George, Alder (Ed.). *Buddhist Insights* - Essays by Alex Wayman, Motilal Banarasidass, Delhi.

George Francis Allen, (Trans, Ed.). *The Buddha's Philosophy*, George Allen and Unwin Ltd., London, 1959.

Gombrich, F. Richard. *Precept and Practise*, Claerdon Press, Oxford, 1971.

Govinda, A. B. *The Psychological Attitude of Early Buddhistic Philosophy*, Nag Publications, New Delhi, 1975.

Goyal, S. R. (Ed.). *A History of Indian Buddhism*, Kusumanjali Prakashan, Meerut 1987

Grimm, George. *The Doctrine of Buddha*, Motilal Banarasidass, Delhi, 1982.

———*Buddhist Wisdom*, Translation Carroll Aikins, (Ed.). M. Keller Grimm, Motilal Banarasidass, Delhi, 1982.

Guenther, Herbert, V. *Buddhist philosophy in Theory and Practice.*

Guenther, Herbert, V. *Philosophy and Psychology in the Abhidhamma*, Motilal Banarasidass, Delhi, 1974.

Haldar, Aruna. *Some Psychological Aspects of Early Buddhist Philosophy*, Based on Abhidhamma, Calcutta Asiatic Society, Calcutta, 1981.

Hardy, R. Spencer. *A Manual of Buddhism*, William and Norgate, London.

Hoffman, Yoel. *The Ideal of Self*, East and West, 1937.

Holmer, Edmond. *The Creed of the Buddha*, The bodley Head, London, 1949.

Humpherys, Christmas. *Buddhism*, penguin Books,.........,1972.

———-*The Way of Action*, George Allen and Unwin Ltd., London, 1960.

Jayatillike, K. N. *The Message of the Buddha*, George Allen and Unwin Ltd., London, 1975.

———*Facets of Buddhist Thought*, Buddhist Publication Society, kandy, 1971.

———-*Early Buddhist Theory of Knowledge*, Motilal Banarasidass, Delhi, 1980.

Johnsson, Rune, E. A. *Pali Buddhist Texts*, Scandinavan Institute of Asian Studies, Monograph Services, No. 14, Curzon, Press, Londo, (1973), 1981.

———*The Psychology of Nirvana*, George Allen and Unwin Ltd., London, 1969.

Johnston, E. H. (Trans.). *Asvaghosa's Buddhacarita or Acts or of the Buddha*, Motilal Banarasidass, Delhi, 1978.

Johis, L. M. *Studies in the Buddhist Culture of India*, Motilal Banarasidass, Delhi, 1977.

Kamaleshwar Bhattacharya. *The Dialectical Method of Nagarjuna, Vigrahavyavartani*, Motilal Banarasidass, Delhi, 1978.

Kalupahana, D. J. *Buddhist Philosophy: A Historical Analysis*, University Press of Hawai, Honolulu, 1976.

———Causality, the Central Philosophy of Buddhism, University Press of Hawai, Honolula, 1975.

Kapil, N. Tiwari. *Suffering Indian Perspectives*, Motilal Banarasidass, Delhi, 1986.

Kashyap, Bikkhu. *Abhidhamma Philosophy*, Mahabodhi Society, (2 Vols.) Saranath, 1942-43.

Katsumata, Shunkyo. *A Study of Citta Vijñāna Thought, in Buddhism.*

Katz, Nathan. *Buddhist Images of Human Perfection*, Motilal Banarasidass, Delhi, 1982.

Kern, H. *Manual of Indian Buddhism*, Motilal Banarasidass, Delhi, 1984.

Keith, A. B. *Buddhist Philosophy in India and Ceylon*, Clarendon Press, Oxford, 1923.

Kloetzli, Randy. *Buddhist Cosmology*, Motilal Banarasidass, Delhi, 1983.

Kochu Muttom, Thomas, A. *A Buddhist Doctrine of Experience*, Motilal Banarasidass, Delhi, 1983.

Lakshminarasu, P. *The Essence of Buddhism*, Thacker & Co., Bombay, 1948.

Law, B. C. *A Study of the Mahavastu*, Bharatiya Publishing House, Varanasi, 1978.

———(Trans). *A Manual of Buddhist Historical Traditions (Saddhamma-Sangha)*, University of Calcutta, 1963.

Law, N. N. (Ed.) *Gautama Buddha, 25the Centenary Volume*, Publishers J. C. Sarkhel, Calcutta, Oriental Press, Calcutta, 1940.

Malala Sekara, G. P. (Ed.) *Dictionary of Pali Proper Names*, (2 Vols.), J. Murry, London, 1930.

Maitra, S. K. *Fundamental Questions of Indian Metaphysics and Logic*, University of Calcutta, Calcutta, 1974.

Michael, Edwards. *In the Blowing out of a Flame*, George Allen Allen and Unwing Ltd., London, 1976.

Mizuno, Kogen. *The Beginnings of Buddhism*, Kosei Publishing Co., Tokyo, 1980.

Mookerjee, Satkari. *The Buddhist Philosophy of University Flux*, Motilal Banarasidas, New Delhi, 1975.

———(Ed.) *The Nava-Nalanda-Mahavira*, Research Publication, Vol. I, Calcutta, 1957.

Murthy, T. R. V. *The Central Philosophy of Buddhism*, Geroge Allen and Unwin Ltd., London, 1960.

ñyanamoli Bhikku (Trans.). *The Path of Purification Buddhaghosa's Visuddhi Magga*, Buddhist publishing Society, Kandy, 1979.

Nagao, Gadjin, M. *Madhyamta Vibhanga Bhasya*, Suzuku Research Foundation, Tokyo, 1964.

Nakamura, Hajime. *Buddhism in Comparative Light*, Islam and The Modern Age Society, New Delhi.

———-*Indian Buddhism: A Survey With Bibliographical Notes*, Motilal Banarasidass, Delhi, 1987.

Nanamoli, Thera. *Pathways of Buddhist Thoughts*, Buddhist Publishing Society, Kandy, 1963.

Narain, A. K. (Ed.). *Studies in History of Buddhism*, Motilal Banarasi Dass, Delhi, 1980.

Nariman, J. K. *Literary Sources of Sanskrit Buddhism*, Motilal Banarasidass, Delhi, 1972.

Nayak, G. C. *Analytical Studies in Buddhist Philosophy*, Publication of Department of Philosophy, Utkal University, Bhubaneswar, 1984.

Nyana Ponika, Mahathera, Venerable. *The Pathways of Buddhist Toughts*, George Allen and Unwin Ltd., London, 1971.

Oldenberg, H. *Buddha: His Life, His Doctrine, His Order*, Translated by William Hoey, The Book Company Ltd., Calcutta, 1927.

Pande, G. C. *Studies in the Origin of Buddhism*, Motilal Banarasidall, Delhi, 1983.

Paul, Carus. *Buddha and Buddhism*, New Age Publication, New Delhi, 1980.

Paul, Carus. *Karma/Nirvana*, Asian Publications, Delhi, 1978.

Piyadarasi Thera. *The Philosophy of Change*, Dharmodaya Sangha, Kathmandu, 1956.

Poussin, De. La, Vallee. *The Way to Nirvana*, (Six Lectures in Ancient Buddhism as a Discipline of Salvation). The University Press, Cambridge, 1917.

Premasiri, P. *The Philosophy of the Atthakavagga*, Buddhist Publication Society, Kandy, 1972.

Radhakrishnan, S. *The Dhammapada*, Oxford University Press, Madras, 1982.

Ramesan, N. *Glimpses of Buddhism*, The Government of Andhra Pradesh, 1961.

Rhys Davids (Trans) *Abhidhamma Sangha-Compendium of Philosophy*, Pali Text Society, London, 1910.

Saddhatissa, H. *The Life of Buddha*, George Allen and Unwin Ltd., London, 1976.

————Buddhist Ethics, George Allen and Unwin Ltd., London, 1970.

Saher, P. J. *The Conquest of Suffering*, An Enlarged Anthology of Geroge Grimm's Works on Buddhist Philosophy & Metphysics, Motilal Banarasidass, Delhi, 1977.

Sangha Rakshita, Bhikshu. *Survey of Buddhism*, Indian Institute of World Culture, Basavanagudi press, Bangalore, 1959.

Sila, Lynn Ade. *The Problem of Self in Buddhism and Christianity*, Macmillian, 1979.

Silananda Brahmachari. *An Introduction to Abhidhamma*, Jadab Barua Publications, Calcutta, 1980.

Samkrtyayana, Rahula. *Buddha-Darsana* (In Hindi), Allahabad, 1962.

Singh, Jaidev. *An Introduction to Madhyamika Philosophy*, Motilal Banarasidass, Delhi, 1978.

Sobti, Harcharan Singh. *Nibbana in Early Buddhism*, Eastern Book Likers, Delhi, 1985.

Soma, Thera. *An Old Debate on Self*, Buddhist Publication Society, Kandy, 1962.

———*Treasures of the Noble*, Buddhist Publication Society, Kandy, 1965.

Sorkar, A. K. *Changing Phases of Buddhist Thought*, South Asian Publications, New Delhi, 1983.

Stcherbatsky, Th. *The Central Conception of Buddhism and the Meaning of the Word 'Dhamma'*. Motilal Banarasidass, 1979.

———*The Conception of Buddhist Nirvana*, Motilal Banarasidass, 1977.

Suzuki, B. L. *Mahayana Buddhism*, George Allen and Unwin Ltd., London, 1959.

Suzuki, D. T. *The Outlines of Mahāyana Buddhism*, George Allen and Unwin Ltd., London, 1978.

Tachibana, S. *The Ethics of Buddhism*, Curzon Press, London, 1975.

Takausu, Junjiro. *The Essentials of Buddhist Philosophy*, Motilal Banarasidass, Delhi, 1975.

Thomas, E. J. *The Road to Nirvana*, A Selection of Buddhist Scriptures, J. Murrey, London, 1950.

Tucci, Gueseppe. *Minor Buddhist Text*, Motilal Banarasidass, Delhi.

U, Nu. *The Buddha*, Kamala Lectures, University of Calcutta, Calcutta, 1961.

Venkata Ramana, K. *Nagarjuna Philosophy*, -As presented in the Mamaha Prajnaparamita Sastra, Motilal Banarasidass, Delhi, 1978.

Verdu, Alfonso. *Early Buddhist Philosophy*, Motilal Banarasidass, Delhi, 1975.

Varma, V. P. *Early Buddhim and Its Origins*, Munshiram Manoharlal Publishers Pvt. Ltd., Delhi, 1973.

Ward, C. H. S. *Buddhism*, Vol. I. Hinayana 1947, Vol. II. Mahayana, 1952, Epiworth Press, London.

Warder, A. K. *Indian Buddhism*, Motilal Banarasidass, Delhi, 1980.

Warren, Henry, Clarke. *Buddhist Discourses*, Asian Publications Services,

Wood Ward, F. L. (Trans.). *Some Sayings of Buddha*, Oxford University Press, London, 1973.

Wijisekera, O. *Knowledge and Conduct*, Buddhist Publication Society Kandy, 1963.

Winternitz, M. *History of Indian Literature*, Vol. II, Part-I (Buddhist Literature), Translated and Revised by Bhaskara JnA, Bharatiya vidya Prakasman, Delhi, 1987.

Yamakami, Sogen. *Systems of Budhist Thought*, University of Calcutta, Calcutta, 1912.

JOURNALS

International Philosophical Quarterly, Co-edited: Forham University New York. Berchmans Philosophyicum Heverlee - Louvaian

Vol. IX. No. 1, March 1969.

Kenneth K. Inada. "Some Basic Misconceptions of Buddhism", pp. 101-119.

Vol. IX, No. 1, March 1969.

Donald W Mitchell. "The no-self doctrine in Theravāda Buddhism", p. 248-260.

Indian Philosophical quarterly, Journal of Pratap Centre of Philosophy, Amalner, and Department of Philosophy, University of Poona, Poona-7.

Vol. 11, No. 1, October 1974.

S. R. Bhatt. "The Concept of Māyā", pp. 65-70.

T. T. Kalghatgi. "Jaina Ethics", pp. 77-86.

Kamal Chand Sagani. "Jaina Ethical Theory", pp. 177-184.

Philosophy of East and West (O) A Journal of Oriental and compararative thought.

University of Hwaii Press,

Honolulu, 14, Hawaii.

Vol. IX, No. 1 & 2, April, July, 1959.

S. K. Saksena, "Relation of Phisosophical thought to the practical affairs of men", pp. 9-10.

T. M. P. Mahadevan, "Indian Ethics and Social Practice", p. 62 & 63.

Paul Mus, "The problematics of the Self, East and West", pp. 75-76.

Vol. IX. No. 3 & 4. October 1959, Jan 1960.

David White, "Moksa as value and experience", pp. 145-160.

Vol. IX, No. 1 & 2.

Charles, A. Moore. "Philosophy as distinct from religion in India", pp. 3-26.

Vol. XI, No. 3, October 1961.

Alex Wayman. "The Buddhist 'Not this, Not this", pp. 99-114.

Vol. V, No. 2, July 1955

Alex Wayman. "The lamp and the wind in Tibetan Buddhism", pp. 149-54.

Vol. VII. No. 1 & 2, April, July 1957.

Alex Wayman. "The meaning of Unwisdom (Avidya)" pp. 21-26.

J. A. B. Van Buitenen. "Dharma & Mokṣa", pp. 31-40.

Daniel, H. H. Ingalls. "Dharmma and Mokṣa", pp. 41-48.

Vol. VIII. No. 1 & 2, April, July 1958.

Kalidas Bhattacharyya. "Classical Philosophies of India and the West", pp. 17-36.

Vol. XIII, No. 1, April, 1963.

Edward Conze. "Buddhist Philosophy and its European parallels", pp. 9-24.

V. P. Verma. "The origins and Sociology of the Early Buddhist Philosophy of moral determinism", pp. 25-48.

K. B. Rmakrishna Rao. "The guṇas of Prakṛti according to the Samkhya Philosophy", pp. 61-71.

Vol. XVIII, No. 1-4, Jan-Oct, 1967.

G. P. Malalasekara. "Transference of merit in Ceylonese Buddhism", pp. 85-90.

Yoshifami Veda. "Two main streams of thought in Yogacara Philosophy", pp. 155-166.

Vol. XVIII. No. 1 & 2, Jan-April, 1968.

Kenneth K. Inada. "The ultimate ground of Buddhist purification", pp. 41-54.

Vol. XIX, No. 4, October, 1969.

Richard Taylor. "The anattādoctrine and personal Identity", pp. 359-366.

Vol. XX. No. 4, October, 1970.

R. Puligandla and K. Pushakka. "Buddhism and revolution", pp. 345-354.

Vol. XXI. No. 1, January, 1971.

Donald W. Mitchell. "Analysis is Theravāda Buddhism", pp. 23-32.

Vol. XXI, No. 4, October, 1971.

Herbert Morris. "Guilt and suffering", pp. 419-434.

Vol. XXII. No. 1, January, 1972.

Raymong Panikkar. "The laws of karman and the historical dimension of man", pp. 25-44.

Vol. XXII, N o. 2, April, 1972.

John M. Koller. "Dhamma: An Expression of University order", pp. 131-144.

Vol. XXII, No. 4, October, 1972.

Donald K. Swearer. "Two types of saving knowledge in the pāli Suttas", pp. 355-372.

Vol. XXIII. No. 4, October, 1973.

Donald K. Searer. "The structure of Buddhist Meditation in Pāli Suttas", p. 435-456.

Vol. XXV., No. 4, October, 1975.

Kenneth, K. Inada. "The metaphysics of Buddhist experience and the White Headian encounter", pp. 465-488.

Vol. XXVII, No. 4, October, 1977.

David J. Kalupahana. "The notion of suffering in Early Buddhism compared with some reflections of early Wittgenstein", pp. 423-432.

Vol. XXVIII, No. 1, January, 1978.

peter Porrest. "Reincarnation without survival of memory or character", pp. 91-98.

Vol. XXX, No. 4, October, 1980.

Wayne Alt, et al. "There is no paradox of desire in Buddhism", pp. 521-534.

Vol. XXIX, No. 1, Jan., 1979.

A. L. Herman. "A solution to the paradox of desire in Buddhism", pp. 91-94.

Vol. XXIX, No. 2, April, 1979.

Kenneth, K. Inada. "Problematics of the Buddhist nature of self", pp. 141-158.

Vol. XXXII, No. 4, October, 1982.

Jeffrey, D. Watts. "Necessity and sufficiency in the Buddha's causal scheme", pp. 425-38.

Vol. XXXIII, No. 2, April, 1983.

Henry Craise. "Early Buddhism, Some recent misconceptions", pp. 149-166.

Vol. XXXIII, No. 4, October, 1983.

David Day. "The difference between saṁsara and Nirvāna", pp. 355-367.

The Mahābodhi,

Journal of the Mahabodhi Society,

A monthly journal of International Buddhist Brotherhood founded by the Venerable Anagrika Dharmapāla in 1892, Calcutta.

Vol. 48, No. 9, September, 1940.

C. L. A. De Silva. "Nibbāna", pp. 309-313.

H. De S. kularatna. "The path to Buddhist Sainthood", pp. 324-327.

Vol. 56, No. 1-3, Jan-March, 1948.

Ven. Narada Thera. "A simple introduction to Abhidhamma", pp. 8-23.

Francis Story. "Anatta in modern thought", pp. 74-76.

Vol. 67, No. 5, May, 1959.

Edward Conze. "The Buddhist 'personalities'", pp. 118-126.

Vol. 73, No. 5, May, 1965.

Miss Sujata Soni. "Place of Sīla in Buddhsm", pp. 137.

Vol. 74, No. 7-8, July, August, 1966.

Moni Bagchie. "The Conception of Nirvāna", pp. 161-64.

Vol. 75, No. 3, March, 1967.

Ven. Dr. U. Dhammaratna. "The Four Noble Truths", p. 66.

Dr. H. Saddhatissa mahathera. "Ethics of the Buddhist", pp. 70-73.

Friedrich V. Lusting. "The pure Conduct", p. 87.

Vol. 75, No. 5-6, May-June, 1967.

Dr. H. Saddhatissa Mahathera. "The emigma of the theory of Anatta", pp. 171-74.

Prof. Madhusudun Mullik. "The law of causal gensis in Buddhism", pp. 221-25.

Vol. 75, No. 9, September, 1967.

John D. Ireland. "The stages of the path", pp. 306-7.

Dr. Y. Kusmadasa. "The Buddhist doctrine of Impermanence", pp. 213-219.

Vol. 77, Nos. 4-5, April-May, 1969.

Dr. Nallinakṣha Dutta. "The Buddhist theory of flux or Becoming", pp. 119-21.

Dr. H. Saddhatissa. "Concept of rebirth in Buddhism". pp. 135-37.

Vol. 78, No. 5-6, May-June, 1970.

Rev. Nikkyo Niwano. "Eightfold path", pp. 133-34.

Ven. Narada Maha Thero. "What is it that is reborn? pp. 138-140.

Nrs, A. A. G. Bennett. "Samādhi", pp. 154-56.

Vol. 79, Nos. 5 & 6, May-June, 1971.

Ven. Dr. Walpola Rahula. "Bodhisattva Ideal in Theravāda and Mahāyāna", pp. 139-43.

Vol. 79, No. 1, Jan., 1971.

Prof. K. N. Jayantilleke. "Nirvāna", pp. 2-7.

Mr. Neville Gumaratna. "A Philosophical approach to the doctrine of karma", pp. 8-13.

Vol. 80, No. 10-11, Oct. -Nov., 1972.

Ven. Narada Maha Thera. "The Bodhisattva Ideal", pp. 481-85.

Vol. 81, Nos. 2-3, Feb. - March, 1973.

Bhikkhu Silacara. "The Noble Eightfold path", pp. 71-79.

Vol. 81, No. 7, July, 1973.

Anagarika B Govinda. "The cause of suffering", pp. 351-55.

Vol. 81, Nos. 11-12, Nov. -Dec., 1973.

pandit Rahula Sankrityayana. "Hinayāna and Mahāyāna compared", pp. 423-427.

Vol. 82, No. 1, Jan., 1974.

Bhikhu M. Prajnananda Sri, "Bondage", p. 19.

Ven. Narada Maha Thera, "Nibbāna", p. 19.

Ven. Narada Maha Thera, "Nibbāna", p. 20-22.

Vol. 82, No. 2, Feb. 1974.

Ven. Narada Maha Thera. "What is karma"? pp. 50-54.

Vol. 83., Nos. 8 & 9, Aug.-Sept., 1975.

Dr. Karunadasa. "The Philosophical basis of Early Buddhist thought", pp. 349-55.

Vol. 84, No. 1, Jan., 1976.

S. N. Goenka. "This is duh/.kha", pp. 6-13.

Vol. 84, No. 4-5, April-May, 1975.

Dr. R. L. Soni. "The Ego, Its raise and fall", pp. 101-104.

Vol. 84, No. 10, October, 1976.

V. V. S. Saibaba. "The nature of Nirvāna in Sutta Nipāta", pp. 359-61.

Vol. 85, Nos, 2-3, Feb. -March, 1977.

Ven. Dr. V. Jagarabhiwamsa. "What is Nibbāna", pp. 20-24.

Vol. 86, No. 1, Jan., 1978.

Ven. Buddhadasa Bhikkhu. "Three Universal Characteristics", p. 2-8.

Rabindranath Basu. "Bodhisattva in Buddhism", pp. 30-31.

Vol. 87, Nos. 1-3, Jan.-March, 1979.

Francis Story. "kamma and Causality", pp. 11-16.

Vol. 87, Nos. 4-5, April-May, 1979.

Anukul Chandra Banerjee. "Nibbana-Its concept in Buddhism", pp. 65-66.

Vol. 89, Nos. 7-9, July-Sept. 1981.

R. Sri padamamaban. "The Buddhist doctrine of Kamm", pp. 182-84.

Ven. L. Ariyawansa. "The four noble truths", pp. 205-207.

Vol. 92, Nos. 7-9, July-Sept., 1984.

Ven. Dr. Rewata Dhamma. "The fundamental forces of the Mind", pp. 137-45.

Vol. 93, Jan. -March, 1985.

Dipak K. Barua. "Consciousness or citta as Revealed in the early Pali texts", pp. 9-11.

Vol. 93. Nos. 4-6, April-June, 1985.

Richard Josephron. "The importance of precepts as a foundation for meditative development", pp. 76-79.

Vol. 94, Jan-March, 1986. Nos. 1-3.

A. K. Bandyopadhyay. "Buddhist Ideal of an Arhant (according to Dhammapada)", pp. 29-33.

Buddhist Studies (yearly)

The Journal of the Department of Buddhist Studies,

University of Delhi, Delhi

(A Yearly Research Journal)

No. 2, April, 1975: 2. G. G. Gyatso, "A Study of the Non-soul doctrine", pp. 3-7.

No. 3, May, 1976: 6. peter Della Sabina. "The treatment of the self (ātman) in Madhyamika philosophy, pp. 22-31.

No. 4, May, 1977: 2. Ankul Chandra Banerjee, "Life and teachings of Mahāvira", pp. 20-26.

No. 5, May, 1978: 1. Ankul Chandra Banerjee, "Pāli literature-A critique", pp. 1-5.

No. 6, May, 1979: 3. Mahesh Tiwari, "Meditation in Theravāda", Buddhism, pp. 19-35.

Arivind Sharma. "The Concept of a person in Buddhist Ethics", pp. 62-69.

Vol. VII, May, 1983: Swati Ganguli, "A Study on Pratityasamutpāda", pp. 21-26.

Abbreviations

Ang.	:	Aṅguttara-Nikāya.
B. B.	:	Buddha Bharati.
B. V. B.	:	Bharatiya Vidya Bhavan.
D.	:	Dīgha Nikāya.
Dh. P.	:	Dhammapada.
Dhs.	:	Dhammasangani.
Dhs. A.	:	Dhamma-sangani Aṭṭhakatha
IṪ	:	Itivuttaka.
It. A.	:	Itivuttaka-Aṭṭhakatha.
Ja. A.	:	Jātaka-Aṭṭhakatha.
Kg.	:	karmagatha.
M.	:	Majj. Nikāya.
Mp.	:	Milinda-Pañha.
Mv. (Vin).	;	Mahā-vagga.
N. Bh.	:	Nyāya Bhāṣya.
N. S.	:	Nyāya Sūtras
Ps.	:	Paṭisambhidāmagga.

P. T. S. : Pali Text Society.

Sam. : Saṁyutta Nikāya.

S. B. B. : Sacred Books of the Buddhists.

S. B. E. : Sacred Books of East.

S. D. S. : Sarva darśana Saṁgraha.

S. K. : Sāṅkhya Kārikā.

Sn. : Sutta-Nipāta.

S. T. K. : Sāṅkhya Tattva Kaumudī.

Ta. : Theragāthā.

T. Su. : Tattvārtha Sūtra.

U. A. S. : uttarādhyayama Sūtra.

V. bh. : Vibhaṅga.

Vis. Magga. : Visuddhimagga.

Y. S. : Yoga Sūtras

Pāli Dic. : Pāli English Dictionary.